ADVANCE PRAISE

"I just finished your book and am in awe of your courage, bravery, passion and never-ending quest in always choosing love on your path. Your gift for storytelling is so deeply inviting that it was hard to put down. Through so many trials and tribulations. It is a true tale of the power of the human spirit, this memoir is forever indelible in my heart and mind and is a story that the world needs to hear!" — LISA WYNN SALVATORE, Certified and Licensed Wellness Mentor, CT, USA

"Your manuscript arrived today and I can't put it down. I cannot stop reading this story of survival and blooming of the woman who shines such an incredible light. Thank you for this treasure. In awe and admiration for a journey of fortitude and triumph." — GAIL LeBAUER, NC, USA

"Betty, your story provides such strength. You are an amazing woman to have lived the life you have lived, so far and I know there is more to come. Your resilience is inspirational." — MARY SUE RABE, TX, USA, author of *Stand There and Look Pretty Darlin', Don't You Worry Your Pretty Little Head About Nothin'*

"This aptly named memoir is grace and courage personified. Betty's memoir is an inspiring reminder that when we view the larger story of our life, the challenges we face come again and again as we learn the lessons we were meant to experience. Throughout, I was rooting for Betty to love and stand up for herself and find the helpers who would lead her to the right next step. She shares courageous lessons of forgiveness and love in the most inspiring ways. Perhaps one of the most noteworthy is Betty's persistence in continuing to fight to write even when faced with tremendously daunting obstacles. This is a book to treasure; a gift to the world." — JANE RAMSEY, CA, USA, author of *Vision Quest: a Journey to Happiness.*

Resilience

MY LIFE OF FLIGHT, FEAR, AND FORGIVENESS

Betty Ann Connelly

RESILIENCE
My Life of Flight, Fear, and Forgiveness

by
BETTY ANN CONNELLY
www.bettyannconnelly.com

———————————————

ISBN: 978-1-7780409-0-0

EDITING, DESIGN & TYPOGRAPHY:
D. Patrick Miller ◆ Fearless Literary Services
www.fearlessbooks.com/Literary.html

TABLE OF CONTENTS

PART I

FAMILY LIFE

PART II

FOLLOWING A NEW COURSE

PART III

THE ACCIDENT

For

Ann Brittain

November 7, 1915 – January 4, 2014

PART I

Family Life

1

A Walk Away from Home

THE YEAR was 1956 and it was a hot summer day. Mom, depressed, was taking a long afternoon nap in her bedroom, leaving us to fend for ourselves. My two sisters, one older and one younger, and I were playing on the kitchen floor, crawling around on the cracked, dull grey linoleum with our dolls. My sisters liked their Barbies, with their ridiculously big breasts and tiny waists, and they dressed them up, combed their frizzy hair and acted out all kinds of scenarios. I preferred soft dolls, the stuffed and cuddly ones with the big plastic heads that I could drag around by the arm or hug when I was scared.

But I wasn't scared that day. I was bored. The kitchen door had been left open and brilliant rays of sunshine danced through the open doorway into the kitchen. The sunshine was a personal invitation to adventure, to the great outdoors, calling me to come see the world. My love of travel and adventure was about to be born.

Three years old, dressed in a T-shirt and shorts, my thick black hair tied up in a ponytail with an elastic band, I stepped outside.I don't know if I was going anywhere in particular. I don't think so. I stayed on the sidewalk as I wandered along. Cars passed by in both directions and when I came to a cross-street, they stopped for me to get to the other side. I boldly kept going, enjoying every minute of my newfound freedom, soaking in all the activity around me. People walked quickly on both sides of the street, bicycles whizzed past, cars sped along. I was so excited that I laughed as I walked.

I sauntered along for two or three blocks before a woman

stooped down to ask me where I was going. She was beautiful, with blond hair piled up on top of her head, sparkly earrings, and a flowered dress. She seemed very kind as she picked me up and carried me to her home. I loved the feeling of her arms around me. They felt safe and warm and caring and I snuggled my face against her neck. I didn't ever want her to put me down. She carried me up the sidewalk to her house, dug in her purse for her key and opened the front door.

I was amazed by what I saw. Her house was enormous and elegant, with pretty bowls on side tables, paintings on the walls and fancy blue drapes covering a big picture window. I was sure she must be very rich. She took me into the kitchen and sat me on a chair while she made a peanut butter sandwich, then sat down beside me while I ate it. After that she took my hand and walked me down the hallway to the bathroom. She filled the tub, put me in the warm water and soaped my entire body, including my face and hair, before rinsing me off and wrapping me in a big towel.

"These clothes used to belong to my kids when they were your age, and they won't mind my giving them to you," she said as she dressed me. She made a phone call and we sat in a big, overstuffed chair by the window, me in her lap, as we watched out the window for the police car. It pulled up a few minutes later. She carried me down her front steps, hugging me and saying goodbye before passing me into the arms of a police officer. He was tall and imposing in his blue uniform and had a big belt with a flashlight and other things on it. In spite of his smile and gentleness, he was a bit scary, really. I didn't want to go with him, to leave the hugs and attention and warmth of the lady. But I didn't tell him that.

The police station was busy and I sat on the counter eating a candy bar, watching all the excitement. Police officers stopped by to say hello and tell me how cute I was. I loved the candy and the attention. I always had a smile on my face for anyone who smiled at me. I loved and trusted everyone equally.

A woman came over and said she was a social worker. She looked the same age as my mother and wore a print dress with a dark sweater over it. Smiling, she said she and a police officer were going to take me home. I don't know how they knew where home was because I didn't, but soon we pulled up in front of my house. She held my hand as we walked to the front door. Dad, tall and lanky, was sitting in the living room smoking a cigarette and reading a newspaper. Mom, who, at five-two appeared so small next to my Dad, was up from her nap. She came rushing out of the kitchen, a worried look on her face, still wearing her apron and wiping her hands on a kitchen towel. The social worker and police officer were invited to sit on the sofa facing the two chairs that Mom and Dad sat in. I hovered against the wall. I could see my older sister Margaret, five, peeking around the corner into the living room, but not my little sister Carol, two, who must have been napping. The social worker lectured them both about how to take better care of me, telling them to watch me so that I couldn't just walk away. Dad promised her, "It won't happen again."

As soon as the officials left, I could feel my parents' fury—and I was scared.

Mom was rigid with anger, the frown on her face reducing her eyes to small slits as she glared at me. She spit her words out like nails. "You ran away on purpose. You're a bad, bad child."

Dad furiously agreed, saying, "I will not let you destroy this family." His slap slammed my head backwards into the wall.

I knew that my parents weren't happy to see me and didn't want me back. Through my tears, my young mind interpreted their reactions as anger that I'd been returned to them. My feelings were hurt and as soon as it was safe to do so, I ran sobbing to my favorite hiding spot, squeezing into the small dark space between the dresser and the wall in the attic where I knew no one would find me. I didn't understand that they weren't angry I was returned; they were angry that I'd brought social services and the police to the house. I would find out years later that it wasn't the first time, as the neighbors sometimes called in complaints of abuse and neglect. Margaret would later tell me repeatedly, "You're bad. You're so bad." But over the next year, I would go on more adventures, drawn outside by the sunshine and blue skies, each time forgetting the price I would pay when I got home.

For years, my Dad, in his drunken stupors, told my sisters and brother that I was bad, I was destroying the family and that it was up to him to protect them from me. "I am going to break you," he would say to me. "You were born bad and, if I have to, I will kill you. You will not destroy us." In his drunkenness, his sorrow at having to perform such a task was obvious. He told me that he sincerely hoped he wouldn't have to kill me but, if he did, it would be my fault, not his. He blamed me for everything. When his car was repossessed, it was my fault. If it snowed, it was my fault.

I never understood why the entire family seemed to feel I was such a burden. I felt confused and terrified, encircled by anger and unjustly accused. When Dad's anger subsided and he left the room, my sisters would tell me to "stop being so bad." When I asked them what I was doing that was bad, they didn't have an answer.

My very existence seemed to send Dad over the edge. And though I didn't know it then, it's obvious now that my mother and siblings were angry only because they feared that Dad's rage would escalate and everyone would get hurt.

In my attempts to escape all the hostility I isolated myself, escaping to my hiding spots for hours, day after day. My sadness was enormous. As an adult, one of my younger sisters told me, "When we were kids, I could never find you." Fear had always driven me into hiding.

2

A Real Monster in the Night

"**B**ETTY, GO TO BED."

I was four years old and Mom's voice rang out much too early for my liking. I'd been sitting in the living room in my pyjamas with my Dad and older sister, watching our brand new, black-and-white television set. In between the sofa and the TV was a wooden coffee table with open ends and sides that held a full set of encyclopedias. I liked the encyclopedia even more than I liked the TV and often picked a book at random to take to a quiet spot to look at the pictures on its glossy pages. But, tonight, I was just sitting quietly. Mom was in the kitchen cleaning. My younger sister Carol, the third child and baby brother, Mark, number four, were already asleep.

I never wanted to go to bed. But I slowly climbed the steep stairs to the attic alone. It was dark on the stairs and there was no railing, so I hugged the wall as I climbed. The cavernous attic held two double beds and a dresser wedged against the alcove, with plenty of room left over for us to play. Dolls and clothes were scattered on the floor. Margaret and I shared a bed, while Carol slept on the other side of the attic. Next to the small window was a hole in the wall the size of a baseball and the clothes hanging on a nearby rod swayed when the wind howled through the hole, creating moving shadows that I knew for sure were terrifying ghosts.

But it was not the ghosts that scared me the most.

As I crawled into bed, I thought about how I could stay awake. I tried to stay awake every night, to stay sitting up instead of lying down, to be prepared in case he came into my room. But with the darkness of the night and the warmth of the bed, the terror of falling asleep wasn't enough to keep me awake.

I awoke abruptly from a deep sleep as my body slammed against the wall. Panic pounded at my heart as I cringed on the floor. Dad towered over me, laughing at my distress and confusion. I didn't dare cry out or I would be kicked, so I remained silent, curled up on the cold linoleum floor, frozen by terror that his rage would escalate.

It was funny, my Dad told me through his laughter, to come to my bedside in the middle of the night, pick me up while I was sound asleep and throw me against the wall. He called it a game, one that he won if he was able to catch me by surprise. Night after night, he caught me by surprise. In spite of his laughter, there was something steely and angry in his demeanor and when he turned to leave after hurting me, he seemed satisfied. I waited until I heard his footsteps descending the stairs before crawling back into bed, my heart still pounding. Margaret was sound asleep in the bed we shared, as was Carol in the bed across the room, or at least they pretended to be. I wondered, years later, how anyone could sleep through my Dad's booming voice and loud laughter and suspected they'd been awake the whole time. But in the mornings, they never said a word about the previous night's events. And at the time, I didn't say a word either, ashamed by the violence, believing I had done something really bad to deserve it. But I didn't know what.

I wasn't sure what hurt more: the pain of hitting the wall or the fact that he laughed and so enjoyed my distress. In my house, there were no monsters hiding under the bed. The monster was six-two and standing over me night after night. He was my own personal monster, as I never saw him go after my sisters at night. There was no one to comfort me and tell me that monsters weren't real. There was only my real dad, telling me what a bad child I was. I absorbed every word of his hatred as if it was fact set in stone.

THERE was another game Dad liked to play.

His smell, the strong odor of cheap alcohol and stale cigarettes, clung to his clothes and hair, often pulling me from my sleep as he stood silently beside my bed. I hated that smell. It made me want to throw up but I would hold my breath, pretend to be asleep and freeze into stiffness. I knew what was coming next as he leaned closer and his hands touched me.

And then my mind would just float away, like a cloud in the sky. All awareness of ugliness and pain was left behind, blocked out completely, other than in brief flashes of memories that made no sense to me at the time. They did not return until many years later.

In the mornings, I remembered no details of what had happened the night before, only my Dad's words: "You are evil and if you don't stop making me do this, I will kill you. I promise I will kill you." I had no idea what I was doing wrong and I was terrified that he really would kill me.

When it was time to get up in the morning, Dad stood at the bottom of the narrow stairway yelling, "Rise and shine!" at the top of his lungs. Suddenly jarred awake, I hurriedly tumbled out of bed, exhausted and afraid of angering him by being too slow to get up. Even though I remembered nothing of the night before except his words, I couldn't understand why his smell sent a surge of panic through my entire body whenever he came near me.

But every night as I began to fall asleep, I would suddenly jerk awake in panic, knowing it wasn't safe. When I did fall asleep, my dreams were terrifying. In the dark, I was running from someone or something, a big, black, angry shadow. It was right behind me, nipping at my heels, grabbing at me. Barely escaping its grasp, I knew I would be dead if it caught me. But just when I thought I was safe and could slow down, it reappeared, and I took off running again. Every night the shadow appeared and every night I never quite got away. Every morning I awoke feeling like I'd spent the night in a war zone. That shadow chased me every night, without fail, for the next forty-five years, as vague bits of memories haunted my dreams.

I never questioned why Dad picked on me so constantly, as I believed him every time he said that I was born a bad child and he had to protect the family from me. It would be many years before I understood that his calling me evil was just his attempt to blame me for his terrible actions.

DAD WAS a mechanic in the Air Force. He was posted to the Distant Early Warning Line in the Arctic, a joint military venture between the United States and Canada. Because of this he was often away on long tours of duty. An alcoholic, he drank away most of his paycheck, leaving little for food, clothes or shelter for his growing family. Mom struggled to cope, trying to feed seven children and struggling to explain to the landlord month after month why there was no money to pay the rent. Hunger was a companion we were all familiar with. I constantly craved milk and food.

When he was home, Dad always seemed to be in a rage. He was tall and slender, and his movements reminded me of a snake's. He would go in for the kill suddenly — often with a smile on his face — slamming my head hard and fast into the wall as he walked by. If he was napping on the sofa and I got too close, his foot could abruptly fly out, kick me in the stomach and send me flying backwards onto my butt, sometimes with my head hitting the edge of the coffee table.

I deserved the kicks, I felt, because I was dumb enough to walk too close to a snake. I knew better than that.

At dinner, I was jarred when he would be smiling and laughing about something that had happened that day but then suddenly lash out with his fork to hit my knuckles, or with his hand to slap me upside the head. He did this to all of us kids and never apologized for losing his temper. When his rage subsided, he'd warn us never to make him so angry again. His children were not people; we were his property, and he was certain that each of us deserved exactly what we got from him. Mom often agreed with him that we were bad but even when she didn't, she wouldn't dare reach out to us — or she would be next.

There were times when Mom did try to protect us. Whenever Dad brought his drunken friends home, Mom watched closely to make sure none of them got too friendly with us. She would sometimes hide us in their bedroom, whispering, "Dad's friends are here. Don't make a sound. Not a peep." After she closed the door behind her we would lie sprawled out in our pyjamas on the bed or floor in the tiny room, sometimes whispering, but mostly silent and bored. The bedroom was right off the living room and we could hear ranting and yelling. We knew there was danger present, especially as the men got drunker, their language rawer and the conversation angrier. They raged about the state of the world and about their wives. I couldn't understand much of what they were saying because their words were slurred and they kept interrupting each other, but I could tell that they hated women and blamed them for everything.

It was amazing how quiet seven small children could be but there were times when the silence was broken, like if my brother farted and the rest of us burst into laughter. Then Dad would charge into the bedroom, yelling and screaming, grabbing kids, throwing us into walls and kicking anyone he could reach. His rage was enormous and our laughter turned into screams of pain and fear.

When we screamed, Mom would run into the room and he turned on her. We scrambled to the attic for safety as we heard Dad screaming, "You bitch. You fucking bitch! How dare you hide them?"

The screaming seemed to go on for hours, accompanied by the sounds of pots and pans hitting the wall. The mornings after, Mom would tell me that she'd called the police but when they came, they just rolled their eyes and whispered to Dad, "Women!" in a buddy kind of way and told him to "cool it" before leaving.

THOSE early years were marked by long periods of relative peace when Dad was away, and bursts of chaos upon his return. His presence always demanded attention. With each visit home, he became more violent as his drinking increased. Mom seemed to slip into the background the minute he walked in the door. He never treated her as anyone of consequence, ignoring her when she spoke and waving his hand in dismissal. We began walking on eggshells as soon as he got home, and for me, life became terrifying once again. His nighttime visits to my room resumed, along with his threats to kill me.

For some unknown reason, Dad particularly hated Mark, his only son. He never went after any of his other children with the constant viciousness with which he attacked Mark and, to the day Mark died, at 38, I was never able to understand it. It drove Dad nuts that Mark adored him. Mark mimicked every move that Dad made, sitting beside him on the sofa, crossing his legs when Dad did, slouching and then sitting up when Dad did. He constantly snapped at Mark. "Stop it! What's wrong with you?" Or, "Why are you so stupid? Get away from me." Sometimes his irritation became anger.

One hot, lazy morning when I was seven, I was in one of my hiding spots, squeezed between the dresser and the wall in the attic, trying to get away from the chaos. It was the only safe place to be that day. Outside the heat was sweltering and the earth was scorched dry. In the attic, Dad's rage was taking over. I crouched down even further as I saw him corner my brother just a few feet in front of me. He yanked his belt out of his pants, then screamed and hit Mark with increasing fury. Dad didn't slow down even when the belt hit the bare lightbulb overhead and smashed it.

Peeking out from my hiding place, I was unable to turn my eyes away, feeling each lash as if I were the one being hit. The pain burned inside me and I searched in vain for a way to cope with the violence. Eventually, the sound of Mom's screams reached Dad and he stopped, picking Mark up off the floor and putting him in the car for the drive to the hospital. He was four years old.

While they were gone, I tried to talk to Mom about it but she calmly told me she hated Mark because he looked so much like Dad. I was upset that I couldn't protect Mark. I wanted to wrap my arms around him and comfort him, but I couldn't. To do that would be to acknowledge what had happened. That was not allowed. Soon Mark's pain was too much on top of my own, and I had no option other than to disconnect from him, unaware of the hurt and isolation I was causing him by doing so.

Later that day, I was again crouched in my hiding spot as I listened to Dad, sitting downstairs at the kitchen table, ranting as he got drunker and drunker, cursing the world and everyone in it. I pressed my hands against my ears, trying to shut out the sound of his raging voice. Suddenly, an explosion of thunder drowned him out. I jumped up, anxious to hear the next blast. I was not disappointed. Menacing piles of thunderclouds had been rolling in for the last hour. *Cumulonimbus.* I had looked it up in the encyclopedia.

Scrambling from my safe spot, I bolted down the stairs and flew out the door, onto the front porch and into the yard. The wind howled as the clouds changed quickly from grey to black, rolling and blowing and billowing across the sky. I watched every bolt of lightning and counted the seconds between the flashes and the cracks of thunder to determine how far away the lightning was striking.

The rain started. Soon, huge drops splashed on my head. I held my face up to the downpour, arms spread wide above my head. Twirling happily, I laughed out loud as I spun around and around in circles, stopping only when, staggering like a drunk, I fell down on the wet grass. Everyone else had run for cover but I wanted to be in the middle of the storm, to feel the wind blowing against my body, the rain pouring down. Even as the rain turned to hail, I challenged myself to bear the icy, painful strikes, never wanting it to stop.

I marveled at the force of nature and the power of the storm — the wilder and louder the better. These storms confirmed to me that there was something bigger and stronger and more powerful than my father. For a few brief moments they took away that ugly, frightening feeling of powerlessness inside me. I was in awe and the joy inside me bubbled over.

Somehow, through it all, I knew that I would be okay. I knew in my heart that I was not evil, that I only had to wait it out until I was older. I knew in my heart that I would survive.

3

Skating on Bacon Fat

DAD CAME by his anger involuntarily; alcoholism ran in his family and his past was dark, full of neglect and violence. Dad's sisters were quite open about the sexual abuse they endured at the hands of their father and I suspect Dad wasn't exempt. The children weren't fed properly; they grabbed food when they could and often went hungry. No adult seemed to care. They went to school if and when they felt like it, as education didn't seem to be valued. Dad made it to grade four although, as an adult, his enormous intellect — not to be confused with the common sense he sorely lacked — and interest in what was going on in the world hid his lack of education. In those days, teachers and neighbors never pried into "private family matters" and there was no protection for children. His past was a dark vortex that he was seldom able to rise above, although he declared regularly that he would quit drinking and smoking. I wonder if he hated himself each time he failed.

One beautiful summer afternoon, Grandpa visited. I'm not sure why because Grandma wasn't with him and Dad was away. Dad's parents were overbearing and nasty to Mom and she found it hard to stand up to them because Dad usually took their side. But she politely chatted with Grandpa while she cleaned up after lunch and Grandpa sat at the table with his coffee. After about an hour, he told Mom he was going to the bathroom, but when he didn't come back, Mom decided to look for him. He was nowhere in sight. Neither was one of my sisters. Going from room to room, she found them in my brother's room. Grandpa's pants were undone and his hands were on my sister, who was crying. Mom went nuts, screaming at him to get out, that she was calling the police. She chased him as he struggled to zip up his pants and run to his car. Then she phoned the police. Grandpa and Grandma lived on a farm two-and-a-half hours away and the police told Mom they would go out there the next morning. When they arrived, they found him hanging by a rope in the barn. Mom bragged for years that she "murdered the old man."

Either Mom didn't know that Dad was doing many of the same things to me or she was unable to cope with what she knew. There was an unspoken rule of silence in our house, upholding the constant pretense that nothing was wrong and that our lives were normal. I tried to express the intense pain and fear I was feeling to Mom and my sisters, but I got shut down every time. They were angry with me for even trying to discuss it. They told me to shut up, that what I was saying wasn't true, that it had never happened—and then they walked away from me. This was even though they had seen the same things I had, even though they slept in the same room that I did. How could they not acknowledge it? I felt horribly alone in a house full of people.

ONE MORNING when I was nine years old, I woke up with a fever and red spots all over my face. Dismayed, Mom announced that I had chicken pox. She knew that very soon her six other children would also be sick. My fever raged on and I whimpered in my discomfort and itchiness. Dad picked me up and wrapped me in his rayon-lined coat. It felt cool to the touch and I fell asleep in his arms. My Dad had never held me before, or hugged me or comforted me, so this feeling was new and surprising. Maybe Dad didn't really hate me after all. Maybe he didn't really think I was evil. I loved my Dad.

But he didn't make loving him easy.

The next morning, Mom announced that she was going out for

a few hours. The minute she was out, Dad promptly went back to bed, ignoring the children he was supposed to take care of. Mom and Dad's bedroom was near the entrance to the kitchen and my sisters and brother were playing quietly near it. I was reading a book in one of my hiding spots. Most of us knew better than to make any noise when Dad was sleeping but our baby sister didn't. Cathy was less than a year old and, when her diaper got wet, she started crying loudly.

I ran downstairs and peeked into the kitchen when I heard the commotion. Dad's anger was obvious from the frown on his face as he came out of the bedroom and into the kitchen. He was furious when he realized what the crying was about. He yelled at her that it was time she quit diapers. Her crying reduced to whimpering as he roughly ripped off her wet diaper, put her in a pair of panties and ordered her not to wet them. Then he disappeared back to bed.

Of course, she wet herself again and her crying woke him up a second time and he charged angrily out of his bedroom. Cathy was crawling on the kitchen floor, a few feet from the wall, and Dad came up behind her and kicked her like a football. We heard the crack of her head hitting the wall as she screamed in shock and pain.

None of us dared comfort her — we were all too frozen with fear. We just stood there while she screamed. We had learned at an early age that there was a price to pay for trying to help each other — an increase in Dad's anger.

Dad laughed and told Cathy he hoped she'd learned her lesson. Then he retired to his bedroom and I retired to my hiding spot. I curled up in a ball on the floor and rocked back and forth for hours.

For years, Dad bragged that he had toilet-trained Cathy.

Each time Dad returned to the Arctic, relief poured through me. But my anger didn't leave with him. With no place for that anger to go, it got heaped onto the only safe place available: my mom. I had learned from my father's example that it was okay to be disrespectful to my mother.

One afternoon when I was about five, Mom told me to go

outside and play. "No!" I yelled at her angrily. "Don't tell me what to do."

Mom was furious. As she lurched toward me, arm stretched out to grab me, I easily escaped her grasp and ran around the kitchen table, laughing at her.

"Stop it," she ordered. "Stop now!"

My anger unleashed a sense of power in me. As she chased me around the table, I began screaming at the top of my lungs, as if I were being murdered.

She became distraught. "Stop. Please. Stop. The neighbors, what will the neighbors think?"

I didn't stop, not until she fell into a chair, head in her hands, and began weeping. Staring at her brokenness, I was horrified at what I'd done, at how mean-spirited I was being. My shame was visceral. I slunk off to my hiding place and cried.

Mom struggled to raise seven children, mostly on her own, with no family support nearby and very little money. She relied heavily on my older sister, Margaret, to take care of us and help around the house when she was overwhelmed, which was often. Margaret helped so much that she lost her childhood, always looking after the rest of us — putting Band-Aids on cuts, giving baths and getting us off to bed, taking us to the park and, when she was older, babysitting and giving the money to Mom to help feed us. She cleaned and cooked and worked just as hard as Mom did. For the rest of our lives, every one of us respected and were in awe of the sacrifices she made.

When Dad was away, we were unafraid to laugh and have fun. In hindsight, it's amazing to me how quickly, as children we bounced from fear and pain to fun and laughter.

Early one morning when I was five years old, while Mom was still sleeping, we found the jar full of bacon fat that she kept under the sink. The kitchen was the biggest room in the house, bigger even than the living room, and we learned that lard made the huge kitchen floor wonderfully slippery. If we spread it all over, we could easily slide back and forth on our bums. Our own little skating rink! We had races, each of us trying to be the fastest to slam into the wall on the far side of the kitchen. Mark won every time. We were having a blast.

Mom woke to the laughter of little kids sliding around on the greasy kitchen floor and to the sight of her children with bacon fat making our hair stick out in all directions. Our pyjamas were cemented to our bodies like glue. We didn't want to stop but she gingerly picked up each slippery child and put us into the bathtub two at a time, then began the arduous task of scrubbing the lard out of the floor. She didn't seem to be mad. She seemed to be trying not to laugh along with us which made us laugh even more.

MOM suffered from depression and talked constantly about suicide. She would often tell me, "It's your fault that I want to die. You ruined my life. You're a bad child, always causing trouble." I felt her intense hatred as if it were a sledgehammer, but I could never understand it.

"If it weren't for you, I could have left your father," she'd tell me. "I told him to get out many times but he would only go if he could take you. I told him 'No.'"

That confused me. Dad always said how much he hated me so why did he want to take me with him? And if Mom hated me so much, why didn't she let him?

Mom believed that life was a chore, something of no value and thus easily thrown away. In turn I felt that I was of no value to her. I have no memory of her ever hugging me and I wondered if she ever had any normal "mom" feelings for me, if she ever looked at me and liked what she saw. If so, she never told me.

One freezing winter day, when she was sick with a cold, Mom told me that she was going to stand outside in hopes of getting pneumonia and dying. Coughing heavily, she stepped outside the kitchen door, cigarette in hand, into the blowing wind and -30°

temperature, and closed the door behind her. I sat at the kitchen table feeling helpless and numb, wondering what I could change about myself so that my Mom wouldn't want to die. But I was unable to come up with an answer. How terrible a child must I be to make my mother want to die?

A week later, she did get pneumonia and eventually she called for an ambulance. As she was being taken out of the house, she whispered to me, "I want to die and it's your fault." I absorbed every bit of her vitriol as if it were gospel and believed it for the next forty years. As a child, I didn't understand that Mom wasn't really committing suicide by getting sick or she wouldn't have called for an ambulance. But I knew that, to some extent, her wish to die was real; I'd heard it too many times. As an adult, I still don't understand why she chose to blame me in particular for her problems, other than the fact that I had already been labelled a bad child by my Dad, and often by my sisters. And I wondered if, in the back of her mind, she knew what my Dad was doing to me at night and hated me for it.

I learned well from my mother and, as the years passed, death became ingrained in my psyche as a viable option for me to look at every time life became difficult. It would be many, many years before I was able to rid this idea from my mind and begin to understand that life is a valuable gift to be treasured.

Mom didn't get her wish to die. In between bouts of depression, she worked hard: scrubbing floors on her hands and knees, doing laundry with an old wringer washing machine and then hanging it outside to dry no matter the weather; cooking three meals a day and sewing late into the night and early morning. Her sister lived in a beautiful home in Vancouver and, every once in a while, she would send us a large package. We were excited as Mom cut it open, gathering in a circle to watch as she pulled out the contents. There were clothes my cousins had outgrown and we all scrambled to try them on, arguing over who got what. There were also old draperies that were just as exciting. We knew Mom could work magic with a sewing machine and, sure enough, she spent many hours over many days sewing matching dresses for us. They were beautiful and, though I joked about wearing my 'curtain', I was so proud of my new dress that I wanted to wear it all the time.

Mom also worked hard in the yard and we were all enlisted to help clear a patch for a garden. I hated having to pull the tall weeds because sometimes there were wasps in the grass and I got stung. Once it was all cleared, Mom planted early potatoes and carrots and peas. For weeks we hungrily watched for signs they were ready to eat until, finally, one warm evening, Mom and Margaret would go into the garden to get some new potatoes. Mom fried them in lard and we sat around the kitchen table in excited anticipation. When they were finally ready, perfectly browned, crisp on the outside and soft on the inside, Mom sat down with us and we began to eat. She informed us how lucky we were, pronouncing our meal "fit for a king." We all felt the solemnity of the occasion as we devoured their deliciousness. We were indeed royalty.

4

"I'm Not Green!"

I WAS about six years old when, one evening after an absence of several months, Dad suddenly burst through the door, angry and upset, announcing he was no longer in the Air Force. Mom whispered to me later that he'd been so drunk he'd left a wooden block in the wheel well of an aircraft and the plane nearly crashed on take-off. He was immediately discharged from the military. Mom cooked his favorite food in an attempt to calm him down, then got us all into our pyjamas and told us to go to bed. Later, I heard pots being thrown and Mom begging him to stop. As I crept partway down the stairs, I heard her pleas on the phone to the police and her anger at being told they were too busy to come. The next morning, it was as if nothing had happened.

Just because he was unemployed didn't mean that Dad would stay home much. We didn't know what he was up to until Mom started getting phone calls from women desperately trying to reach him. Apparently, he was giving ballroom dance lessons at a local studio and preying on lonely, vulnerable women who were recently widowed — life insurance beneficiaries and inheritance recipients. He showered them with attention while stealing their life savings. Some of them called the police. When it came to pressing fraud charges, the police didn't mind showing up at the door regularly.

Gone for months at a time, Dad took off on drunken binges, living with other women and bouncing from place to place, sometimes spending nights in the drunk tank. We never knew if or when he was coming home. Hunger became an even more familiar companion.

Mom refused to go on welfare, explaining that it offended her sense of dignity — so when there was no money coming in, we just went hungry. I felt like telling her that it offended my sense of dignity that her dignity was more important than our empty stomachs. But I never did. I didn't find out until years later that she had applied for welfare but was refused because Dad was still around and sometimes worked, although he never gave Mom much money. I was constantly thinking about food, hungry for fruits and vegetables and even milk. Mom used to buy skim milk powder and mix it with water but sometimes we didn't even have that.

One day, I was looking for food, anything at all that would ease my hunger, and I opened the refrigerator door. Lo and behold, there was half a glass of milk. Mom was sitting nearby with her back to me, visiting with Mrs. Wells, a neighbor, and I decided to sneak the milk. I took a sip and nearly threw up. It was sour and lumpy. I went running to the bathroom to spit it out while Mom sat there laughing at me. "Why do you think you deserve milk when no one else has any?" she asked. She had known what I was doing and decided not to warn me that the milk was sour to teach me a lesson about being greedy. Lesson partly learned.

Another time, my father returned from a trip to the Okanagan, western Canada's fruit country, with a large box of fresh cherries. Mom and Dad said we could have as many as we wanted and my siblings and I were beside ourselves with excitement. Fresh fruit! As much as we wanted! We all pigged out while Mom and Dad said not a word to us. Later, when we were all running for the toilet with diarrhea, they sat there laughing, telling us we deserved to be sick because of our greed. Lesson learned.

IN SPITE of the chaos in our house, Mom and Dad felt that school was important and expected us to bring home good grades. Most detailed memories of my school years are missing, such as who my teachers and classmates were, but I remember one particular teacher. Mr. Cooper, my grade four teacher, was unusual among my teachers because of his mean-spiritedness. He constantly asked me, "Are you an Indian?" in a derogatory, sneering way. He wasn't the first to ask me that but he was the nastiest. I always said, "No," but he kept asking.

One day, I was sitting in the front row of Mr. Cooper's class. My desk was much too large for me so my legs dangled off the chair and my arms barely reached the table. Mr. Cooper told the class that we were going to study animals, specifically monkeys, and he pointed at me and said, "Get up and show the class how a monkey acts."

"I am not a monkey," I replied, sitting stiff as a board. My classmates were laughing as I sat there, humiliated and afraid.

"I told you to get up and show the class how a monkey acts! Crawl under your desk like a monkey would. Make the sounds a monkey makes." Then, when I didn't move, "If you do not do what you are told, you have to go home."

I stood up with all the dignity I could muster, silently picked up my books and pencils and walked out the door. I didn't stop until I arrived home. Mom eyed me suspiciously as I walked in and I flew into a panic about how much trouble I was going to be in. I explained what had happened, expecting her to be furious, but she was oddly calm. She promised she would walk me back to school after lunch.

"No, you are not a monkey," she said. "You did the right thing to come home." I think she was shocked that I, so afraid of my own shadow, had stood up to my teacher the way I did.

When we got to school, she took me right to the principal's office. I sat in a chair outside the room while Mom talked with him. When she came out, she told me it would be okay now and then headed home. The principal took me to my classroom and asked to speak to the teacher in the hallway while I got seated. When the teacher came back in, he apologized to me in front of the class for calling me an Indian. He never did it again.

I was confused on many levels. What was wrong with being an Indian? No one ever explained that to me. And why did Mom protect me? Was it okay for my family to say awful things to me but not for strangers to do so? Why did she defend me at school but not at home? She told me constantly how much she disliked me, but why was it not okay for others to agree with her? None of it made any sense to me.

That evening, I asked Mom why people asked me if I was Indian. "It's because you have olive skin tone."

"I'm not green!" I yelped and stomped out of the room, insulted. I could hear Mom's laughter as I climbed the stairs to the attic and crawled into my hiding spot, picking up one of my books. I loved reading and especially liked getting to take books home from the school library. Nancy Drew and the Hardy Boys stories and books about other people who lived in different countries and times fascinated me. History and memoirs and novels transported me from my hiding place to their worlds. I pretended I was the hero or the detective or the princess. The reality of my world was left behind and I was happy as my mind traipsed through the lives of others. Books were my saving grace.

I was seven when I made a friend at school. JoAnn was cool and she liked me in spite of the fact that I was not. We giggled constantly, finding the same things funny. Her mom, Ann, was kind and thoughtful, and I instantly loved her. She wrapped her arms around me in a big hug every time she saw me and I just knew that she loved me too — even though deep down inside there was not a doubt in my mind that it wasn't possible for her to really love me, because I was totally unlovable. But Ann and JoAnn didn't know that because I never let them know who I was on the inside; I knew they could only love me if they didn't know me. But I was desperate for "mothering" so I latched on tight to what Ann offered me.

JoAnn's house was a few blocks from ours. She had her own bedroom filled with dolls and toys and we spent hours playing. On Saturdays, Ann sent us to the movies with money for popcorn and soda while she caught up on errands. What luxuries! I thought I was in heaven. Lots of times, I spent the night. I was fed, loved and, best of all, able to go to sleep without fear.

But the pain inside me had created a rigidity, a vacant, hollow emptiness and a fear of feeling pain—my own or anyone else's. It left me unable to have any real, deep feelings for others.

As Mom sank deeper and deeper into depression, she talked more often about suicide and warned us not to make the same mistakes in life that she had made. She told us over and over again never to repeat her situation with a violent husband and too many children. She believed that a woman needed to be married but she told me never to have children and never to trust any man. She offered advice about not sharing a bank account with a man and about how to be independent so that it would be easy to leave any situation that became unbearable.

Unfortunately, her advice was so tinged with bitterness and anger that I tuned it out. Mom believed that all men were scum but, if a woman looked good, then she could have some control of the scum. Appearance was everything and, having told me for as long as I could remember that I was ugly, she despaired about my future, sincerely asking me, "Why do you have to look so ugly? No man is ever going to want you." How does a child explain her ugliness to her own mother?

So my love for JoAnn and Ann was quite superficial, although it was the best I could offer at the time because I had no familiarity with what love really looked like. Ann never shared her feelings, never told me she cared for me, although her actions spoke volumes. JoAnn sometimes, occasionally, shared with me when she was upset. But I instantly tuned her out. It wasn't that I didn't care; it was that I was terrified I would be expected to empathize — more than I was capable of — and thus lose her friendship. It would be many years before I stopped running from other people's pain the minute they shared it. But, at the time, I thought this was normal and had no understanding of it.

Ann would ask me why my parents never called to check up on

me. I knew why but I didn't tell her. I didn't want her to know that they didn't care where I was or if I was okay. I was afraid that if she knew what they thought of me, she wouldn't let her daughter play with me. It was a big secret for a seven-year-old to keep.

Thus began a split within myself. I was two people: the happy, laughing girl I pretended to be when I was away from home and the bad girl that my family told me I was. As much as I wanted the pretend girl to be real, I knew that she wasn't. So firmly affixed were my family's definitions of me that I knew the bad girl was the real one. It was confusing, but I no longer knew what else to believe.

Often when I returned home from JoAnn's house, the chaos and clutter would send me running to one of my hiding spots with a book. Sometimes Mom was angry, calling me princess or brat or saying things like, "You little bitch! You think you're special just because you get to go to the movies." My sisters would perfectly mimic her words and tone of voice. Most of the time, however, no one said anything to me, not even hello. I was invisible, less than a shadow.

When I was twelve, reality crashed in on me when Ann re-married and she and JoAnn moved to a farm a couple of hours away. I was devastated and couldn't stop sobbing. Even though they invited me to visit them often, I felt abandoned and angry and hurt. The feelings of rejection overwhelmed me. I missed them and cried my eyes out for months. How could the only people who really loved me move so far away? The fragile bit of trust I had in the world being a safe place evaporated. It was a painful shock that took years to heal from and I never really regained my sense of trust.

It was a lesson that affirmed for me that no one could ever be trusted and that was just the way life was. I felt stupid for ever having trusted anyone that way in the first place. How could I have been so dumb? So I pushed the pain to the back of my consciousness, compartmentalizing it as I did all the other pain, blocking any awareness that it had ever happened. All was forgiven and forgotten.

Then JoAnn invited me to come over for a long summer visit.

I was bouncing with excitement as I sat, along with JoAnn, in the backseat of her new dad's car. As we got closer to their farm, I was astonished to see fields of tall, bright yellow flowers swaying in the wind. There was nothing but yellow as far as the eye could see and it was the most beautiful sight I'd ever seen. Howard, JoAnn's new dad, proudly explained to me that they were canola flowers and that canola was a new, modified version of rapeseed that created a healthier cooking oil than any that had ever existed before. It was all new science and canola was just getting started in world markets. Howard said that it would be hugely successful, a prescient prediction in 1965.

The farm was exciting, with lots of old, empty buildings to explore and machinery to climb on. The only animals were cats that lived in the barn and JoAnn and I spent lots of time with the new kittens that had just been born. We had fun and were constantly giggling and laughing, sometimes until our stomachs hurt. Everything was hilarious to those young girls.

As I got to know Howard, I began to love him. He was a big, affectionate teddy bear who hugged me a lot and told me what a good girl I was. He was the first man I felt entirely safe with and he always made me feel welcome. For many years to come, I would visit them on the farm, once every few years, even long after JoAnn had moved away. I loved them and they were always happy to see me. In hindsight, I wish I'd visited more often. But, at the time, I was so desensitized by trauma that I was a shell, unable to reach inside myself, unable to do more than survive.

As an adult, I would see a young person on TV who had done something horrible, like murder or rape, and hear people wondering how a child could do something like that. I knew exactly how a child could do terrible things. I knew the numbness and separation from reality that caused that lack of humanity. I never did anything terrible like that, but I could have because I had no sense of belonging to the world, no sense of other people's pain, no feeling of being alive inside. My life was an act, a pretense.

I'd never appreciated the deep love my friend's family offered me, unable to believe anyone could really love me in more than a superficial way. It turned out that I was the one who loved in only a superficial way. It would take many years before I realized that they weren't just pretending to care, before I finally understood how much each visit meant to them and that their love was real and that I did matter to them. I would eventually feel sorrow for taking so long to understand what an enormous gift their love had been in my life.

5

I Will Survive

CHRISTMASES were interesting in our house. Mom did her best to get each of us gifts. She worked hard baking and cleaning for the big day and she made sure we always had a Christmas tree. Every year, as the big day approached, the tension in our house rose anticipating whether Dad would show up. When he didn't, we all started to relax. But unfortunately, after having been away for months, he would usually burst through the door on Christmas Eve. He was proud of the fact that he came home for his family but he didn't seem to understand that the "good dad" impression was negated by spending the previous months running around with other women and not sending any money home to feed and clothe his family. When he walked in the door each Christmas Eve, Mom looked crestfallen and whispered to me, "Oh no, your Dad's home." He tried to stay sober so that he wouldn't destroy our Christmas and sometimes he succeeded. But often the situation descended into drunken rages and violence.

Even as a kid, I believed he tried his best even when things descended into chaos. Every kid wants a parent that at least tries to be a good parent and I craved "normal," without even knowing what normal was. On these rare occasions, he seemed to be trying to make things normal.

One spring, when I was twelve, the Salvation Army people came to the house to ask Mom about giving me singing lessons. She was genuinely puzzled. "Why would they choose you when they have all the other kids in this house to choose from? Why you?" I never found out why they chose me but I later suspected that one of my teachers at school knew a battered child when she saw one and asked the Salvation Army to reach out to me.

At any rate, off I went to have my voice tested. I sang along to the piano notes and it took about two minutes before they decided to pack it up and take me home. "She's tone deaf," they informed Mom, "so there will be no singing lessons."

Tone deaf? I thought I could sing just fine, thank you very much.

Two months later they were back, wanting to take me to the YWCA summer camp at Sylvan Lake, Alberta. "Why her?," Mom asked. "There are other kids in this house, you know. And who's going to pay for this? And how is she going to get there?"

"We'll take care of the bill and we'll drive her back and forth," they offered.

Mom grudgingly agreed to let me go but, for the next few weeks she told me repeatedly, "You don't deserve this, you know. Margaret deserves this more than you do. You don't deserve something this nice."

All I could say was, "I know, Mom. I know I don't deserve it but I'm the one they invited."

I never did understand why they chose me over any of my siblings and I knew that it hardened their resentment toward me. But I was not one to look a gift horse in the mouth. This was to become a pattern that repeated frequently in my life: receiving unexpected gifts, usually when my world seemed so dark that I wondered if I'd survive. So I learned to welcome these surprises without question.

On arrival, I was so excited I could hardly stand it. The huge lake, a shimmering emerald green, and the surrounding forest were the most beautiful I'd ever seen. A log cabin with my very own bed was home for the next several days. I chose the top bunk, feeling safe and secure as I imagined myself sleeping close to the stars. We canoed and swam and played games; we sang songs around the campfire while we roasted marshmallows. Sometimes we slept out under the stars. There was laughter, giggling and plenty to eat, and I got lots of hugs from the counsellors because I tagged along behind them. This was a whole new world. For over a week, I was just the same as every other girl there.

At the end of camp, the Salvation Army people showed up to drive me home. They had the patience of saints as they listened to me regale them with tales of adventure and fun during the hour-and-a-half drive. I was still busy talking when we pulled up to my house... only to realize that it was no longer my house.

The front door was locked. We peeked in the windows and saw that it was empty. My family had moved while I was away, without telling me or the Salvation Army.

There was a bit of panic. Calls were made and the police arrived. They tracked down my family and drove me to where they now lived. When I walked in the door, they acted as if nothing had happened, as if I hadn't been gone. No one said a word to me. I found out later that Dad had returned home from one of his long absences and decided he didn't like where we were living. He had immediately moved everyone to a house on the other side of town.

It wasn't the last time my parents would ditch me.

DUE TO the move, I started in a new school in the fall. Some of the girls in my class invited me to go to church with them. They were Mormon and went every Sunday. I wasn't sure why they invited me but I was happy to be asked to go anywhere so I joined them. I was astonished at what I saw. I'd always thought that Ann's hugs and kindness were an aberration but here were parents hugging their kids, being kind and gentle with them, and families laughing together. I couldn't believe my eyes. The love was obvious. I hadn't known there were families like that. I watched the small children running around, hurling themselves at their parents, knowing that they would be safely caught in their arms. Not one of them huddled in a corner in fear, trying to shrink into invisibility. Sometimes my friends' parents even hugged me. I couldn't remember ever being hugged by my parents, other than when I had the chickenpox.

And so, I decided I wanted to be a Mormon. I didn't really understand what it meant but I liked the idea of being part of this group. I asked the Mormon elders if I could be baptized and they told me they needed to talk to my parents. "That won't be a problem," I said. "They don't care what I do."

Wrong! Dad went nuts on them, saying they were brainwashing me. But he let them in the house, seemingly convinced that he could convert them out of their Mormonism. The two missionaries came by frequently to discuss it, sitting in their black suits with white shirts and black name tags, on the sofa across from my Dad, refusing the coffee Mom offered them every time. Dad put up quite an argument but eventually, gave up and let me be baptized. I took it very seriously and was so happy to belong to a group of families so loving that they seemed like angels to me.

When I was fifteen, I met a boy at church that I liked. Michael was kind and interesting and fun. We hung out a bit, not actually dating, but spending time together with other kids from church, watching movies on TV, listening to music, stealing kisses when no one was looking. I had no memory of my father's touch and so no hesitation about Michael's kisses, which were gentle and caring.

After one such evening, Michael drove me home. I didn't want to go inside, and I didn't want to be seen in the car, so I lay down on the seat and put my head on Michael's leg while we continued talking. Suddenly, Dad's voice filled the air. I sat up, afraid that Dad was coming to yank me out of the car. But he wasn't. He was saying goodbye to a friend who'd been visiting. I had no idea until years later what it must have looked like to see my head pop up from Michael's lap.

The rage on Dad's face said it all. Terrified, I froze. Now I really didn't want to go into the house. After his friend was gone, Dad stood on the front steps and began yelling. His screams echoed through the neighborhood: "You slut! You goddam whore! You get inside NOW!" I ran inside, tense with fear, barely saying goodbye to Michael. Dad kept me cornered in the kitchen, yelling until he was hoarse. As soon as it was safe, I escaped to the room I shared with Margaret in the basement, too afraid to sleep, wondering if this was the night he would follow through on his threats to kill me.

The next morning at school, Michael told me he was sorry but he needed to break up with me. He couldn't stand the way my Dad treated me. My shame overwhelmed me and I was heartbroken. Michael had made me feel safe and I sobbed uncontrollably for days. I missed his gentleness and thoughtfulness. In my depression, I hid as far away as possible from everyone else. When I ran into him at school a few weeks later, he told me that he'd met someone else, someone who "isn't as nice as you but has bigger breasts and, after all, I'm only sixteen so I can't help myself."

It was my first glimpse into the mind of a sixteen-year-old boy and I wasn't impressed. But it made me laugh too. My sisters had teased me for years about my flat chest, telling me not to "make mountains out of molehills" and offering Band-Aids to use as a bra.

IT TURNED out that the man visiting Dad that night was from Alcoholics Anonymous. Dad had decided to sober up! We all rejoiced, thinking life would get better.

It didn't. It got worse — for me, at least.

Dad quit drinking but he was more arrogant than ever, telling us that he didn't need to follow the AA steps. He struggled to stay sober, each evening becoming edgier and more miserable; we wondered if that would be the night he would reach for the bottle. He stopped visiting my room at night but his hatred for me increased and he lashed out more often, slapping me on the head or shoving me into walls, yelling at me and telling me that I was evil. It was one thing to be hated by a drunk; it was a totally different thing to be hated by someone completely sober who knew exactly what he was doing. I could no longer blame the alcohol instead of my father himself for the abuse. Realizing that his hatred was real, and perhaps justified in some way that I didn't understand, made me more terrified than ever. I just couldn't figure out the 'why' of it all and I had no clue that perhaps his guilt was the reason for the hatred. That understanding was a long way off.

The nightmares became more frequent and more violent. Night after night I ran from my father, sweating, my heart pounding, never able to escape. He caught me and slammed my head into the wall, knocking me out before choking me to death in a rage, screaming at me that I made him do it. But sometimes I was the aggressor. These dreams always started the same way: I was Superman, flying alone at night in the peaceful, starlit sky, calm and safe. Then I spotted my father walking along an empty street. He looked up at me and laughed, that same laugh he had when he was hurting me. Calmness turned into rage and I swooped down to attack him, punching him, stabbing him, cutting him into pieces, stomping his body into the ground so that he could never, ever get up again. I was powerful and in control. Relieved that he was dead, I flew off, regaining my sense of calm and admiring the stars and the lights of the city below. But then I looked down and again saw my father walking along, looking up at me and laughing. It never ended. I kept killing him and he kept reappearing as soon as I felt safe again. The vividness of the nightmare never left me.

When I was invited to hang out one evening with a girl from school, I went to her house after supper, knowing that I had a curfew. Diane's parents were nice and said hello as we headed to her room to do homework together. We talked about everything under the sun, laughing and joking as we worked on our math problems and history lessons, and I forgot the time. When Diane's mom came into her room to say it was getting late, I panicked. I ran all the way home, huddled in my parka against the cold, slipping on the snow and ice, and walked in the door about twenty minutes late. There were no lights on as I tiptoed in. I thought I was safe, until Dad's voice cut through the silence.

"You are a whore and I'm going to kill you. You are destroying this family and I'm not going to let that happen. I have warned you for the last time. Now I have to kill you."

He'd been sitting in the dark kitchen on a chair up against the wall, full of quiet rage, waiting for me. With icy calmness, he stood up and leaned over me, cornering me. In the past, Dad had always been drunk when he threatened my life but this time he was sober. He was truly out of control and, for the first time ever, I knew he was serious. I ran to bed in a panic, not knowing what to do, unable to sleep at all. Terror seeped into every part of my body, stiffening every muscle, making my heart pound. I was alert to every sound, jumping every time the furnace came on or the house creaked.

The next morning, exhausted and afraid, I sat hunched over the old grey Formica kitchen table, eating a breakfast of oatmeal and brown sugar with my sisters and brother, when Dad quickly walked up behind me and screamed at me, "You stupid whore!" He grabbed a handful of my hair and slammed my head into the table. The corner of the table nearly took my eye out. Stunned by the suddenness of the attack, I ran out the door as fast I could to the safety of school.

Once there, I didn't go to class; I was too embarrassed to be seen. I cowered in the corner of the girls' bathroom, crying, scared and confused. What was I doing wrong? I couldn't understand the rage that was directed at me. I just couldn't make sense of it.

The school counsellor, Mrs. Brown, came into the bathroom looking for me. I was unaware of how badly bruised I was, of how my eye and the right side of my face had started to turn purple. She gently took my arm and led me to her office. She'd asked me before about the bruises but I'd always lied and said I fell down the stairs or bumped into something. Dad had always told me, "If you tell, no one will believe you." Now I was scared to death but I knew I had to tell the truth. My fear of anyone knowing how bad I was and how I was punished for it was overwhelmed by my fear for my life. So it all poured out of me.

Mrs. Brown listened, then told me there was someone I needed to talk to about the violence. She made a phone call, then gave me a bus ticket and directions and sent me off.

Nervously sitting near the bus driver, I watched for the building I'd been told to go to. The driver told me where to get off and I approached the offices of Social Services, slowly climbing the stairs from the street as if I were going to my execution. A receptionist took me to a Mrs. Williams' office, where I was asked many questions. I was afraid to tell the social worker my story but more afraid not to.

I told her everything, except for the sexual abuse. That was just a blank spot in my mind, a horror too ugly to face. I wouldn't have known how to survive if those memories had poked their ugliness through my consciousness. I felt as if I was barely surviving as it was, that I was as small as a mouse in a big world.

And now I was setting in motion something I had no understanding of. But, in spite of my fear, I felt that I was doing the right thing. I wanted to be protected but I also wanted my brother and sisters protected. I couldn't bear the thought that some of the things Dad did to me might also be done to them. I wanted Mrs. Williams to help us all. All the memories just poured out of me, all the things I wasn't allowed to talk about at home. I talked for a long time and she made a lot of notes before saying, "You need to go home now. I'll call your Dad and tell him not to touch you. It'll be safe for you now."

"My Dad won't listen to you. He doesn't listen to anyone. He'll kill me," I sobbed. But she insisted. I got back on the bus to school and went to see Mrs. Brown who reassured me over and over that I would be okay. I had no choice but to go home.

As I walked in the door, the phone rang and Dad answered. When he hung up, he turned to me and said, "What have you done?"

I scurried down to the basement, hiding for the rest of the day. When nighttime arrived, I was too afraid to sleep. I sat up in bed, knowing that the door would open at any moment and I would have to pay a horrible price, perhaps the ultimate price, for telling. Every sound spooked me and every movement snapped me to attention. I was terrified. But the door never opened and, the next morning, it was as if nothing had happened. Mom cooked breakfast as usual and no one but me seemed to know what was happening in our midst.

When I arrived at school that morning, Mrs. Brown met me at the entrance and took me into her office, telling me to sit beside her. Sitting in chairs that had been arranged in a half-circle in the small office were a police officer and Mrs. Williams, the social worker. Just then Dad walked in, taking a seat across from the police officer. When I saw him, I trembled and my heart pounded.

The police officer explained to Dad that it was illegal to hit me in the face, or to kick me or throw me into the wall. Dad was defensive. "She's lying. She is a bad child. I've been trying for years to break her but she's a bad child and she's destroying my family," Dad said, hitting the arm of his chair for emphasis.

"Why do you think she's a bad child?" the police officer asked.

"She just is."

"What does she do that's bad?" Mrs. Williams asked Dad.

"She's just bad, through and through. I'm a good father and I'm trying to control her but she's a bad child. She's lying. She belongs in reform school."

I will never forget the moment when the police officer pointed at my bruised face and said, "She's not lying. Look at her."

I was stunned. Dad said no one would believe me, but they did. They believed me. Then Mrs. Williams spoke up. "She will be removed from the home and you and her mother will be charged with criminal child abuse."

It was Dad's turn to be stunned.

Mrs. Williams and I met again a few days later. She told me that she was having trouble finding me a home to go to so I asked her if I could live with one of the Mormon families. And suddenly one of the families had Social Services knocking on their door, asking if they would take me in. They didn't really want me but, after great hesitation and a lot of discussion, they accepted me.

Their home was heaven — quiet and chaos free. They hugged

each other all the time. If someone was crying, both the mom and dad were there to listen and try to help. Sometimes the sisters fought, but only with words and not to the death, like in our house where one sister had been known to take after another with a butcher knife.

I was safe. I got a break. I was the luckiest person in the world. I was fifteen years old and I knew now, for the first time in a long time, that I would survive.

6

The Age of Aquarius

AT FIRST, I rarely opened my mouth. My new Mormon "parents" never yelled at each other but any time a voice was raised even a little, I disappeared into hiding. When I wasn't scared, I was clingy, wanting to be close to them, as if some of their normalness could rub off on me. They weren't registered foster parents and had no training in living with a foster child so they had no idea what was going on with me. My actions must have driven them crazy. I was nervous because I didn't know how to act in a normal family and I never knew when I should step up or what I should do to help out. I didn't know how to cook or clean, or even about personal hygiene. I felt like I'd been raised in a cave.

They told me I had to get good grades or I would be given back to Social Services so I worked extra hard on my homework. The threat of being told to leave was constant and I gradually became aware that my attempts to ingratiate myself weren't working. In fact, they were having the opposite effect. The family seemed to be irritated by my every action. I didn't blame them. My own family had been irritated by everything about me as well.

I continued in the same school as before and sometimes ran into my sister Margaret, who was furious with me. "Dad will probably start drinking again, thanks to you," she told me. "You've ruined everything for the rest of us."

After that encounter, each time she saw me she walked right by as if she didn't know me. I suspected that the upheaval frightened my siblings as much as it did me. Another sister told me years later that Dad had told them he'd thrown me out on the street and they'd better behave or the same thing would happen to them. He told them I was cold and hungry and alone, with no place to go. Sheer terrorizing seemed to be the only form of discipline he knew.

In spite of my efforts, after about a year my new family told my social worker that I had to leave. They couldn't afford to keep me. Mrs. Williams told me she was sending me back to my parents. She had nowhere else to place me. Panic overwhelmed me.

"My Dad will kill me," I cried. "You can't send me back there. He'll kill me."

"Both your parents were supervised while you were gone and they're still being supervised. Your dad has been ordered to buy food for the family and not to touch any of you. You'll be okay. I promise."

I didn't believe a word she said. I knew that Dad had been fighting long and hard against the criminal charges and was threatening to sue everyone involved. When the charges were eventually dropped, I was heartbroken. Dad was so powerful that he could even get out of criminal charges! I asked Mrs. Williams why things had turned out this way and she said the lawyers and judges didn't like to have kids testify in court. Her answer made no sense to me.

I was crushed. The pain of my new family's rejection and the fear of being sent back to my parents were as sharp as a knife cutting into my soul. I felt raw and vulnerable, torn into little pieces. Why was this happening? I knew I wouldn't survive. I knew the hatred I was going to face again, day after day. If the Mormons abandoned me, it must mean that even God had abandoned me. I must be the worst of the worst for God to abandon me. All hope was gone.

It wasn't that I believed I was worthless; I knew I was worthless. I knew that any kind word or compliment that ever came my way was only because that person didn't know me. A compliment was proof that my pretenses were working, not that I was likable or lovable or good. I knew that. Any nastiness that came my way was only more proof of my worthlessness, proof that I'd been seen for who I truly was. I no longer questioned negative comments in any way, whether they came from family or strangers. So, terrified, I went home.

Some things had changed. There was food on the table. Dad's anger seemed muffled. He kept his distance, as did Mom and my siblings. No one spoke much. The next year went by in a haze. I felt useless and irrelevant, with just a dark void inside me. I dragged myself through school, full of rage and bitterness, jealous of those who seemed normal and furious with the world in general.

AT SEVENTEEN, for the first time in my life, I got drunk. One of the girls at school had issued an open invitation to a party at her house and I decided to go. Arriving with a cheap bottle of sparkling pink wine, I sat in a corner watching the party swirl around me and drank until I got sick. I wanted to numb the pain but all it did was increase the anger about the pain. The next morning when I'd sobered up, I decided to be tough — to have no compassion for anyone, no sympathy. If I could survive what I'd been through, then others could survive their stuff on their own. The shell around me became so thick that nothing could penetrate. I ran away from people who wanted to be friends or to date me. I knew that I didn't deserve to be treated well and was afraid of others knowing that.

Even so, I tried telling myself I was fine. I compartmentalized everything that had happened to me. Every shameful event got locked away in its own space in my mind and those events were somehow separate from my day-to-day life. But this approach left me without any real perspective on my life, no understanding of the whole picture. And still I subconsciously blamed myself for everything. How could it not be my fault? I couldn't bear to look inside myself. What if my family was right? What if I was really, really bad?

Because I didn't know who or what I really was, I let everyone else define me. My mood depended on every other person I encountered. Everyone else was better than me. I constantly looked for someone to emulate, to demonstrate the life and social skills I didn't have. Any small compliment sent me over the moon (even though I didn't really believe it) and any slight frown in my direction had me depressed for days. That sense of worthlessness and invisibility was a constant companion, one that I was so used to that I barely recognized it was there. There was no peace in my heart, only turmoil. I put one foot in front of the other and dragged myself through my last years of high school, full of anger and bitterness, exhausted from pretending to be normal and trying to fit in with everyone else. Always afraid, always pretending.

Graduation day arrived along with an order from my parents: "Get out."

I was seventeen years old, robotic, living but not alive, pretending the best I could to be normal and fit in. I had subconsciously blocked out the darkness of my past and started my new life with a superficiality that I wasn't even aware of. I thought everyone lived in survival mode.

I began my job search immediately, suddenly needing to pay for rent and food. Canada had a severe labor shortage in the early 1970s and, within days, the Royal Canadian Mounted Police, Canada's federal police force, hired me to work in their Alberta headquarters as a stenographer. I enjoyed my job, which involved typing and bookkeeping. It was in the days before computers but we were supplied with the latest technology: electric typewriters, a rarity in any government office at that time. The office I was in had three other civilian workers who did the same type of work I did, typing letters and doing some accounting work. Our desks were gunmetal grey and our chairs were designed long before anyone knew what 'ergonomically correct' meant. We were each in our own corner of the room, facing each other. The people I worked with seemed nice but I was so afraid. What if no one liked me? What if they recognized how bad I was? I was cautious with each person I met, smiling at everyone but not really letting anyone in.

With my first paycheck, I went apartment hunting. Finding

a small, one-bedroom basement suite, I slept on blankets on the floor until I could afford furniture, slowly accumulating kitchen stuff and towels each time I got paid. I filled the cupboards with canned food and macaroni, vowing never to be hungry again, at least not the kind of hungry where you can't focus on anything else. I was unaware of how deep this fear went inside me — and that it would be decades before I was able to stop buying more food every time I was upset about something.

It was scary to be alone. I realized that I had no clue how to cook, clean, shop, handle money or take care of myself in the most basic ways. But I was optimistic about my new beginning. I kept rejoicing. *You're safe now,* I told myself. *You don't have to be hurt ever again.* I felt as if a huge weight was slowly being lifted off me.

Gradually I began to fit in and to feel safer with my colleagues. They all seemed kind and thoughtful and, as time went by, I lost some of my wariness and felt an unexpected ease with each of them, aware that they weren't going to attack me. It was a huge step for me to let a bit of my guard down.

Shortly after I started work, my boss called me into his office to discuss my security check. He gently told me of outstanding warrants against my Dad for fraud. Some of the women he had cheated were still pressing charges. My boss also told me that he had records from social services detailing the child abuse charges against my parents. It would not affect my job, he told me. He was only mentioning it because I was being given top security clearance and they wanted to make sure no one could blackmail me about my past.

I didn't like that others knew my awful secrets. Shame flooded through me. I was unaware then, of course, that this was only the first of many times throughout my life when my past would echo in the present.

Gradually, with a safe place to live and a secure job, I blossomed. It was 1971 and the Age of Aquarius had begun with its ideas about personal transformation, empowerment, and consciousness. There were self-help books and workshops everywhere. Despite the derision surrounding this lifestyle by an older generation who saw the concept of personal transformation as self-centered and radical, I devoured the information. I intensely disliked who I was and was constantly searching for ways to become a better person. Desperately wanting to leave my past behind, I read many books that talked about forgiveness, of others and oneself, as being the only way to stop being a victim and move on.

I also signed up for yoga classes and, although the nightmares still interrupted my sleep every night, the panic attacks began to ease, along with my anger and depression. Sometimes I was asked on dates, and occasionally I went on one. But my newly developing self-confidence was fragile. I tried hard to be normal and to fit in but I felt stiff and awkward and usually couldn't wait to get home.

Dating was confusing. I'd been sexualized at a very young age and left with the belief that my only purpose in life was to be used, that it was all I was good for and that I had no other value. But without any specific memories of the sexual abuse, I had no way of putting any of that in context or understanding normal sexual desires. I had no boundaries and no understanding that sex was meant to be part of a caring relationship, that it was an expression of love and closeness with another person. I thought of sex in an animalistic sort of way, as a normal bodily function, and I had no inhibitions, never feeling shy about being naked in the locker room at the pool or the gym. There'd been no sex education at school and I certainly wasn't given any information at home. When I got my period at seventeen, I hadn't even known what it was.

One day, when I was in grade eight, a classmate had confided in me how angry she was with her best friend for having sex with a boy she went out with once. "Why would she do that?" she ranted. "Good girls don't do that."

They don't? I didn't know that. It was the first I'd heard of boundaries and social stigma, or that I could say "No." I was really glad she told me.

A few months later, another girl in grade eight, fourteen-year-old Sandy, told me she was pregnant. When I got home, I told Mom. "Sandy's pregnant."

Mom was shocked. "Who is the father?"

I was indignant. "There is no father. She told me she never let a boy touch her."

"There has to be a father. Who is he?"

I was furious. "She's not like that. She said there's no father and I believe her." I stomped off to my room.

I'll never know why my mother didn't take that opportunity to enlighten me about sex but she didn't. She kept silent. And I stayed ignorant. Eventually, Sandy confessed to sleeping with her boyfriend and I forgave my mother for thinking badly of her.

Besides social stigma, there was one thing that kept me from being sexually active: I hated being touched. Kissing was okay but any other affection scared me. If a date went to put his arm across my shoulders, I jumped, thinking I was about to be hit. I hated holding hands, feeling like I was on a leash and couldn't run away if I needed to. My body language probably spoke loudly: Don't Touch Me. Once in a while, I'd date someone I really liked and would let my guard down a bit but, as soon as he got close, I'd push him away in fear.

Still, I wanted a relationship, someone I could be close to and confide in, someone I could be with forever, someone who would love me and never hurt me, someone who would protect me from the dark, dark world. I wanted the fairy tale to be real.

There was a police officer I worked with, Marty, who asked me out. I liked him and we started dating. He was nice and treated me respectfully and kindly, and I enjoyed our dates. Eventually, after a few months, I let the relationship go further and we spent the night together. I liked the sex but not the affection and discovered that I couldn't be open and honest with anyone, I couldn't get close in any emotional way. It was too scary. The relationship didn't stand a chance and gradually ended.

7

Forgiveness

AT NINETEEN, I decided I wanted to travel and I saved every penny from my paycheck that I could. Young people were traveling around Europe in droves and I wanted to do that too. It didn't cross my mind that few young people heading to Europe went alone, and I didn't recognize that part of the reason I wanted to go was because I was subconsciously running away from my dark past and from myself. It was the beginning of a lifelong pattern of temporarily escaping the reality of who I was. I would travel to other lands to pretend I was someone else, someone better than the real me, someone without the burden of pain and self-recrimination that I couldn't escape at home.

I remembered all the books I'd read from my attic hiding spot describing different parts of the world and the adventures that could be had there. I also recalled the discussions about faraway places that Mom and I had had as I was growing up. I wanted to see those places. I loved history and wanted to make it come alive by seeing museums and ruins and famous places.

I have no memory of telling anyone in my family my plans. I was feeling wonderfully free. I had no close adults in my life to offer wisdom or advice and no friends to confide in. Most of the time it was painful to have no one but now I suddenly understood how free I was; there were no limits on how high I could soar. I studied every piece of information I could find about where to go and how to stay safe. I trusted, naively, that my instincts, honed by years of knowing when to run into hiding and when it was safe to come out, would guide me.

My boss, on the other hand, was decidedly nervous about my plans. He poured out numerous warnings about staying safe, telling me about kidnappings and disappearances of young girls in Europe. I was also warned that the Cold War was in full swing and spies were supposedly everywhere. As someone with a top security clearance, I was given a list of places I was not allowed to visit. I could not, for example, go to any communist countries and was cautioned to be wary of anyone asking me about my work. But I knew this wouldn't be a problem; I took my security clearance and the oath of secrecy very seriously. I didn't even speak to RCMP officers or other staff about any confidential material entrusted to me.

Loaded with information, excited and nervous, I boarded a flight to London all by myself. It didn't occur to me that I was doing anything unusual or daring and, if I had any real fear at the time, I have no memory of it. Years later, I would be asked by several different people how I'd had the courage to do this trip at such a young age. Each time I thought, Really? Courage? I didn't understand risk the way that others might. Going to sleep each night as a small child took courage. Telling Social Services and the police about my parents took courage. Heading out into the scary world all alone at 17 to look for a job took courage. By comparison, traveling by myself didn't require courage.

I was immediately entranced by the flight attendants, so glamorous and sophisticated in their uniforms and makeup. I caught snippets of conversations about trips to London, Paris, Rome. They seemed to exist in another world, one I wanted to be a part of.

Stepping off the plane, I instantly fell in love with London. I was unaware that I was seeing it through a kind of fog, as if I were in a movie theatre and watching it on a screen. In retrospect I know that I was not immersed in the moment, as I maintained my usual distance from life. But even on that detached level, it was colorful and exciting, bursting with energy.

When I got off the train from the airport into the city, no doubt looking a bit lost, a guy about my age approached me and introduced himself. Peter was an American traveling with friends and told me of a small hotel that was cheap and clean. He walked me over to it and then told me of a group of travelers getting together that evening at a pub and invited me to join them. I did and had a good time. In the days to come, I often joined them on various explorations of the city.

It was easy to meet other young people and I felt no trepidation about joining them. In hindsight, I don't know if I was being brave or dumb, but it was the perfect adventure for someone who never went beyond the shallowness of superficial relationships. I loved the feeling of freedom from the past, as if I had been released from some invisible chains. There was a whole world out there, far beyond the small, dark world I'd been existing in, one that I could get lost in and be anyone I wanted to be. It was bright and glorious and welcoming. No one here knew anything about me and I was happy, without a care in the world. Secretly, I felt proud of being so adventurous.

At one point, Peter and I were walking along the street, chatting and relaxed, when he turned to me and looked into my eyes.

"I see such sadness in your eyes. Huge sadness," he said.

I was shocked and upset. Instantly, a wall went up. I'd thought I'd hidden my infinite aching loneliness. The relaxed feeling I'd had with him disappeared and I decided to spend less time with him. I'd liked him a lot. He was thoughtful and considerate, never asking me for anything I wasn't willing to give, leaving me with a chaste kiss at the end of each day. But I couldn't let him know more about me; it didn't feel safe.

It was easy to travel around Europe and I was well-prepared with lots of information I'd gathered before leaving home. From London, I flew to Paris. Museums, art galleries, shops, restaurants.... Sometimes I explored alone, sometimes with others I'd just met. I saw the Eiffel Tower and walked along the Champs-Elysées, the most beautiful avenue in Paris. I met Tomas, a Parisian who spoke seven languages, a handsome, thoughtful and intelligent person. We had wonderful conversations about the politics and economics of his part of the world as we walked through parks and shopping areas, laughing and joking. We had exotic, romantic dinners and he, the perfect gentleman, asked for nothing in return. He seemed to understand instinctively that pushing my boundaries would only make me turn and run.

In restaurants, Tomas ordered food that this Canadian prairie girl had never even heard of, like octopus, which I'd read about in the encyclopedia but didn't know that people actually ate. I didn't tell him that it tasted like rubber. One evening, as we enjoyed yet another wonderful meal, I noticed that the waiters were speaking a foreign language amongst themselves. As we were leaving the restaurant, Tomas said to them in Arabic, "Thank you for your good service." Their jaws dropped. Speaking in Arabic, Tomas was letting them know that he'd understood every word they'd been saying about the customers they'd just served. We laughed. Tomas made Paris so much more fun and informative than it would have been otherwise and I was sad to say goodbye.

I had a EuroRail pass and Munich, Germany was next on my list, as I boarded a train to travel through the majestic Swiss Alps. The mountain peaks were covered with snow and, in the valleys, we wove through thick forests of various shades of green. There were many small towns and villages off in the distance looking picture-book perfect.

Two American girls sat in the seats opposite me and they introduced themselves. Susan and Gail were students from the University of Massachusetts. We talked about their studies as I pushed down a twinge of envy at their higher education, and where they had travelled so far on their trip. After a short time, they asked me if I wanted to share a bed-and-breakfast room with them when we got to Munich.

"Yes!" I was happy for the company.

The timing of our arrival was perfect. It was Oktoberfest. We left our bags in our room and headed out to dance, party and develop a taste for German beer and bratwurst. We cut loose, dancing up a storm and meeting young people from all over the world. The next morning's hangover was well worth it.

AFTER two days spent exploring various tourist spots with Susan and Gail, I boarded a train to the Dachau concentration camp, ten miles northwest of Munich. Susan and Gail weren't interested in joining me, which I would later be grateful for, since I wanted to be alone as I absorbed the intensity of what I was seeing. All the reading I'd done about the Second World War had not prepared me for the reality of the death camp, for the profoundly dark energy that permeated the actual site. As we gathered at the gate, our guide informed us that we were about to walk the same path that the prisoners had walked as they'd entered the camp on their way to forced labor, torture or death. I shivered as I traced their steps. Horror hung in the air, still strong more than thirty years later.

The camp had originally been built on the site of an old munitions factory. Prisoners had been forced, under brutal conditions, to tear down the factory and construct the concentration camp they would live in. There were bunkers, showers, a kitchen and a laundry facility, as well as a crematorium with gas chamber and gallows. Thousands of prisoners were worked to death during the construction.

Many buildings had crumbled over time but there were enough remaining to make it possible to picture how the site originally looked. The living quarters were very basic, with dirt floors that probably turned to mud every time it rained and endless rows of bunk beds crammed together. There didn't seem to be any source of heat and I wondered how many weakened prisoners had frozen to death. Modern memorials set up at Dachau displayed shocking photographs of gaunt, starving people in grey-and-black-striped pyjamas as well as images of corpses stacked outside the crematorium, piled one on top of the other.

My mind wouldn't take it in. I couldn't accept that human beings had done this to other human beings. I stared at the buildings and the photos and the descriptions of the lives of the people who lived there over and over again, trying to absorb the enormous barbarity. It was too much.

After several hours, I boarded a train back to Munich, my thoughts roiling with a new awareness and a deeper understanding of the human spirit. Before leaving Edmonton, I'd read several memoirs of Jewish camp survivors who had somehow been able to forgive their torturers. This seemed almost inconceivable to me. Now that I'd actually seen the atrocity of a concentration camp, the stories of survival and forgiveness indicated a magnitude of courage and grace and dignity that overwhelmed me with its power.

For the last year or so, I'd been in the process of trying to understand what real forgiveness meant. The Mormons had taught me about Jesus and the words He used as He was dying on the cross: "Forgive them, Father, for they know not what they do." (Luke 23:24) Even while suffering violence and death, Jesus had asked God to forgive his killers. I wasn't sure exactly what I believed about all the stories in the Bible but I wanted to believe those particular words of forgiveness. They told me that anything could be forgiven, no matter how horrific. No act was too large or too small. The only limits on forgiveness were those we each created.

The Jewish survivors taught me by the example of their forgiveness that those particular words of Christ were a universal truth. I now began to understand them in a deeply personal way as I realized how perfect and practical they were. They weren't just words in a book. They were a message of love and guidance, an instruction for how to live, how to overcome and rise above, how to be totally free.

Forgiveness seemed to be the path to releasing the pain that kept me chained to the past and to anger and judgement. If I could forgive, I could let go of all that. I realized that nothing I'd gone through would require me to surrender my dignity. The pain and terror created by the violence in my life still felt fresh and overwhelming but now I knew, for the first time ever, that these emotions and memories didn't have to control or define me. Grace was possible for me.

As I considered all this on the train back to Munich, a sense of power and strength buoyed me up. At the same time, I felt humbled as never before. The seeds had been planted but I had no idea just how many years would pass before these feelings took root, before I understood these lessons deeply and totally.

8

The Flight Attendant

AFTER my tour of Europe, I knew that I needed to move away from Edmonton. The smallness of my world and the memories of the past felt too limiting. I wanted a fresh start and new possibilities, so I asked the RCMP for a transfer to Vancouver.

Bundled up against the minus-ten degree cold of Edmonton, I arrived in Vancouver on a warm, sunny day in March 1974. Bursts of color were everywhere: yellow daffodils brightened the avenues alongside trees covered in pink and white cherry blossoms. The brilliant sunshine seemed emblematic of my release from the cold darkness of the past.

As prearranged, I arrived on the doorstep of a couple I'd met in Europe who'd invited me to stay with them until I could find an apartment. I spent a few days touring the city before arriving at the Vancouver RCMP Subdivision headquarters for work.

My new boss was Robert Simmonds, Officer Commanding of Vancouver Subdivision. He was a wonderfully kind man who told me I reminded him of his daughter. He eventually went on to become the Commissioner of the RCMP in Ottawa. I settled in, enjoying my job and happy I'd decided to transfer. It took a while before I learned how protective the police were of me. There were whispers from other staff that I was getting special treatment but I had no idea what they were talking about. It seemed that whenever a very violent case was being investigated, the officers ensured that I never saw it. Over time, it became obvious that my boss in Edmonton had filled in my boss in Vancouver about the violence in my past. Robert Simmonds was just as protective as my old boss had been. Once I understood this, I was grateful for it.

It wasn't long before my colleagues accepted me and I became part of the team, occasionally joining them for a drink after work, or going on a date, although I never discussed anything personal with anyone. I felt a sense of freedom in Vancouver and, as I explored the parks and hiking trails and pathways, I fell in love with this beautiful city surrounded by mountains. I felt I had absolutely made the right choice to move.

Peter was in the drug squad, working undercover when I first met him. He approached me at work one day and asked me out for dinner. I liked him. He was about 5'9", stocky, with dark hair, an easy smile and a casual wittiness. He was funny and people were always laughing when Peter was in the room. When I mentioned to a colleague that he'd asked me for a date, she said that, when I'd first arrived, he told everyone he was going to marry me. Wow! Someone wanted to marry me? I liked that.

He had a kindness and attentiveness I'd never experienced before. Within a few months, we were a couple, spending most of our time together, practically living together. I never let him know anything about who I really was on the inside and he knew little of my family and childhood so it must have confused him that I jumped and pushed him away every time he touched me. But gradually, I began to feel safer with him and less edgy, although I was never able to relax enough to sleep properly at night, and the nightmares never let go of their tight grasp on my psyche. Through the numbness inside me and in my own shallow way, I loved him, although he terrified me.

I'd never opened my heart to anyone before and, every once in a while, I'd panic. Feeling vulnerable, I lashed out at him for small irritations, criticizing him and telling him he wasn't good enough. I went for the jugular, knowing deep inside that I was the one who wasn't good enough, not him. I knew that when he figured that out, he'd have to leave me.

Then, feeling terrible for how I'd treated him, I'd tell him how much I loved him and was as kind and as thoughtful as I could be. My mood swings scared me and I didn't like myself for being so unstable. But I didn't know how to fix it. In hindsight, I can't imagine the pain I caused him. He seemed as patient as a saint through all of it.

I attended the Mormon Church several times, enjoying the closeness of the families there, but I was beginning to understand the teachings more, some of which I had trouble dealing with. Among other difficult aspects of the theology was the patriarchal nature of their beliefs and the consequences of challenging them. I read about a woman in the US, a member of the Mormon Church since birth, who had just been excommunicated for declaring herself a feminist. I was quite shocked by the extreme measures the Church had taken and, the more I learned about it, the less I was able to reconcile it with my sense of fairness. Eventually, I stopped attending.

Months later, one morning while having coffee with some of my co-workers, I complained about some minor thing; I can't recall what it was but I do remember that one of the older women looked at me and said, "You'll never be happy. You'll always find something to complain about and you'll never appreciate what you have."

Her words hit me hard. For the first time I was aware that, in spite of being happy with my move and my life in general, I still complained a lot. Even after what I'd learned on my recent trip to Europe, I still had bitterness and mistrust and, whenever a distant memory from the past was triggered, I was edgy and snappy with others. I had blocked so many of my memories that I was usually unaware of the triggers. I vowed to pay more attention to what was going on inside of me, to understand what was upsetting me and deal with my pain in a healthier way. But it took a monumental effort to force myself to look at each insecurity as it popped up.

I never told my colleague how much I valued what she said to me, how much that one comment changed the way I saw myself. I wish I had.

Shortly after my move to Vancouver, Mom and Dad also moved to B.C., to Vancouver Island. I'd no idea why they moved west but I visited them a few times, mainly to ensure that Mom was okay. She was so small and broken by so many years of violence and poverty and, in spite of how she'd treated me in the past, I felt protective of her. Somehow, I managed to see her lost, lonely, frightened soul and I wanted to help her, not just for her sake but for mine as well. I desperately wanted a family, particularly a mother, to fill that gaping hole inside me. But on my visits, she never really opened up to me and my Dad seemed like some distant relative that I barely knew. I kept my walls up and was polite but not open. After one visit, Dad walked me out to my car to say goodbye and shocked me with a question: "Are you ever going to forgive me?"

He'd never before given a hint of acknowledgement of what had happened in the past and I couldn't believe he was speaking of it now. But I wasn't ready; it was too enormous and I didn't under-stand it. My memories were jagged, unclear and painful, and I wasn't about to go traipsing through them right then. So I said, "I already have."

We both knew that wasn't true. I only said it because I truly wanted to forgive him and had put a lot of thought into it. He just smiled and said goodbye.

On another visit, I took Peter with me as a buffer to avoid any more probing questions. It worked and they were extra polite with him there. They seemed to like him, although that didn't really matter to me, and they invited him back anytime. He'd wanted to meet my parents but I wonder now if he was shocked by the coldness that was normal in my family. If he was, he never said so. He'd taken me to meet his parents, who lived on a farm in Sas-katchewan, and I'd loved both of them. His mother gave me big hugs (mom hugs were always welcome and I, in fact, craved them) and she welcomed me warmly. When she was making dinner, I offered to help and she never said a word about how truly lost I was in the kitchen. I wondered if she worried her son might starve to death if he stayed with me. If so, it never changed the warmth of her hugs and her welcome.

As much as I loved my work with the RCMP, spending eight hours a day in an office was not my idea of fun. I wanted to travel and constantly be doing new things. What I really wanted was to learn how to be sophisticated, to have a sense of etiquette and style. I'd been watching TV to see how people who appeared confident walked, talked, dressed and acted. Alone in my apartment, I stood tall, shoulders back, walking back and forth and practiced swaying my hips a bit, pretending I had a sexy dress on. When I saw someone who seemed particularly gracious, I imitated that graciousness, vowing to learn it for real.

Maybe it was inevitable that, after my trip, as I spent long days at my desk, my mind lingered on memories of my London flight and the glamorous flight attendants. I decided to send applications to all the airlines. When I approached Bob and told him what I was doing, he said he didn't want me to go.

"The airlines are a harsh place to work," he told me. "I have a friend in the airline and it's a tough job. Here, everybody cares about you and looks out for you. You won't find that in the airline. But, if that's what you want, I'll support you completely."

But I was careless with his and my colleagues' feelings. It was too difficult for me to believe that they really did care, in spite of the evidence, because how could they? At that point, I was still so numb inside that my feelings for others were very superficial and so I believed that everyone else felt the same way. I thought that was normal.

Bob kept his promise to support me. Two police officers drove me to the airport in a police car for my interview and waited for me, before bringing me back to the office. They were happy for me when, within a month, I was hired by Canadian Pacific Airlines. I got the call at work and my elation knew no bounds. Jumping up and down, I ran around the office telling everyone, "I'm going to be a flight attendant!"

I wanted this more than I'd ever wanted anything. Everyone congratulated me, telling me how excited they were for me, and that they would miss me. For days, I was too excited to sleep. What I didn't learn until many years later was that Bob's airline friend had played a part in my getting hired. I'm glad I didn't know. I wanted to believe I'd done it on my own.

Peter wasn't quite as excited as I was when I told him the news. I think he worried he was about to lose me. He tried to convince me to stay with the RCMP but I wasn't having any of it.

But on my first day of training, as I sat in class and looked around at the other twenty women, I was subdued. They all seemed so poised and assured, with their nice clothes and their hair and makeup perfectly done. They exuded confidence in their right to be there among the chosen few. I think I believed that being a flight attendant would help me deal with my insecurities. These women already seemed to have overcome theirs. Most spoke more than one language. I spoke only English and was so short that I barely fulfilled the height requirement. I couldn't stop staring as panic rose inside me. What was I thinking? What on earth made me believe I could do this? They're going to see right through me and kick me out of here.

Mom's familiar voice began to drown out what the instructor was saying. "You are so ugly. Why do you have to look so ugly?"

We were each asked to stand, introduce ourselves to the class and say a bit about ourselves. I snapped to attention as bile rose in my throat and my stomach churned with fear. Pretend you belong here, I told myself. Keep pretending. But when my turn came, I crumbled. My pretend self was totally gone. Standing up, with all eyes on me, tears streamed down my face and I barely managed to get my name out before quickly sitting back down. The instructor moved on as everyone in the room stared, dumbfounded, at me and I spent the rest of the day ashamed, wondering if I would be asked to leave.

But I wasn't. I went home exhausted, but determined, and the next day my pretend self was back, stronger than ever.

Many of our classes were in the traditional style of lecture and exam but, sometimes, we left the classroom for the hangar that had North America's first flight attendant aircraft simulator. We ran repeated, timed drills on this. We evacuated through simulated smoke and flames, mechanical problems and plane crashes. It often felt very real and very scary as we cracked open the doors of the aircraft and helped everyone to get out before jumping down the slides ourselves. At one point, to more fully capture the experience, we went to a pool and slid down the aircraft slides into the water, then climbed into life rafts. We were tasked with describing, from memory, all the equipment contained in the life raft and how to use it. We also learned first aid, including how to deliver a baby and what to do during heart attack and stroke.

Of course, we also practiced service procedures. It was driven home to us that the passenger was always right and always got what he asked for. After watching television commercials showing beautiful, perfectly attentive flight attendants leaning over busi-nessmen, tucking blankets over them as they went to sleep, I couldn't help but hope that they wouldn't always get what they wanted. Because what if they wanted me? It was my only moment of silent rebellion.

Makeup artists showed each of us how to do our makeup and we had our hair styled in the latest fashion. I felt no qualms as my long black hair was exchanged for a pixie cut. We were taught to never stop smiling, even when in pain or tired or throwing up, to never let on that anything was bothering us. This was easy enough. I was already good at hiding things.

Over the next two months, the class size was gradually whittled down as trainees were told they weren't suitable for the job. Each day that I went home without being fired was a good day.

Graduation day was exciting. We all proudly lined up in our uniforms for a photo in front of one of the aircraft with big, expectant smiles on our faces, laughing and joking as we wondered what exciting places we would head to first. It was all surreal and I went home amazed that I'd actually made it through. We later met at a local bar and proudly celebrated our accomplishment. The next day, I called my family to tell them I'd graduated. Mom gave her usual warning. "You just wait. They'll figure out who you really are and they'll hate you."

Dad was angry. He asked me how much I was paid during training and, when I told him, he said that I'd been taken advantage of because the pay was too low. It bugged me that he made it about his indignation instead of my accomplishment.

I wasn't close to my siblings and their reactions were muted, as they were coping with their own issues at the time.

I let their reactions diminish my excitement and sense of achievement, as had happened so often in the past and I was mad at myself for calling them. I should have known better.

After graduating, reality quickly struck home. The work was physically demanding. The time changes, jet lag and turbulence were difficult to cope with. On my first flight, the aircraft was bouncing and swaying so much that I dumped a tray of twenty glasses of orange juice all over a woman in a business suit. Crying, I kept saying, "I'm sorry. I'm so sorry." The soaked passenger spent the next several minutes trying to calm me down. She was pure graciousness.

Gradually, the job got easier and I started to fit in with my seasoned co-workers. I joined many of them on layovers for shopping in exciting international spots. We bought cashmere sweaters in London, copper and brass in the flea markets in Amsterdam, electronics in Hong Kong and Tokyo, alpaca fleece in Lima and, years later, pearls in Beijing. We lay on beaches in Mexico, Hawaii, Fiji and Australia. We toured museums and historic places, usually meeting up for dinners at restaurants recommended by previous crews. Sometimes, one of the first-class passengers invited us to an event they were attending. Every chance I got, I returned to the Royal Albert Hall in London to listen to the classics. The music still touched my soul and the world felt right when I was immersed in a performance.

On these trips, I opened up. I was in some ways a far cry from the girl who had grown up in that tiny, crowded house in Edmonton, who huddled in hiding spots, terrified of every sound and movement. I gained courage as I socialized with wealthy, sophisticated people who seemed to come from another world. As I learned how the other half lived, I began to attain a comfort level with people from all walks of life.

Peter disliked the changes in me, including my new haircut, and we began to drift apart. I disliked the fact that he was undercover for long periods of time, doing dangerous work with a rough criminal element.

One day, he had a day off and picked me up at the airport after my flight. I introduced him to one of my colleagues who stood chatting with him whle I went to the office for a moment. The next day, she told me that he'd asked her for her phone number. It was the end of the road for Peter and me. I don't remember the details of our breakup but I clearly remember the pain inside me and the feeling that I was losing my mind. I was afraid of being on my own again and that no one would ever love me again the way he had. He'd helped me navigate the world and I missed him terribly.

Within weeks, he married a woman that he'd apparently been seeing while I was away on flights. The pain of his betrayal was so overwhelming that it would be well over two years before I ventured out on a date again.

9

An Actor in a Play

IN SPITE of all the glamour, I was practical enough to know that a flight attendant's lifestyle was surreal and I avoided getting caught up in excessive drinking, partying and shopping. For the most part, I saw past the illusions. And, of course, when I arrived home, I faced the more mundane aspects of life. I really didn't make much money and life wasn't nearly as exciting at home as it was on layovers. At home, the mask of my pretend self slipped and I got confused, often feeling like I was two separate people.

When I was wearing my uniform, I was strong, self-assured and organized. I managed the timing of the food and bar services well and I was good at calming people down and being patient and understanding. I felt strong when I was doing my job and able to stand up for myself when people became rude or demeaning. But when the uniform came off, my sense of wholeness left me and the real me appeared, the one who would never in a million years stand up to someone trying to hurt me, the one who felt undeserving of respect. The years of trauma and insults didn't allow me to believe that my pretend self could possibly be real or that I could ever earn anyone's respect if they knew the real me. And so I spent most of my time at home alone, reading and watching TV, not wanting to get close to anyone who would see through my pretenses.

After six months of flying, I received employee passes allowing me to fly standby virtually anywhere for a small fee. Tickets were issued through the employee travel department and it would be many years before we were allowed to share them with friends or family, so I often travelled alone. I listed myself each time on flights that looked promising, and had open seats on them as I searched for the bargain basement hotel and restaurant deals around the world that were offered to airline employees.

I'd been so impacted by my tour of Dachau a few years earlier that my first major solo trip was to Israel, in 1977, to see the land the Jewish people called home. At Masada, I learned about the history and peoples of centuries ago. I was stunned at the advanced technology used in the construction of the ancient city, like heated floors in the homes and efficient use of sun and shadows in the courtyards.

At the markets, because of my black hair and olive skin tone, Arabs spoke to me in Arabic and Jews spoke to me in Hebrew, neither of which I understood. I had the obligatory picture taken of me sitting on a camel and I toured museums and art galleries.

I also took in the beautiful underwater caves on the Lebanese border, natural grottos formed by ocean water eroding the soft rock beneath the cliffs on the Mediterranean. As we were walking out of the caves, an explosion rocked the air. My heart pounded for a few minutes but, suddenly, we were surrounded by soldiers with machine guns. Helicopters flew overhead — they looked like they'd come straight out of the brand-new Star Wars movie. But we weren't in danger: the explosion turned out to be far from us and involved a gas line. The incident was quite the eye-opener. Maybe the Israelis were used to having soldiers appear around them at a moment's notice but it shocked me. The fact that they were so ready to respond made it clear that people there lived in a state of vigilance, always braced for the worst.

Back home it only took about a minute before I wanted to escape again and I started saving money. Once in a while, I got bumped as flights I'd listed on would unexpectedly fill up and I'd be left sitting in an airport somewhere trying to figure out an alternative plan. But, for the most part, I got to my destinations without trouble. Palm Springs and Phoenix became favorite choices every time I had a few days off. I soaked up the sun and joined people I'd just met for dinner and drinks. I was no longer shy as I ran away from my real life and became my pretend self, the self who was sophisticated and charming and fit in anywhere, anytime. I was acting in a play, choosing a character that I wanted to be in real life.

In spite of all the fun, I was unable to shake the feeling of hollowness and emptiness that haunted me even when I travelled, whether I was alone or in a group. I'd often look around at others and wonder who they really were on the inside. Did they have families and lives that were totally different from mine? Did they have secrets too? I felt no envy because my imagination was unable to take me beyond my own circumstances. Just curiosity. I marvelled at their seeming ease and lack of self-consciousness and wondered how they could be so self-assured. And, of course, I tried to imitate it. Until, once again, I returned home and reality crashed over me like a wave of darkness.

When the bills came in, I worked overtime as much as I could until I'd saved enough for my next adventure. I was having a blast and, apart from being perennially broke, it seemed that this part of my life had become magical. With each journey, my confidence grew and I felt less and less like I was pretending to be someone else. I felt more whole and self-assured, both at home and at work. I enjoyed my work, feeling a new calmness and finding it easy to chat with passengers and tease the children who were usually bored and restless. I loved holding the babies and calming the ones who were crying, often taking them up to the flight deck to show the pilots how cute they were. Most of the pilots missed their own kids during long trips and loved meeting the children I introduced them to.

But, once in a while, things turned more serious. On a flight from Vancouver to Whitehorse, Yukon Territory in Canada's far north, a passenger approached me in the galley and complained that the man with two young children in the row ahead of him was hitting his small son in the face. He wanted me, as the in-charge flight attendant, to do something about it. My heart pounded and

I felt panic as I mulled over how to deal with the situation. I definitely did not want any part of it but I knew that I had a responsibility there. Then another passenger seated in the row in front of the family complained that one of the children was kicking his seat. I approached the father and asked him to please remove the child's footwear so that he wouldn't kick the seat but, before I finished speaking, he slapped the boy hard across the head.

"Sir, it's not okay to hit your child. It's illegal."

"Get lost. It's none of your business," he replied.

"Please don't do that again," I said and walked back to the galley. The passenger who first complained followed me, saying that the man was still hitting his son. After thinking about it, I told him, "I'll file a complaint with the police but they will need you to come forward as a witness."

He agreed, telling me that he was flying to Whitehorse for a conference on preventing child abuse. My witness was an expert. I couldn't believe it.

Approaching the captain, I explained why I wanted him to contact the police and arrange for them to meet the flight. "If this is how he treats his children in public, what does he do behind closed doors?" I asked the captain. He agreed.

An RCMP officer and a social worker met the flight and I introduced them to the witness before pointing out the father and sons as they deplaned. Later, the captain and I saw the police and social worker with the family in the airport terminal. When the man's wife, who appeared to have just arrived at the airport, saw us, she started screaming. "You f***ing jerks. Who do you think you are? You had no right." We quickly walked away.

Back on the aircraft, the captain told me he was glad we called the police. "We did the right thing. Thank you for your courage," he said.

I didn't tell him my stomach was churning or how shaken I was on the inside and just how much courage it had really taken for me to deal with the situation. It had touched a nerve in me that felt exposed and raw and it took me several hours to calm down.

As I reflected on this incident over the next several days, I realized that not long before, I wouldn't have been able to deal with it. I would have walked away, unable to cope with the memories dredged up by the man's violence and the pain of seeing a small child get hurt. It would have given me nightmares and my own pain from the past would have seemed fresh and recent. When I was small, I wondered why no one did anything to stop the violence. I felt that I must have deserved the pain and it must have been my fault and that's why no one helped me. But now, because of the confidence I'd gained from my job, I felt like I'd done something to help those children. I did what I'd wanted others to do for me so many years ago.

On another occasion, I was on the crew bus that drove us from the aircraft hangar where we checked in for our flights to the airport. There were about fifteen pilots and flight attendants on board heading out on different flights. One of the pilots was joking about an incident on a flight and I made an innocent comment about it, at which he seemed to take offense. He turned to me, saying loudly, "I know your type. You were an only child, totally spoiled, with everything you ever wanted given to you."

"How did you know?" was my only response. He smiled, happy that he'd been right.

As we got off the bus, a flight attendant who knew a bit of my story asked me why I'd let him think he was right.

"Because I'm delighted that my past and my insecurities aren't showing and that someone could really believe that I've had a normal life." For the first time, I understood that my inner pain didn't show in my face.

It turned out that he was the captain on my flight and we spent the day on a milk run of northern airports, ending up on a layover in Edmonton. As we gathered for dinner at a Mother Tucker's restaurant near our hotel, I was seated on an outside edge of a large, horseshoe-style booth and he was near the center. A man walked into the restaurant and was seated at a small table near me. We began to chat and, after we all finished our meals, we got up to go and I said goodbye to the man.

The captain sidled up beside me. It seemed my earlier response still bothered him and he was edgy. "So, you're picking up men in restaurants, are you?" We were walking out the door of the restaurant, out of earshot of the rest of the crew, and I turned to him. "I know that man."

"Sure you do," he said in disbelief. "Who is he?"

"One of my foster parents."

He looked shocked. "Are you serious?"

"Yes."

It was interesting to run into my foster parent. We'd had no contact after I was moved back to my parent's home. But now he told me he was happy to see me and was glad that I was okay. I asked how each of his family was doing, and I enjoyed hearing what they were up to. It was a fun, light-hearted conversation and brought closure that I wasn't aware that I'd needed, as I understood just how lucky I was for the temporary escape that his family had provided me.

I'm not sure why I told the captain the truth because I rarely spoke of my past at work. Nothing else was said about it but he was calm and subdued for the rest of our trip the next day. I caught him staring at me several times and he showed a thoughtfulness that he hadn't shown before.

10

The Pilot

I MET Gary on a blind date set up by a flight attendant and her pilot boyfriend. The four of us gathered for dinner at a small local restaurant. Gary was a pilot temporarily laid off from CP Air but now flying for Buffalo Airways in the Northwest Territories. He was an intelligent man with a quick wit, a kind smile and an uninhibited laugh. He was straight out of central casting: 6'2", blond, blued-eyed and handsome. He looked stylish in a dress shirt, a light jacket and casual brown pants and I was feeling sexy in a printed summer dress and sandals.

The evening flew by as the four of us spent hours over dinner talking and laughing. The next day, Gary returned to the north but we spoke almost daily on the phone. He was observant, with something funny to say about everything from what was on the news to the latest movies to the social escapades of colleagues and family. We laughed constantly. He briefly visited Vancouver several times and we went for dinner and got to know each other better. I was very attracted to him.

A few months later, he invited me to visit him in Fort Smith, his NWT base, and I flew to the far north to meet him. He showed me around Buffalo Airways, with its large, rustic aircraft hangar, and introduced me to his colleagues. Then he guided me over to a DC3, the propeller-driven aircraft considered to be the workhorse of the north, and with him at the controls we taxied out and lifted off. He was my own personal tour guide as we flew over Wood Buffalo National Park, where herds of buffalo scattered at the noise of the engines, and over clear, deep green lakes, lush boreal forests and grassy wetlands that went on forever. It was a beautiful, open and rugged landscape, different from anything I'd seen before. That evening we joined friends of his for a fun, relaxing dinner at their home.

I woke the next morning to the inviting smells of bacon and eggs, toast and coffee. Over breakfast, Gary explained that he wanted to show me his favorite spot in the area. We both dressed for the fall weather — jeans and sweaters, heavy winter jackets and boots — and drove to the airport again where we boarded a helicopter with Gary once again at the controls. Pointing out the Slave River, he followed its winding path as I looked down on the trees and wildlife far below us. We moved in over a spot in the river and began to hover before slowly dropping down over a massive rock about three times the size of the helicopter in the middle of the rapids. After gently touching down and shutting the ignition off, we climbed out. The only sound was the water cascading over the rocks which were worn smooth over time as the river crashed forward.

My pulse slowed as my body accommodated the different energy and I gradually relaxed every muscle that I hadn't known was tense. The force of the water was beautiful and surreal as I lifted my face toward the healing negative ions created by the moving water. I was reminded, once again, of the powerful thunderstorms I ran into as a child and the reassurances that something stronger than any of us was in control. This was another world, in sharp contrast to the noise of Vancouver, with ringing phones and barking dogs and noisy traffic. We stayed on that rock, enjoying the rushing water all around us, for about an hour before heading back to the airport. That evening — and almost every evening — we watched the northern lights put on a stunningly brilliant show, with vast bands of blues, reds, greens and yellows illuminating the sky.

Gary and I seemed to understand the world in the same way, and our humor meshed perfectly. It wasn't long before we seemed to fit together like a glove. It was all very magical and romantic. I fell in love — deeply and passionately — for the first time ever.

Gary had grabbed hold of my heart in a way that no one else ever had and I loved him with an intensity I'd never experienced before. It was as close to unconditional love as anything I could imagine and I gave myself, heart and soul, to him.

That said, I may not have always been cognizant of potential warning signs. For example, once, as we were doing the dishes together in his kitchen, he casually mentioned that I wasn't in very good shape. I ignored it, sure that I must have misunderstood.

I returned home to Vancouver with my head spinning, totally in awe of how wonderful he was. Just by being chosen by him, I saw myself differently: as someone worthwhile. I so desperately wanted to be loved, to have someone fill that awful emptiness inside me, to prove that I wasn't unlovable.

I'd dated other men a few times since my relationship with Peter but those relationships were more "like" than love. There was still a numbness inside me that I'd thought was normal. My feelings were always superficial and I'd never worried about hurting a man's feelings because I honestly believed men had no feelings — other than anger, of course. And I always ran away when problems cropped up because I was so afraid that, if I stayed, disagreements would eventually turn into physical violence. Fear had ruled me.

It wouldn't be until many years later, after discovering a teaching called A COURSE IN MIRACLES, that I would finally understand the numbness and begin to come truly alive inside. I would learn just how profound my lack of self-awareness had been and how, in an effort to shut out the terror of my past, I had deadened my ability to feel fully alive. And I would wonder about the effect on Gary of having had a lover who was so emotionally distant and closed off. But I had no idea at that point that I had done that. Gary paid the unseen price.

I had trouble letting my guard down. Adjusting to having a man in my life again was no simple process for me. I'd never slept soundly but I was even more on edge with a man nearby. In spite of my love for Gary, he was no exception. My nightmares continued, as they always had, and I woke from every little sound. I was afraid to drift off to sleep and, if he touched me while I was sleeping, I was instantly startled, heart pounding, every muscle in my body freezing before it registered that I was not being hurt.

I tried to hide my edginess but I wasn't totally successful. Being jumpy and not sleeping was normal for me but Gary hated it. He complained that I wasn't affectionate and that he couldn't hug me while we slept. I didn't know how to show affection and I didn't understand what he wanted. He knew that I loved him but not why I was unable to trust him. I was too ashamed of my past to try to explain my fears and I had no understanding of them myself, so I pretended all was fine.

CP Air eventually called Gary back to work and together we bought a brand new house in White Rock, near Vancouver. It was beautiful, with white siding and lots of yard, front and back. The interior was open design with plenty of light and space. I couldn't wait to decorate it, blissfully unaware at the time that Gary would never allow me to spend money on furniture or decorations and that it would sit half empty the entire time we lived there. It would even take an intervention by his friends to convince him to put grass in the yards nearly two years after we moved in. He only agreed because the neighbors kept complaining.

But my desire to believe in perfect love — and fear about my own lack of value — led me to ignore the flaws, and in my mind my life had become wonderful, a fantasy. I enjoyed every moment of this passionate, exciting relationship. There were times when Gary was harsh and critical, mean-spirited, and I tuned out the warning signs that should have led me to question how much he really cared for me. The fact is, I did not have the courage to look honestly at our relationship.

Gary was an extrovert. He loved to spend time with other couples, to go out for dinner and to movies, parties and social events. He also liked to cook for friends and together we had dinner parties for eight to ten people at a time. We had a dining set that seated twelve, a gift from friends of his. There were many times when I sat at that table, looking around at our friends and at Gary laughing and joking, and felt exhilarated. I was happy in this relationship—ecstatic in fact—and I did everything I could to show Gary, catering to his every wish, sublimating my needs to his as if he were the only one who mattered. When he had early morning flights, I'd get up, no matter how tired I was, and cook him a hot breakfast at 4:00 a.m. Gary bragged about it to other pilots to the point where their wives asked me to stop. But I didn't. To me it was evidence of my love for him and my way of compensating for all that I could not be.

To him, apparently, it was evidence of subservience, and he gradually began to look down on me. At first, I didn't notice the subtle changes in our relationship as Gary slowly became more distant and controlling, ordering me around. He was affectionate and loving in front of friends but, the minute we got home, he pushed me away and his criticisms escalated.

"Why did you say that? It sounded really dumb."

"Why did you wear that dress? It made you look like an old lady."

At first, I wondered if I was being too sensitive. When I told him I was offended, he apologized, saying he was 'just joking'. But he was the only one laughing.

Deep inside, I believed his criticisms were true. On some level, I believed he was seeing through my pretenses and that terrified me. He was kind and thoughtful to others, to our friends and their families, and he was loved by many so I knew the problem had to be me. I tried harder to be exactly what he wanted and, in the beginning, it didn't matter how mean he was. Compared to what I grew up with, my life still felt like pure fairy tale. I blocked the negatives from my mind and told myself they didn't exist.

I thought I had somewhat succeeded when, two years after we'd met, I was standing at the stove cooking dinner, waiting for Gary to arrive home from a trip to Munich. I heard the front door open and he walked into the kitchen with a bouquet of long-stem red roses and a bottle of champagne. He motioned me over to the kitchen table where I sat staring at him as he got down on one knee. "I love you," he said, "and I want to spend the rest of my life with you. Will you marry me?"

"Yes," I instantly replied, remembering Mom's words from the past: No man will ever want you. You'll never be married. Who could stand you?

I was so happy to prove her wrong.

Several months later, we had a small wedding with about thirty guests at a church in Calgary where Gary's mom lived. I hadn't wanted a wedding. I hated the very idea of a wedding and all the complications that could arise by getting together with family. I wanted to elope but Gary wouldn't hear of it. He wanted my parents there, even though he'd never met them and knew little about them. I knew it was the right thing to do but I was afraid of bad memories arriving with them and spoiling my big day. I was afraid that Mom would say, "Is that the nicest dress you could find?" Or "Why does your hair still look so ugly?" Or "You're lucky you found someone to marry you."

I was afraid that others would see through my pretenses of normalcy, which were way harder to maintain with my family present, and see who I really was on the inside. They would see that the 'me' I showed them was nothing but a sham. But, apparently, it was a fear that I would have to face this time.

Gary's mother wanted the wedding to be bigger and kept inviting more people but, each time she told me that, I'd mention that maybe we should elope and she backed off. I was not considerate of her feelings as panic rose inside me. I put my foot down firmly when it came to one issue. I just couldn't let my father walk me down the aisle and demanded that Gary and I walk down the aisle together. I told others that I was a feminist and that I would not allow one man, my father, to give me away to another man, my husband, as if I were a piece of property. And so Gary and I would walk into our future together. People told me how courageous I was. But it wasn't courage or feminism. It was me trying to walk out of the past and into the future, escaping once and for all. If only it could have been so simple.

I hoped this marriage would be a new beginning. It wasn't. After the wedding, a chasm seemed to open up between Gary and I. We no longer shared our thoughts and feelings. I felt shut out and couldn't understand the abrupt change in him as he became more contemptuous of me, snarling at me when I tried to talk to him. He took to saying, "You are my wife now and you'll do as you're told."

Before long, Gary didn't even pretend to have any respect for me, no longer apologizing when I told him he hurt my feelings. I wondered now if he'd ever had any respect for me, if maybe it had been just wishful thinking on my part, simply a fiction in my own mind. His criticisms escalated. I was too ugly, too fat, too stupid. I couldn't do anything right. He didn't like what I wore, what I did or what I said. He was always telling me, "Why don't you just shut up?" He laughed at me, rolling his eyes as if I was too stupid for words. Sarcasm became his favorite style of communication.

I didn't know what to do. I panicked. My insecurities raged and the migraines I'd had as a child came back full force. The self-esteem I'd gained from my job and travels proved to be very superficial. I couldn't figure out what Gary really wanted but his words were echoes of the past and I knew he was right. I wasn't good enough.

I'd always had a habit of pretending everything was fine in every relationship, including friendships, and ignoring the small issues. It was too scary to complain about small things like rude comments, just in case the other person just walked away. I was so insecure that I was always amazed that another person would want to be a friend or lover and so I blocked out all red flags until it was too late to fix the problem. Each relationship was a fairy tale until it was not. But I was unwilling to let go of this fairy tale at that point.

Desperate for his love, I dieted to a dangerously low weight. I tried to cook and clean and look and act the way he demanded, but the criticisms never stopped. It felt like he hated me and was trying to make me leave him. I wondered what had happened to the intense passion we'd felt for each other such a short time ago. The thought briefly occurred to me that maybe he was seeing someone else. I pushed it to the back of my mind, unwilling to look at it but it was clear he had no interest in me and he pushed me away when I tried to get close. The rejection left me in despair, feeling hollow and empty. It hadn't taken long for Gary to decide that I could not live up to his high expectations. It would have taken so little effort on his part to help me let my guard down, to feel loved and secure in our relationship. But, instead, he attacked. It seemed he had a very low tolerance for imperfection.

Gary and I continued to put on a happy front for our friends. Life went on as we each got on our respective aircrafts, heading for different parts of the world for long periods away from each other. Running away was my modus operandi. Apparently, it worked for Gary too.

But things continued to get worse. Gary became more controlling, lambasting me in front of other crew members for spending two dollars on a magazine to read on a layover. When he saw me talking with a male colleague at work, he blew up: "What's going on? Are you cheating on me? You stay away from him."

At one point, I asked Gary to go for marriage counseling, telling him I couldn't live with things as they were. He only sneered at me and said, "No. You would never have the guts to leave all this."

He waved his arm around, indicating our home and lifestyle, as if he considered me bought and paid for. With those words, I felt stabbed in the heart, insignificant, dismissed as if I were nothing. I felt cheap, as if he was saying I'd sold myself for what he could offer. I knew then that Gary had not viewed me as someone, but as something; that he believed that a wife was a possession, someone to be owned and controlled. In refusing to allow my father to walk me down the aisle because he viewed his children as something he owned, I hadn't understood that I was marrying a man who held the exact same beliefs.

In truth, I didn't know what a loving relationship was supposed to look like. I'd been unable to recognize early on when normal kindnesses were lacking and to see the warning signs present before Gary had asked me to marry him. My naïveté led to my fairy tale dream becoming a nightmare. After predicating my sense of self on Gary's validation of me, it now seemed that my very existence was in peril.

I wasn't entirely passive. Although Gary never hinted at physical violence, I lashed out as if he were threatening my life. With terror raging inside me and my heart pounding as my sense of self was shredded again and again, my pain turned into scorn. I grew disrespectful, bitter and edgy, throwing off nasty comments: "You're useless and boring and you can't do anything right."

I criticized every mistake he made and blew out of proportion small incidents that happened at work. Nothing hurts a pilot more than someone criticizing his flying expertise and I went for the jugular: "I heard you hit the runway pretty hard on landing yesterday and the passengers complained about it." I often snapped at him, disagreeing when he voiced an opinion and, feeling overwhelmed, I complained when he wouldn't help around the house or cook a meal. He laughed at me. But, in my mind, this wasn't a game. It was life and death. My very being was under threat. I had wanted Gary to define me but I could no longer live with his awful definition.

I didn't even believe the negative things I was saying to him and intensely disliked myself for trying to hurt him, but I didn't know how to stand up for myself in a healthy way. I'd never let my guard down with any man before and it brought out raw pain that was new to me. He'd hurt me in a way I'd never been hurt before. How could he say he loved me and then try to destroy my very sense of self? In the past, when my parents had hurt me, they never said they loved me, so I never confused love with pain. But now, Gary was saying he loved me even as he hurt me in a way that was deep and intense and soul destroying. I didn't know how to cope with it.

In spite of my love for him, I was furious. How dare he tell me he loved me while he destroyed me? So, I fought back in the only way I knew how. I'd never fought back before. I'd never stood up for myself before. It felt empowering to hit back, to identify a strength I'd never seen in myself before. And even though it felt awful to be so mean to him, it felt good to know I was capable of stepping outside my powerlessness and passivity, even though I didn't really understand it at the time.

I never told anyone at work the truth of our situation but my coworkers sometimes shared with me what Gary was up to when we were apart. When I was on one particular charter flight to London with an unusually long, seven-day layover, some of the flight attendants let me know something I'd already had suspicions about. Gary was cheating on me when he was on his own layovers. They even went so far as to say that I should cheat on him in retaliation. But I couldn't cheat. It went against everything I believed in.

I'd deliberately chosen that long trip to London so I'd have enough time to try to sort out my feelings and I thought long and hard about how I would handle this mess. Spurning tourist attractions like museums, parliament and Big Ben, I wandered around shopping districts in my jeans and t-shirt, looking like any other tourist, window-shopping and stopping for coffee at sidewalk cafes to people-watch as my mind worked overtime trying to sort things out.

The confirmation of his infidelity had only added to the list of reasons our relationship wasn't working and, as I mulled over my options, I came to what was probably the only viable one. I knew that if I stayed with Gary, there would soon be nothing left of me. I felt that he had seen right through me, toying with my emotions and laughing as he'd caused me some of the most agonizing pain I'd ever felt. My relationship with him seemed to have confirmed every negative thought I'd ever had about myself and self-loathing raged inside me.

I had to leave him. It seemed to be a do or die situation. If I didn't do something now, I would be forever destroyed, as my mother had been. I could give up or I could muster every last bit of courage inside me and stand up for myself. It was now or never. I didn't know how I'd be strong enough as I suspected that our mutual friends would side with Gary since they'd been his friends first, and thus I'd be alone, without support, as we separated. But I kept telling myself that I could do this; that I was strong and capable.

In the midst of my anguish, as I spent days on the other side of the world from Gary, I thought long and hard about how I would find the strength to get through this. A familiar thought came to mind: forgiveness. I decided to try to separate the intense pain in my heart from my anger at the person who'd caused it. I wanted to let go of the anger and forgive Gary, even as I was still struggling through the pain. I knew it seemed crazy to think this way but I knew the forgiveness was not for his benefit. It was for mine. For my survival and my sanity.

In the past, when I'd hung on to anger, it had enveloped me with an ugly darkness, spoiling every moment of every day, causing me to hate the person who had hurt me. When Peter had hurt me by cheating on me, I'd hidden from the world for the next two years before letting go of my anger against him. But I had learned a lot about forgiveness since then and I no longer wanted to hate anyone. I still loved Gary and I wanted to rise above the petty emotions, for both our benefits. By choosing not to be his victim, I could let go of some of the self-contempt that I was immersed in and the control I felt he had over how I saw myself. As I thought it through, I found a tiny shimmer of light in the darkness.

Gary may have sensed the vacuum inside me, the insecurities, the fears, the weaknesses. But he hadn't created those things. They'd been there all along. Something in Gary had taken advantage of them and he'd viciously attacked me. And the depth of my love for him had made the pain even more intense. So, in trying to forgive Gary, I wasn't thinking it meant everything was okay. It just meant that I was choosing not to hate him.

It was a difficult balancing act. But it was too dangerous to let the anger take control. If I did, I sensed I'd never find my way out of it. There was too much pain in my past and it would be so easy to just blame everyone else for my failures. I didn't want to be filled with rage and I didn't want to be a victim. I told myself that it didn't matter why Gary did the things he did. His intentions were irrelevant. All that mattered was that I figure out how to let go of the anger. I had given him power over me and now I wanted it back.

I wanted to understand how things had gone so wrong so that this could never happen to me again. How, I asked myself, could I have been so blind? It would be many years before I understood that you can't ask someone else to respect you when you don't respect yourself, when you think of yourself as so much less than everyone else. It turned out that pretending to value myself was not the same thing as actually doing so.

I thought about how I'd lashed out at Gary whenever I was really hurt. I was ashamed of myself. I'd spent years reading self-help books and taking seminars to help me become the person I wanted to be, someone with dignity and grace, not someone who deliberately hurt others. My lashing out had an ugly familiarity to it, having grown up in a home where mean-spiritedness was the norm and the way to deal with even the slightest pain was to react with rage and violence. I'd always sworn I'd never do that to anyone else. Now I decided that I would never deal with fear and pain in that way again. It didn't matter how bad Gary's behavior was. I would not blame my bad behavior on his. It was the only way for me to break that cycle of abuse.

As I look back now, thirty-five years later, never having repeated that vindictiveness, I realize that I succeeded.

A few days later, as I was wandering through a massive toy

store, it crossed my mind that my leaving Gary was going to create a difficult situation at work, and the gossip might get ugly. I sat down in a plush chair, surrounded by parents with children who were playing with the toys. I was smiling as I enjoyed their excitement and happiness and a memory surfaced. I'd been having lunch a few weeks earlier with my friend Kathy, an ex-flight attendant, who was telling me about a dinner party she and her husband had hosted the evening before in their large, elegant home on the west side of Vancouver. This is what she told me.

"We'd invited several couples from my husband's work and one of the men arrived with a woman who, he quietly told my husband, was an escort. I watched silently and recognized her discomfort as the other guests shunned her, refusing to talk to her and ignoring her attempts to make conversation. As soon as I had a moment, I approached her and welcomed her to my home. I asked her about herself and her interests and invited her to sit beside me during dinner. It turned out that she was intelligent and thoughtful and I enjoyed her company."

It was obvious to me that Kathy had judged neither the woman nor those who ostracized her. I'd been so impressed by her graciousness, by her inner loveliness and courage, that I decided that was the kind of grace I wanted — the kind that goes against what everyone else does and thinks if it's the right thing to do. The kind that comes from the heart and not the social rules, the kind that seems so rare in our society.

And so, as I watched the children playing and laughing, I made the decision to rise above the gossip at work, to maintain a sense of dignity, to stand tall and offer grace in this difficult situation, regardless of how torn apart I felt on the inside. Gary was someone I'd loved deeply, flaws and all, and just because I couldn't live with him didn't mean I wanted to cause him more pain. I decided that, because his colleagues were also my colleagues, I would not hurt or embarrass him in the workplace by discussing our painful breakup, regardless of how he behaved. I would not allow his behavior to determine mine.

I had no idea at the time just how much inner strength that would take.

11

Questioning My Worth

IT WAS 1984. Still judging myself harshly for my failures, I'd
rarely dated in the two years since my divorce. But when I was
invited by a friend to a small gathering at her home, I decided
to go.

One man, Tom, ruled the room. He was short and stocky, all
muscle, with a larger-than-life personality. It was obvious to me
that he loved to laugh and joke and be the center of attention.

He slowly made his way over to where I was standing and
began to tell me about his business, which manufactured industrial
chemicals. When he mentioned the research and development
work he did in order to make his products more environmentally
safe and effective, I asked him if he'd applied for the R & D tax credit
recently offered by the federal government, a credit specifically for
the kind of work he was doing. He hadn't heard of it and wanted to
know more. I explained the details and the evening flew by as we
got into discussions of science and business. I loved the conversation. He seemed very intelligent. And curious about me.

"How is it," he asked, "that you, a flight attendant, are aware of
the details of this new R & D program?"

When I explained my recent accounting training in college, he
gave me his phone number and asked if I would meet him at his
warehouse to discuss business. It was an opportunity I couldn't resist. I'd been missing the intellectual stimulation of attending college and had been debating whether to return. I confess I was also
flattered by his attention and happy for the opportunity to spend
more time with him.

When we met again several days later, he showed me around the huge, cavernous building. It was cold in the warehouse and I was glad that I'd worn jeans and boots and a heavy jacket.

There were two offices, one empty, and a large area containing massive vats that had mechanical arms stirring the contents. It also had an area for storing raw materials and finished product that had been packaged and readied for shipping. As we walked around, Tom explained the manufacturing process and some of the difficulties he was having.

As we wrapped up the tour he asked, "Would you be willing to look over the operations of my company and make some suggestions, just as a friend?"

I agreed, but first I wanted to know if his products were any good. I took home samples of some of the cleaners, tested them and was surprised at how effective they were. None of my household cleaners could match the efficacy of his products. So, having done my due diligence, we started working together. I began by looking at the books. It didn't take long to see that the company was near bankruptcy and that Tom was not in control of either the manufacturing process or his employees.

"First off," I told him, "you need to take charge in the warehouse and fix the quality control problems. Then stop letting your employees show up when and if they feel like it. Next, you need to apply to the federal government for the R & D tax credits you're entitled to. I can put the numbers together but you need to hire a chartered accountant to make the formal application."

Tom agreed with all my suggestions. I couldn't believe that he was willing to just let me make whatever changes I thought needed to be made and I was giddy with excitement. His obvious respect for me was something I hadn't encountered before, and I ate it up. It was intoxicating and empowering, obliterating my common sense. I desperately wanted more of that respect.

The empty office became mine and I spent the next few months gathering information, constantly going between the warehouse and the office to get the details I needed for the R & D application. With over thirty products to analyze, it was a huge undertaking with a learning trajectory that went straight up. Every single chemical addition or subtraction had to be analyzed — first for the cost of various raw materials, then for efficacy. For my secret inner nerd that loved details, this was a dream job and I was truly happy for the first time in a long time. I enjoyed every minute of it, feeling more alive inside than I had in years. I spent all of my days off from flying working hard. Tom also asked for help dealing with lawyers as other issues popped up and what I'd learned in two semesters of business law now came in handy. There was always so much more work to do. But it didn't take long before I felt like I belonged there, like I fit in. It had been a long time since I'd felt I fit in anywhere and the work was the perfect balance to my flying career.

Tom and I became close friends as we worked together, laughing and joking, sometimes sharing dinner as we worked into the evening. He constantly thanked me for my work, telling me how much he appreciated me and how happy he was to have met me. Within a few months, we were dating. I liked his intelligence and thoughtfulness. We laughed easily together and I no longer worried about what I said or how I looked or acted. There was no criticism. We had in-depth conversations about science, politics and the world in general. Tom was gentle, always treating me with respect, asking for and listening to my opinions. I felt valued and loved. Several months later, we moved in together.

Tom shared with me that he was an alcoholic but had quit drinking eight years before. His friends backed up everything he told me, confirming his years of sobriety. He also told me that he grew up in a home with domestic violence and how abhorrent he believed it to be. He shared his values and spiritual beliefs with me, telling me how they'd helped him move out of the past. He'd put a lot of thought into the topic of forgiveness and his interpretations of various spiritual teachings made sense to me. I liked his ideas of

God being gentle and forgiving and loving and I began to accept some of his ideas as my own.

It turned out, as I discovered many years later, that Tom hadn't really believed those ideas. But, for me, they eventually became a prelude to what I would learn from A COURSE IN MIRACLES.

WHAT A difference it makes when one feels loved! I was still afraid to go to sleep at night with a man beside me but, for the most part, I was more relaxed and calmness took over. I felt a new inner peace. The bitterness and anger seemed to recede a bit and others noticed. One of the airline ground staff told me, "What are you doing differently these days? You look more relaxed. You're nicer now."

It was a shock to realize that my previous mask of 'niceness' hadn't always worked. I hadn't known how often I'd been edgy and snappy or that my deep-rooted fear of others that made me keep my distance and prevented me from making friends had come across as snobbishness. Apparently, I was friendlier now.

Tom was the total opposite of Gary. He never once treated me like a servant or took for granted the little things I did for him. He noticed everything, thanked me constantly and told me that I was intelligent and beautiful, that he was very attracted to me. I soaked up his compliments as if they were water for a person crawling through the desert. There was a part of me that would have done almost anything for more of those kind words.

And we had fun together. We took a Caribbean cruise, renting motorcycles and touring the various islands the ship stopped at. We had romantic dinners on board and partied the nights away, once even dancing as the ship passed through the edge of a hurricane.

Another time, I tried my hand at marketing. I contacted the Cousteau Society of France after seeing their ship, The Alcyone, in Vancouver harbor, and suggested they try one of our environmentally safe marine products. Eventually, after much correspondence, I convinced them to apply our anti-fouling solution to a section of the hull of The Alcyone in a test against other companies' products.

They agreed. The ship sailed all over the world for nine months before being raised and examined. The Cousteau Society rated our product number one for effectiveness in keeping barnacles off the hull and published the results in both their English and French magazines. It was a marketing coup of major proportions and my confidence soared.

This led to a seven-week road trip around the perimeter of the United States in 1991. Tom and I, hugely excited, drove from Vancouver to Seattle, across northern US to Boston, down the East Coast to Miami, then across southern US to San Diego and up the West Coast. We called on marinas and boat supply companies all along the way, copies of the Cousteau Society's articles and sample product in hand, and had solid success making connections and sales.

Time flew. The months stretched into years and I kept working at both Tom's and the airline. Looking back, I think a part of me must have felt that, as long as I worked hard, I wouldn't have to assess the parts of my life that were actually deteriorating.

I SEE NOW that I had no idea how vulnerable I still was, how damaged and raw I felt at my core. I was so desperate for kindness from anyone. I suspect my pain and vulnerability were obvious to Tom, though I, of course, can't say whether it was his intention to take advantage of it from the start. For my own part, I ignored the red flags and doubts I had about the relationship. In some little corner of my mind, I knew that I was being used. I was a workaholic and Tom was benefitting enormously. He never talked about paying me for the work I did and I didn't want to ask. I didn't care about the money. Tom even convinced me to begin investing in his company once I was formally listed as a director. I liked hearing all the nice things he said to me and felt too fragile to risk losing his love. I liked being wanted. I didn't want anything to change.

Eventually, though, after about three years together, Tom started drinking again. You would think that living with an alcoholic parent would equip me to recognize signs of trouble but it didn't.

In my eyes, only violent drunks like my Dad were really alcoholics. I believed — or firmly wanted to believe Tom — when he told me his drinking wouldn't be a problem. In fact, I believed everything he said instead of everything he did, not yet having learned the difference between the two.

But. as Tom's drinking grew worse over the next few years, I gradually realized that he had no control over it and our relationship began to fall apart. Tom was no longer respectful. He'd quickly berate me if I said something he didn't agree with. He became more controlling. Under the guise of a compliment, he began to tell me how to dress and wear my hair. At first, I didn't quite understand what was happening. His manipulation was subtle, especially compared to how Gary had treated me — with open insults and degrading comments. I didn't see the damage being done to my sense of self.

Without realizing it, I stopped forming my own opinions. My inner strength seeped slowly away until I again questioned who and what I was or whether I had any real value. And even as the panic rose inside me, I fell back to telling myself that things weren't that bad.

But I could no longer deny that he was drunk most of the time. I was once again living with an alcoholic — this time by choice. I was devastated.

Tom himself grew paranoid, pushing friends away, accusing them of being out to destroy him. He sensed I was unhappy and asked me to marry him. But I was at least aware enough to recognize that he was just trying to keep me from leaving and refused. But I wasn't ready to leave, to admit defeat in yet another relationship. I kept hoping he'd recover and everything would go back to what it was before. So much of my life and self-esteem revolved around the work I did with him and the life we had together that I didn't know how to free myself. Instead, I closed my eyes to what was happening, choosing to believe he'd see that he was throwing everything away and sober up again.

Over the next several years, Tom's drinking affected the business. His employees began taking advantage of him, showing up late for work or not at all, and the quality of the products declined. We were unable to translate the great publicity we'd garnered from the Cousteau Society into major sales. My relationship and years of hard work and investments were going down the drain.

And still the downward spiral continued. I can see now that there was nothing truly surprising about how things played out, given Tom's alcoholism and my own vulnerability. But, at the time, the rapid changes in Tom were confusing and I wondered where his anger was coming from. He misinterpreted everything I said, argued with me over silly things and blamed me for everything that was going wrong. He grew increasingly aggressive, often telling me to shut up while pounding his fist on the wall. Instead of blaming him, I blamed myself, repeatedly wondering: What am I doing wrong? What's happening?

When he first became violent with me, I didn't recognize it as such. I walked by his recliner while he was watching TV and his leg lashed out and struck my back. My response was simply to tell myself to be more careful. You know better than to get close to a drunk. Drunks do this kind of thing.

He took to saying the kinds of things my father used to say to me — ugly things that I had no memory of ever sharing with Tom but identical to what had come from my father's mouth so many years ago:

"You are evil and worthless. You only bring problems to those around you." And most chillingly: "You don't deserve to live."

A terrifying, ominous echo of the past. Deep inside, the old familiar fear surfaced, raging away as panic attacks took over, causing my heart to pound as I gasped for air. The very thought of Tom now scared the hell out of me.

One night, Tom didn't like the dinner I served. He said it wasn't hot enough. "Flight attendant food!" he yelled as he walked up to me in the kitchen, put his hand around my neck and slammed my head backwards into the wall, choking me. "Don't mess with me again," he said, as he let go and walked into the living room, turning on the TV.

In shock and crying, I cleaned up the supper dishes and went to bed, even more afraid to fall asleep than usual. After that, it became normal for him to lash out at me. And every time he hurt me, it crushed me even more until I wondered if there was any me left.

The violence became more intense. Night after night, he cornered me in the upstairs bedroom, where there was no phone I could use to call for help, shoving me down onto the bed, trying to pull my clothes off but too drunk, climbing on top of me and screaming in frustration, "You slut! You goddam slut! You are a piece of shit!"

He'd wrap his hands around my neck, push me down into the bed and choke me, his hands getting tighter and tighter until I couldn't breathe. I'd furiously kick my legs and pull at his hands but he was too strong for me and my efforts exhausted me. Then just when I thought I was going to die, when I couldn't fight anymore and was nearly unconscious, he'd let go and stumble off the bed and downstairs to the kitchen to get another drink. Gasping for air, I'd quietly crawl part way down the stairs and find him, every time, passed out on the sofa with the TV on.

One day, he came home from work drunk, staggering in the door in a rage. I ran for the bathroom and locked the door behind me, screaming in the hopes a neighbor would call the police. No one did. He kicked in the door and slapped me in the face, smashing my head backwards into the edge of the tub, furious with me for trying to escape him.

Sometimes, I called the police and they showed up immediately, putting him in the police car and taking him to jail for the night. He always walked in the door the next morning as if nothing had happened. Other times, I had no warning that he was about to explode and so I couldn't reach the phone in time. His rage continued into the small hours of the night before it was spent. At that point,

I was too afraid to ignite it again by calling 911.

I stayed home from the office whenever I could, trying to get my thoughts together, cleaning the house over and over while listening to classical music. Comforting memories of my trips to London and Vienna bubbled up as I kept cleaning, hoping that, if I kept my outside world spotless, my inner turmoil would lessen.

I came up with a plan. Driving home from a flight one afternoon, I took a detour to look at an apartment that was for rent. The manager seemed nice and the apartment, on the fifth floor, was clean, so I wrote a cheque for the deposit, planning to secretly move one day when Tom was at the office and so make a safe escape. But as I pulled into the driveway at home, Tom pulled up behind me. Roughly grabbing my arm, he twisted it until I cried out in pain and told me to get back in the car. He ordered me to drive back to the apartment, twisting my arm again as he did so. I drove up to the building and he pointed to the fifth-floor balcony I'd just been standing on.

"If you move to this apartment," he said, "I'll throw you off that balcony and tell everyone you committed suicide. If you leave me, I'll kill you."

I believed him. My heart was pounding as I went to tell the manager I wouldn't be taking the apartment. We drove home silently. For the first time, it registered that he'd been following me. There would be no escape.

Later that evening, he was intently watching the news about the murders of O.J. Simpson's wife and friend on TV, laughing as he predicted that O.J. would get away with it. "You know that I can shoot you and tell the police you killed yourself? You're just a wife. No one will care. Look at O.J."

I wondered how many other men would use the O.J. trial to threaten their wives if there was a not-guilty verdict.

I rearranged my schedule at work, going back on overseas trips, choosing particular flights to Nagoya, Japan, because they were five-day trips that gave me a chance to sleep and eat properly. I was too ashamed to tell my colleagues what was going on and pretended that everything was fine.

As I mulled over my situation, I wondered if I deserved what was happening, if there was something wrong with me. I thought I'd chosen so wisely this time, that I wasn't making the same mistakes I'd made with Gary. Now I wondered. Was violence my destiny? For the first time in years, I questioned whether my father was right.

If my whole ugly past was echoing in my present, did that make his words true? Was I evil and worthless?

12

A Visit by SWAT

SEPTEMBER 1993. As I was sitting at my kitchen table with a cup of tea, the phone rang. As soon as I heard my sister's voice, I knew something was wrong. Julie never, ever called me.

"Mark is dead. He hung himself last night."

I was shocked. My brother Mark had been living in Ontario with his second wife and three of his four children for many years, and we'd rarely been in touch. Now sorrow and guilt overwhelmed me. I flew with Mom to Ontario for the funeral, holding her hand the entire way. She was numb and unable to speak. We stayed at the same hotel near the airport in Toronto as my sisters and father did, and I rented a van to get us all back and forth to the funeral home.

The next morning, when Dad showed up in the hotel lobby along with everyone else for the ride to the funeral home, it was the first time I'd seen him in several years. At the funeral home for the viewing, the rest of us mingled but after a few minutes, I found Dad sitting in a quiet reception area. As I stood back and stared at him sitting all alone on that chair, he appeared to be a broken man. He was staring down at the floor, shoulders hunched forward as I went over to say hello and give him a hug. I couldn't imagine how difficult it must have been for him, let alone any parent, to lose a child, especially to suicide. My heart genuinely went out to him. There was still a huge distance between us and I wasn't really comfortable hugging my dad but, once again I compartmentalized, blocking out the old memories, and was able to ignore my discomfort. The pain of the past was just a blur as the pain of the present overwhelmed me. It seemed we were both too shocked by the events of the last few days to converse much at that point. Both Dad and Mom went into denial about the circumstances, unable to accept that Mark's death was a suicide.

There was more than enough guilt to go around although, of course, no one spoke of it. For my own part, I was angry at Mark for choosing death. I asked myself how he could have done this to me. It would be years before I accepted what happened and understood that he hadn't done it to me — he'd done it to himself. It wasn't about me.

And, in truth, I felt guilty too. I felt guilty for not caring enough to get to know him as time passed. Every time I'd thought of Mark, as the years had passed, I felt shame for having abandoned him when we were younger. In my mind, he'd represented the worst of the horrors of our childhood and I'd never had the courage to reach out to him and welcome him into my life. It took years for this guilt to ease.

ONCE back home, life continued to crumble. In a drunken stupor, Tom tried to convince me that I was the one who should have committed suicide. In the midst of my grief, he told me that everyone would be happy if I killed myself, even my family. My mind was in such a dark place that it was hard not to believe him.

As I was sitting in the living room watching the news one evening, Tom staggered up to me pointing a loaded 30-30 shotgun at my head. He was so drunk he could hardly stand. Unsteadily circling my chair, squinting his eyes at me as if I were the devil himself, he told me, "I know who you are. You can't fool me. You think you can destroy me, but I'm not going to let you. I'm too smart for you. If you move, I'll kill you. I'll tell the police it was a suicide, that you killed yourself just like your brother. No one will care."

Sitting stiffly upright, unable to move, to go to the bathroom or call for help, I waited for hours until he passed out, still holding the gun. Even then I didn't know if he was really out or if he would suddenly jump up and start ranting again.

Truly frightened by Tom's insanity, I decided to be more careful. The next time I saw his anger building, I called the police right away. They put him in the police car and one of the officers came back in to talk to me. She said to leave him, that Tom had told them he was going to kill me. She'd heard many death threats before but this one she believed. "Your life is in danger," she kept saying. By this point I was so numb that I could only thank her for her concern. She left very frustrated. The next morning Tom walked in the door without a word about the arrest. Life went on. But I'd heard what the officer had said and I prepared to run.

Tom rarely went to work anymore so my options were limited. But I kept a packed suitcase in the spare room closet and watched nervously for the right time to make a break, aware that the most dangerous time in a violent relationship is when the woman attempts to leave.

Several weeks later, after a particularly violent night, Tom was still very drunk, and I realized that he was incapable of reacting quickly. Grabbing the bag, I ran to my car, slamming and locking the door behind me as Tom staggered towards me screaming, trying to chase me down the alley as I made my getaway.

A few minutes later, Mom opened her door, astonished to see me standing there with my suitcase. She made me tea as I filled her in on the details of what was happening. She'd been unaware of any of it and was stunned at what she heard.

That evening, Tom began calling Mom's number, leaving threatening messages on the answering machine. "I'm coming over and I have a gun. I'm going to kill you."

A police officer arrived within minutes of being called and he sat with us, listening to the messages and calling in on his radio with the information. He asked if Tom had any weapons and, when I said yes, he called in the SWAT team. The police, guns raised, entered the house and found weapons and a large stockpile of ammunition. Mom and I heard the voices of the officers over his radio as they described what was happening in real time. It was surreal and dramatic, something right out of a TV show. Tom had not been on his way over — he was just trying to scare me — but his threats backfired on him and he was arrested and charged with stalking, assault, threatening and weapons offences. Then he was released the next morning.

I applied for and received a restraining order.

A FEW weeks later, the police stood by while I moved my things from the house into an apartment I'd rented in a nearby city. But I was still terrified and couldn't sleep. I took three weeks off work, but it didn't help me calm down. The trauma left me feeling helpless, enveloped by a dark depression. I knew I couldn't survive this. I hated myself for being in this mess and asked myself over and over: How stupid am I that I keep messing up so badly? Other people don't have SWAT teams arriving at their homes. What's wrong with me? Am I insane?

I could barely get out of bed each day. I dragged myself around, pretending to smile when I was at work but too low on energy to carry on normal conversations and always anxious to get home to my new apartment to be alone. Every day when driving home from work, I checked the traffic around me to see if I was being followed, just as the police had advised me to do. When I was out, I looked over my shoulder constantly, expecting him to be there to confront me. Panic attacks made my heart race and I often went running out of stores and other places to the safety of home. Even there, every sound made me jump and I was too afraid to close my eyes at night, afraid that I wouldn't hear him breaking in the door, coming to throw me off the balcony. Even though I was alone, I didn't walk near the balcony doors. And the nightmares raged. Exhausted as I was, I couldn't close my eyes to sleep, thanks to the demons inside me that threatened my sanity, that told me I'd never survive and that I deserved what was happening.

There was an enormous vacuum inside me where Tom's many

years of control had been. I hadn't made a decision for myself in years and was terrified of everyone and everything, not knowing who to trust anymore. A massage therapist I was seeing suggested a self-defense course called Model Mugging and I took her advice. In the classes, a man dressed in a black padded suit with a large helmet on his head pretended to attack individual students and we were to use the moves we'd just been taught to protect ourselves— kicking and hitting and screaming.

When my turn came, I kept repeating the steps over and over in my head but, when the mugger moved towards me, I froze. I just stood there. It was too real for me. It wasn't pretend. I didn't know that I had tears pouring down my face or that my classmates had tears pouring down their faces as they watched, stunned at the intensity of my reaction. The mugger kept acting out the situation and I kept freezing.

Finally, we took a break and everyone sat in a circle and encouraged me. It was amazing. Not one of them knew anything about me, yet they wept at seeing my pain. I understood, in that moment, that in all the times I'd been attacked by my father and by Tom, I had never once raised my arms to protect myself. I just stood there every time because I believed that I deserved what I was getting. This realization shocked me.

I decided to get up and try again.

This time, when the mugger came at me, I hit and kicked and punched as hard as I could. I could hear the cheers of the others in the background. When I finally sat down again, I was totally drained. The experience was wonderful, empowering and liberating. I knew, finally, that I would survive.

TOM received six months' probation for his criminal offences. It took me a lot longer than that to even begin to recover. During a meeting with Crown Counsel about Tom's criminal charges, a woman from Victim's Assistance suggested I call Family Services for help in understanding domestic violence. I called immediately and signed up for a course that teaches abused women about the red flags that indicate when a person may become violent.

I was all for learning that. I'd missed every sign until it was too late to leave safely.

The course was wonderful, with understanding and supportive counsellors and other women who'd shared similar experiences. I felt emotionally safe for the first time in a long time. We all told our stories. Mine was more graphic than some but I didn't care what anyone else thought of me. I just wanted to get the most out of the program.

I had a lot to learn, such as: Just because what happened to me was insane, it didn't mean that I was. That was big news to me.

Sally was one of the counsellors and, after the last class, I asked her if I could speak to her privately. I shared with her something that had been weighing on me. I had seen Danny, one of Tom's friends, at a grocery store the day before. He told me Tom was still threatening to kill me. He said, 'You're in danger. Tom's going to say you committed suicide."

As all this poured out to Sally. I was shaking with fear, crying, certain that I was losing my mind. I'm sure she saw how unstable I was. "Betty," Sally said, "You have to leave the province. You aren't safe here." A police officer had just made the same suggestion.

"I don't think I have the strength to start over again in a new place," I told Sally.

"Then we'll arrange for you to move into a women's shelter."

My immediate reaction was horror. I pictured women sleeping on floor mats in large noisy rooms. But Sally said it wasn't like that. "You'll be with other women who've gone through what you have. You'll be safe. You'll be able to sleep at night and eat properly."

And so, in 1995, afraid enough of Tom, the next day I started a new chapter at a shelter in a Vancouver suburb. The shelter was a large, spotless, brand new house funded by donations and worked on by many volunteers. It was beautifully decorated, like a show home, but cozy and welcoming. It seemed every detail had been well thought out. The kitchen was a brightly lit room with a table that seated about twenty people. There was a counseling room, as well as two large family rooms with televisions, lots of sofas and chairs and, upstairs, several bedrooms. I would share a bedroom with two other women, one with a small baby, where I was given a lower bunk bed. Once I put my bag in my room, I went back down to the kitchen and someone put a cup of tea in front of me. Sitting at the kitchen table with some of the staff, feeling shell-shocked about the sudden move, I found myself saying, "I can't believe that all the people who created this home would care enough about women like me to work so hard, do so much and donate their money. I can't believe that there are people who think I deserve this help."

It just wouldn't sink in. Yet each and every staff member reassured me that I was indeed deserving of their help.

I felt safe at the shelter, but there were challenges at first. It was hard to be doing full-time shift work while trying to come to terms with everything I'd been through and sharing space with so many other people, including a baby who sometimes cried during the night. There were counsellors on shift day and night and I was told to come and talk to them at any time. I did. Danny's recent report of Tom still threatening me made my nightmares worse and, being in a shelter somehow made the danger seem even more real. I couldn't hide from the fact that I was there for a reason. I couldn't pretend that things weren't that bad. They were. Denial was now impossible.

Past and recent nightmares all became jumbled. I found myself waking up on the floor crying, with Dad standing over me laughing because he'd just thrown me into the wall. Or Tom on top of me, screaming, his hands around my neck, choking me as I struggled to push him off. There were even those where I was being kicked backwards but was unsure if it was Tom or Dad who hurt me. Gary was sneering and laughing in my face —or was that Dad? I couldn't be sure. But the worst nightmare was when I was pulled over by a police car while driving home from work. When the cop walked up to the side of my car, it was Tom in a police uniform, holding a shotgun, laughing. "I told you I'd get you," he was saying. The deadly blast in my face always woke me up crying.

Every sound made me jump up in fear, certain that I was about to be killed. Night after night, I slowly tiptoed down the stairs to talk to the counsellor. In the daytime, I was also getting intense counseling from Sally and others at Family Services.

Mom called frequently. She'd been helpful when I was staying with her but now she was furious, telling me repeatedly, "How dare you stay in a shelter? You made your bed, now you lie in it."

When I told her that Tom would have killed me if I stayed with him, she said, "So what? You made your choices."

It was an old pattern with Mom: help one minute, attack the next. I never knew what to expect. It was so upsetting that the staff soon blocked her calls.

When I went to the bank, I learned that Tom had emptied our bank accounts, taking my life savings as well as our joint investments.

I hired a lawyer. Sitting in George's office, I told my story and explained that, as much as I wanted my money back, taking legal action was more about finally standing up for myself. George was an empathetic and kind man who understood what I was trying to do and agreed to help me — even though it wasn't a strong case, in his view. The trauma had left me jumpy and edgy, with large gaps in my memory and I didn't yet know how confused I was.

We learned that Tom had juggled the books in a way that erased the $100,000 I'd invested in the company over the past ten years. Then Tom's lawyer sent George copies of two cancelled cheques from the company made out to me for $50,000 each and claimed that I'd been paid for my work. The cheques had been cashed in our joint personal account but Tom refused to provide copies of the backs of the cheques, which would have indicated who had signed them when they were cashed. It seemed that he'd written the cheques out to me, deposited them in the joint account and then taken the money out himself and hidden it.

He also produced a document, signed by both of us, that removed my name as an owner of the house. It must have been signed during one of the many times he was drunk and violent and ordered me, as a company director, to sign paperwork for the business. I had no memory of having signed it. When I ran for my life that day, all my paperwork had been left behind and so I now had no proof of my investments. It was obvious he'd been planning this theft for a long time.

In spite of George's best efforts, my life savings were gone in an instant and a few years later I was left with a bill for thousands of dollars in legal fees. Even with all the help I was getting, depression overwhelmed me. I was exhausted. The enormity of the dysfunction in my life terrified me.

13

A Shelter, A Move, and a Murder

ONE Friday I spent the day in bed, lost in a heavy darkness I
couldn't shake, feeling like my body weighed a thousand
pounds. Sally called to check up on me, as she did every
day, and when she heard my voice, she was so worried that she
asked me to come in for a counseling appointment, which I did.
For the first time, she was unable to reach through my darkness. I
wondered if it was worth trying to go on anymore. I just seemed
to make a mess of everything. Everyone else seemed to sail through
life just fine, with marriages and families and everything being normal. Not me. I didn't even know how to pretend anymore. She left
for a moment, returning with three other counsellors. We all sat in
a circle as they made suggestions. They were all concerned that I
wouldn't make it through the weekend.

"When the darkness swamps you, go inside where you know
you're safe," one of them suggested.

I freaked out. "I can't go inside. It's ugly in there, too scary.
There are monsters in there."

I had stuffed all my shadows inside me: my anger, fear, insanity,
pain and never-ending sadness and emptiness. It had been one
thing to spend my entire life believing what I'd been told — that
I was bad inside, evil and ugly — but it would be quite another to
actually look inside and know it for a fact. I knew I couldn't live
with what I might see. I didn't have the courage to look inside. It
was too dangerous.

They were shocked by my reaction and made other suggestions.

One was to reach out to the children at the shelter. They thought that seeing the innocence of children and hearing their laughter might be the best medicine for me.

In the end it was the fact that the counsellors cared enough to focus on me that helped lift me up enough to know that I would survive the next few days.

I BEGAN to like living at the shelter. For the first time in a long time, I felt safe and cared for. The resilience of the other women impressed me. Most of them had kids and no jobs, with very uncertain futures since they had left their homes with nothing. But they were supportive and helpful of each other. This was really the first time I had lived in such an environment. When I arrived home from flights, the children ran up to me for hugs. I certainly wasn't used to having kids excited to see me when I walked in the door and their happiness warmed my heart.

It didn't hurt that I arrived home with chocolate. After my flights landed and the passengers deplaned, I took the wrapped chocolate bars destined for the garbage from the unused meal trays.

I was no longer capable of pretending I was okay, or of having boundaries, and I was unable to judge what I should or should not say at work. So I told some of the other flight attendants what I was doing and they were soon scooping up the leftover chocolate bars for me. They loved the idea of giving them to the kids.

One time I found an umbrella that had been left behind. I handed it over to the cleaners to put in the lost-and-found but they said to keep it, that no one ever came back to the airport for an umbrella. I gave it to a woman in the shelter who was taking the bus every day from place to place, searching for housing in the pouring rain with her three small children clinging to her. She cried when I gave it to her.

There was a camaraderie and sisterhood among the women that was new to me and I learned how wonderfully supportive — how loving and kind and thoughtful — women could be with each other. We hugged each other often. There were no mean comments or anger directed at anyone. We each listened without judgement when another needed to talk. We laughed together as we watched our favorite TV shows and cried together during sappy movies. We had to take turns cooking dinner each night, which I wasn't keen on since my mind was often too blurry with exhaustion to focus on the details of cooking. So, the other women who liked to cook often filled in for me.

Of course, that also might have had something to do with self-preservation as they quickly realized that I wasn't a very good cook. In gratitude, when I noticed they were having trouble keeping up with their laundry while taking care of children, I began to sneak down to the laundry room, take their clothes out of the dryer, fold them and leave them on top of the dryer. We joked about who the laundry helper might be, with me pleading ignorance. Every one of these women and children touched my heart. I wished I could wrap my arms around them all and protect them from any further hurts. We watched together as the not guilty verdict came down in the O.J. Simpson trial. Every one of us had heard our partner brag about how O.J. would get away with it because a wife had no value and, now, our worst fears were actualized. We were stunned into silence and each of us relied heavily on the counsellors for weeks afterwards.

Some of the major stores in Vancouver donated new clothes to the shelter. It was a big event for the women and children when these gifts arrived. Several times I came home from a flight to find new clothes on my bed. I protested that because I was working, the other women should take the clothes but they insisted I keep them. They often told me that, if domestic violence could happen to me, it could happen to anyone.

One mother had a three-year-old who'd never spoken a word. The violence little Lisa had seen had so traumatized her that she was unable to speak. Every night, when it was time for bed, the kids all came up to me for a hug. I would say, "Goodnight, sweetie," and they'd say goodnight back as I hugged each of them. Lisa gave me a hug and a smile every time but never said anything. One night, after I'd been in the shelter about three weeks, Lisa hugged me as usual. During a rare moment of perfect silence, we all heard the whisper, "Goodnight, Betty." Everyone, especially her mother, let out a whoop. We couldn't believe what we'd heard. Lisa's first words ever were for me. I felt honored and privileged. Joy bubbled up inside me and the memory still warms my heart as I think of it now.

It took so little to help these kids feel better about themselves. Carol, an eight-year-old, had been watching me crochet and was mesmerized by it. So, I taught her how to crochet. She created a small square, which she ran around proudly showing to everyone, receiving lots of compliments as each woman took a good look at her work. She was beaming as she came back to tell me how everyone liked it.

Andrew, eleven, was doing homework and asked me how to spell a word. I told him to bring me the dictionary and I taught him how to use it. Then he approached each of the women to ask her to give him a word to spell and showed them that he knew how to look it up and spell it. He was so excited by what he'd learned that I told him I'd show him how to use the encyclopedia that had been donated to the shelter. I remembered how enthralled I was as a child when I discovered how to look up anything I wanted to know.

Ashley was seven years old and had been living on the streets with her mother after her mother's boyfriend kicked them out. She hardly spoke and was afraid of everyone, so I quietly reached out to her with smiles and gentle words. She began to relax and, each time she sat down to watch TV, she sat a bit closer to me. The other women noticed this and watched as it unfolded. I spoke quietly with Ashley each time we sat together and I was even able to make her laugh once in a while, although she still rarely spoke.

Her mom told me that Ashley didn't like it when I was away on a flight. One day, arriving home in my uniform with my suitcase trailing behind me, I found her sitting on the front steps waiting for me.

"Can I talk to you?" she whispered.

"Okay," I said, sitting down beside her. "What do you want to talk about?"

"It's not okay for you to be away overnight. You have to come home every night."

I knew that there had been many nights when her mom hadn't come home to take care of her and I suspected that Ashley was vulnerable to whoever came along at those times. I tried to explain to her that I worked in airplanes and would fly to another city and sleep in a hotel. But how do you explain the concept of airplanes and hotel rooms and being a flight attendant to someone who has spent most of her young life on the streets? She couldn't understand what I was saying.

"I'm not being hurt while I'm away," I told her. "And I know you're safe too."

Her next question was, "Why do you wear the same clothes every day? You have to change your clothes every day."

I tried to explain the concept of a uniform and that my clothes looked the same but were clean every day. She didn't understand so I just gave her a big hug and said, "Thank you for caring about me." She relaxed even more and snuggled against me. I loved that little girl.

My time at the shelter was helping me more than I could have imagined. The love shown to me by the women and children and staff, along with that of Sally and the counsellors at Family Services, was new to me. It lifted me up and opened a new world for me, one of loving friendship and caring people. These people told me that they saw me as gentle and compassionate, and that my caring had helped each of them feel better about themselves. No one had ever told me that before. I'd never known what effect I had on others. But now I opened to the idea that others saw something good in me that I hadn't seen in myself. In the past, when people told me they loved me, I hadn't believed them. But now, because they offered love without criticism, I believed these women and it changed me. It opened the door just a crack to me being able to believe in myself. This, I decided, was what family must feel like. Coming from a family that didn't know how to love each other, I found it astonishing that this was even possible. Both their love for me and my love for them was healing and it changed my perspective and expectations, brightening my outlook and slightly lifting the dark shadow of depression that enveloped me.

IN DECEMBER 1995 I walked out of a store one morning and saw Danny, Tom's friend, standing by my car, waiting to talk to me. I'd been having a good day, enjoying the sunshine in jeans and a light jacket and running shoes, feeling a bit more relaxed than usual, so I hung back for a minute, not wanting to spoil my day by hearing any bad news. But then Danny saw me and I walked over to him, bracing myself.

"Tom is telling everyone you're suicidal."

A chill ran up my spine and instantly, the familiar panic attacks made my heart pound and my breath come more rapidly. The sun seemed to dim as we stood in that parking lot.

"I'm not suicidal. I'm fine. Look at me. I'm fine."

He seemed surprised. "Tom's lying. But I believed what he said about you. Be careful. He's going to kill you and say you committed suicide."

At my next appointment with Sally, I told her about the encounter.

"Betty," she said, "it's time for you to leave B.C. We can't protect you from him and you need to start over somewhere safe."

The very idea scared the hell out of me. How could I possibly survive on my own? But she was not the only one pushing me to leave. The staff at the shelter and my police contact were saying the same thing. I had mixed feelings about it. I didn't believe I had the strength to make a move like that and I didn't want to leave the people who cared about me. But I was also tired of looking over my shoulder and I knew I couldn't live in a shelter forever. I trusted Sally's advice and summoned up my courage to start making plans to move a few weeks later. I had lived in Vancouver for twenty-two years and I'd loved it all — the mild weather, the flowers and seafood, the diversity, the mountains and the ocean. It was hard to wrap my head around leaving.

Calgary was the closest airline base to Vancouver, only a one-hour flight away. It was a small, junior base and I would be senior there, which would give me a good choice of flights to work. Sally made arrangements for me to move into the Sheriff King Home for women in Calgary and I began packing my things to go into storage. My plan was to have them shipped to me once I had a place of my own. I tried hard not to hate Tom for forcing this scary move on me, but was unable to bury the bitterness inside me that translated to anger against men in general. What made them all feel so entitled that they hurt or even killed women for no apparent reason? I couldn't understand it.

I was also worried about Mom. Even while I was living in the shelter, I'd visited her frequently and I knew she'd miss me. I asked her over and over again, "Are you sure you'll be okay when I'm gone?"

"Yes, I'll be fine." She listed the friends she'd made since her move to Vancouver and the activities she was involved in. I believed her and I promised to come back to visit her every month, either using my airline passes or driving from Calgary to Vancouver. Either way, I promised her, I would be there whenever she needed me.

JANUARY 1996. Glued to the window of the aircraft, looking at the lights of the city as we approached Calgary airport, I couldn't believe it when the pilot announced that the temperature was a record low of -40. It was too cold for my brain to even register what that meant. I was moving from the beautiful rainforest of Vancouver to the seeming arctic tundra I could see below me. Fear crept in as I looked down at all the snow and ice.

The plane glided into the airport and pulled up to the bridge and I headed to the luggage area to get my bags before calling the shelter to say I'd arrived. A cab was being sent to pick me up, I was told, and I waited, disoriented and scared, unsure that I was making the right choices and wondering what price I would pay if not. After a short cab ride, I was checked into the shelter and assigned a room that I would share with another woman. The shelter wasn't a house like the ones in Vancouver with warm, family-type chaos. It was a large building that was more institutional, where meals were provided buffet style, and everything was strictly organized. But I felt safe there, temporarily hidden away from Tom's omnipotence. I called Sally in Vancouver to tell her I'd arrived safely, crying as I heard her familiar voice.

That night as I lay on my bed, my roommate softly snoring in the bed across the room, I thought about all the changes in my life. Traumatized and exhausted, deep depression took over once again as I looked at the past and wondered if I'd brought the violence with me. Would it follow me everywhere I went? Was it part of who I was? The newness of everything around me, the bitter cold and snow, and the fear that Tom would find me and kill me coalesced into a heavy darkness inside me, weighing me down. It didn't matter if my fear was irrational. After years of his violence and death threats, it felt real to me.

The move was much harder than I'd expected. Without the day-to-day support of the people at Family Services and the Vancouver shelter, I felt completely lost. I tried to talk to the counsellors at my new shelter but they saw me in my flight attendant uniform, suitcase rolling along behind me, heading off to and returning from flights regularly. My career just seemed so exciting. They asked me about exotic places I'd travelled to and my fake smile seemed too real for them to believe I could possibly need their help. I soon gave up.

Two weeks later, embarrassed, I called my old school chum, JoAnn, who had moved with her family to Calgary a few years before. She soon arrived at the shelter to help me look for an apartment. I quickly chose a one bedroom in the downtown area before heading out to buy a bed and a cheap dresser. JoAnn lent me a TV and a chair and helped me move out of the shelter into my new place. She was sympathetic but couldn't really understand how things had turned out so badly for me. I couldn't understand it myself and my shame was enormous. A week later, I flew back to Vancouver to pick up my car and arrange to have my things shipped to Calgary.

BACK IN Calgary, everything seemed foreign to me. I'd never driven in heavy snow before and, when my car slid sideways on the ice, totally out of my control, I panicked. This was before the days of GPS and, when the street signs were covered in snow, I had no way of knowing what street I was on. I got totally lost. After flights, I'd climb into my car to find it so completely frozen solid that I couldn't even turn the wheel. It was like I'd moved to another planet. Sometimes I just sat in my car and sobbed.

My short-term memory was shot. When I parked my car, not only did I forget where my parking space was, I couldn't remember which of the two airport lots I'd parked in. I forgot not just names but faces and I kept introducing myself to people I'd already met, receiving questioning looks each time. At home, I spent hours curled up in a ball, not eating or sleeping or even watching TV. I lost a lot of weight and looked like hell, with dark circles under my eyes. Day after day, I sat alone in that apartment wondering how I was going to pay my enormous legal fees as my lawyer in Vancouver continued trying to get my savings back from Tom.

When my neighbor invited me over for a cup of tea, I poured out every detail of what had happened in Vancouver. She understood violence and listened with compassion, never judging or criticizing, assuring me repeatedly that Tom was not going to follow me to Calgary. She was the only one to whom I talked about my fears, the only one who truly understood the suffocating panic that

I couldn't escape and the paralyzing darkness I lived in. Her wisdom and kindness and humor saved me from total despair. She seemed like an angel that had been dropped into my life and we became good friends for the next twenty years.

When I'd shown up at the airport crew room, ready for my first flight with Calgary crews, I knew that the gossip about my situation would have preceded me. I was terrified that I wouldn't be liked by anyone. There were lots of good people at Vancouver base but a few of them had been nasty, calling me "trash" and other names. Now I felt fragile as I put on a big smile and pretended to be normal.

Fortunately, the crews were close-knit and exceptionally kind, taking me into their circle with compassion and thoughtfulness, never judging or criticizing. They asked a lot of questions which I freely answered, having no ability to set boundaries for myself. Even when what I said was confusing and contradictory, they never lost their compassion, telling me repeatedly how much they admired my courage. They told me that they liked working with me and that they hoped I'd stay in Calgary. I wondered if they had any idea how much their kindness fed my battered soul.

Once in a while, flight attendants would call me at home to ask for advice about domestic violence and I liked that they trusted me to keep our conversations confidential. I did my best to help them understand the dynamics of abuse. A Toronto-based flight attendant told me about her violent relationship, saying, "I'm not as strong as you are. I don't think I can leave him." I told her she surely was as strong as I was and to think about what her daughter was learning from growing up with violence. I told her to call me anytime, hoping I could help, wanting some good to come out of my mess.

But I was edgy and afraid. My default position was that any little slight was intentional and an indication that they were going to turn on me. I blew small incidents, like someone's grumpiness, totally out of proportion. I snapped rudely at one of the flight attendants and she wouldn't accept my apology. A few days later, a union rep approached me and said, "Betty, these people are not going to hurt you. You are misunderstanding things that are said." I thanked him for telling me, vowing to stop being so anxious, something that proved to be easier said than done.

The fear of being stalked did not easily leave me in spite of having moved 650 miles away. I called Danny, Tom's friend in Vancouver, to find out what Tom was up to. I knew that Tom was living with Wendy, a long-time acquaintance of both of ours. Wendy was sweet and fun but she was unable to stay sober and was an easy mark for Tom. What I didn't know was that, a few days before my call to Danny, Wendy had died from a shotgun blast to the head. It happened in the home that I'd shared with Tom and he was with her at the time. No questions were asked, there was no investigation and Wendy's body was cremated without an autopsy.

Danny had been friends with Wendy for a long time and was deeply shaken by her death. "Betty, no one here believes this was a suicide." Neither did I.

Stunned and upset, I called the RCMP. "Have you looked at Tom's record?" I asked.

They hadn't. In spite of all the calls I'd made to report domestic violence when I'd lived in that same house that Wendy died in; in spite of the fact that a SWAT team had removed Tom's weapons and laid criminal charges against him; in spite of all the past threats Tom had made to kill me in exactly the same way that Wendy just died; and in spite of Wendy's calls to 911 for help when Tom was violent — no one had even looked him up in the police files at the time of her death. I couldn't believe it. Neither could the RCMP officer I spoke with. I told her that I didn't believe that Wendy committed suicide. I said that Tom had bragged to me repeatedly about how he could kill me and make it look like suicide, how he had pointed a shotgun at me when making his threats.

An investigation was opened. The police called me several times to ask me questions and, on one call, I was told that Tom was very upset about the investigation and was shocked to learn from one of his friends that I was the one who'd called the RCMP to suggest that Wendy's death was not a suicide. He raged against me to the police as his house was searched. They found nothing. They tried to track the gun that was used but couldn't trace it.

I called Wendy's sister, Karen, who told me that their mother had died just before Wendy did and that Wendy had inherited a large amount of money. Just a few months before her death, Tom had convinced Wendy to make him the beneficiary of her estate. Karen told me that Tom had called her and threatened to hurt her grandchildren if she tried to interfere with him getting the money. She'd hired a lawyer and, in the end, Tom received very little. He didn't follow through on his threats, perhaps because the police were watching him. But they were unable to make a case against him.

It shook me to my core. I'd wavered between not taking Tom's threats seriously because it was all too unreal and being totally terrified because, deep inside me, I knew what he was capable of. Murder was something you saw on TV, not something that happened in real life. There'd been times when I'd thought my move away from Vancouver had been an overreaction, but Wendy's death now justified it. Panic attacks returned full force and the nightmares became worse. I was terrified to close my eyes at bedtime, knowing that when I drifted off, I would remember the feel of his hands around my neck choking me while he yelled and screamed at me for whatever imagined crime I was guilty of. I would see the shotgun he held to my head as he ordered me not to move from my chair. I would remember the times he kicked in the locked bathroom door with a loud crash and found me cowering from his rage. Fear and panic ruled my every waking moment. I was afraid to go to sleep and afraid to wake up. Some days, I was even afraid to breathe. I knew the fear wasn't logical, that Tom couldn't hurt me in Calgary, but I was still too afraid to close my eyes at night. I fought off sleep in spite of my exhaustion and sank back into despair.

The RCMP officer I was in touch with called once in a while to talk about the case, telling me that she occasionally dropped in on Tom at home. She would just show up on his doorstep sporadically to ask him how he was doing. His paranoia was running rampant as the drinking damaged his brain more and more and he began making rambling statements to her about me stalking him and how he'd seen me outside his house and how afraid of me he was.

When she asked me if I'd just been in Vancouver, I always said, "No, I haven't." I wondered if Tom's guilt over Wendy's death was playing out inside his damaged mind since being stalked by me was now his greatest fear.

Wendy's death reinforced the insanity of my life. I wanted the craziness to stop. I so desperately wanted to find a way out of the darkness inside me, from the inner voice that told me that I was so much less than everyone else. It was a voice that told me I was to blame for everything, that I was a failure at this thing called life. I hated myself and I could barely get out of bed each day. I dragged myself around, pretending to smile when I had to, anxious to get home and be alone. My whole life had been about pretending to be normal and trying to fit in. I was so tired of pretending. How was I going to survive? And why did I even want to?

PART II

Following a New Course

Know yourself in the One Light
where the miracle that is you is perfectly clear.

— A Course in Miracles

14

A Love Story

I was desperate. I'd hit bottom so thoroughly that I would have done anything at that point to ease the pain inside me. Little did I know that a gift from the heavens was about to be dropped into my lap.

I'd been in Calgary less than a year when a colleague gave me a book: *A Return to Love* by Marianne Williamson. It explored the teachings of a spiritual program called A Course in Miracles (ACIM). I'd heard about this Course several times in the previous few years and I knew it was a well-regarded program that offered a different way of looking at ourselves and at the world. In this sense, Marianne Williamson's book was incredibly timely. I immediately took it home and curled up on the sofa, reading nonstop until I finished it.

I read about the healing of intense pain: "The only way to heal the wounds of the past is to forgive them and let them go." And about forgiveness: "Forgiveness is like the martial arts of consciousness."

First thing the next morning, I was in my car, heading to the nearest bookstore to buy A Course in Miracles. A miracle, I decided, was exactly what I needed.

I went straight home and, once again, sat on the sofa with my legs curled under me and a cup of coffee in hand, as I looked at my new purchase. The dark-blue front cover of ACIM listed three parts: the Text, the Workbook and the Manual for Teachers. The words "Foundation for Inner Peace" were embossed near the bottom.

Inner peace sounded really, really good. I started reading. It didn't take long before I learned that everything this Course taught was so much the opposite of what I'd believed about myself. It turned my way of seeing the world upside down. And its profound impact on me continues to this day.

There was no sense of dogma in the book and I never felt, for even a moment, that I was being indoctrinated with rules about what to think and how to act and be. It merely offered ideas to be accepted or not, whatever I chose, and I never felt like I was joining an exclusive "club" or that those who chose not to believe these ideas were wrong. The preface clearly stated that ACIM was just one of many paths to truth. The teachings were nondenominational, pragmatic and inclusive, open to any and all who were searching for a better way. Reading this left me with a sense of freedom that I'd never felt with any religious teachings. In spite of the male pronouns used, the Course was not patriarchal and did not view women as less than men. In fact, it did not view anyone as less than anyone else. We were all equally perfect in the view of this Creator, regardless of our histories or beliefs.

The teacher of the Course was purported to be Jesus, but there was no need to have Christian beliefs to practice it. In fact, the understanding of what the crucifixion really meant — it was not a form of punishment — illustrated how the teachings differed from traditional Christianity.

In reality, the teacher of A Course in Miracles is not separate from us; He is truly internal. The entire purpose of the Course is to recognize the power of the mind and help each of us find our own internal teacher.

For years, I had loved the idea of Jesus offering forgiveness to his persecutors and everyone else, even while dying on the cross, and so I was comfortable with the idea of Jesus teaching this course about forgiveness. Still, my guard was up as I looked for any words that didn't come from pure love, which I knew Jesus exemplified. I found none.

The Course described reality as non-dualistic — a perfect Oneness, unchanging, unified and eternal. It defined God as the essence of our being, the pure light of unwavering love and acceptance. I'd always wanted to understand the concept of Oneness but, more than that, I'd wanted to feel it. I'd felt so alone for most of my life. The more I studied the Course, the more I began to understand that, in a deeper sense, I was feeling disconnected from my very source of being. This was a lonely place to be. Understanding this shed light on that awful, empty feeling I'd spent my life trying to escape. And it helped me to see a way forward out of that state.

ACIM described heaven, not as a place, but as an awareness of perfect Oneness. Heaven wasn't an exclusive club for do-gooders, a place we go when we die if we've followed all the rules of religion. Heaven could be discovered in the here and now and finding it could replace the hell of fear and internal pain I'd been existing in for most of my life. I loved this concept.

Similarly, God was not someone physical who existed "out there," somewhere up above, someone who offered His only Son as a kind of human sacrifice to pay for my sins and everyone else's. That traditional teaching of Christianity was a huge burden of guilt I'd always refused to accept and it had kept me wary of any religious teachings. How could I worship a God that deliberately sent his Son to die because of the actions of others? How was that okay?

So, when I read the words of Jesus from the Course, I immediately knew that I was on the right track.

"I was not punished because *you* were bad."

Finally, I'd found my escape. I would use this Course to walk out of hell.

I read about the power of the mind and that tiredness, illness and pain were all the result of our thoughts. I had some familiarity with the power of the mind. As a child I had unconsciously used that power to tune out what was happening to me when I was being hurt, to such effect that some of the memories never surfaced until many years later. I used that power when I was in my twenties and fed up with constant migraines. I began yoga and meditation, effectively ending my migraines for most of the next 23 years.

As I continued to read, it began to dawn on me that the power of the mind spoken of in the Course was, in fact, inner power. It wasn't something outside of me in my brain, like will power, but was a part of my soul. It was part of who I was, a strength that was unchanging regardless of events past or present, a strength that had always been there. Nothing I'd been through had damaged or destroyed it. I wasn't weak on the inside as I'd always believed. I was strong.

I'd spent my life disliking myself so much that it was a concept that was difficult to absorb at first. Me, strong? Really? Who was this person I'd known as me? Apparently not the scared little mouse I'd believed I was. I began to feel less like a failure. My spirits lifted and I felt truly hopeful for the first time in years. Gradually, almost imperceptibly, my old beliefs began to crumble as I learned to look at the world and my past differently. I was as yet unaware that this teaching would eventually help me heal the gulf between my pretend self and my real self, bringing them together into one whole.

I wanted a lot from this Course. I wondered if it could help someone like myself who entirely lacked a foundation and understanding of who I really was, someone who intensely disliked herself as much as I did. The events of my life had caught up to me. I was hollow and disconnected, with a sense of not being part of the world, of just being an observer watching others go about their lives while I tried to figure out what "normal" looked like so I could emulate it. A deep sense of nothingness and emptiness owned me. It took an immense amount of energy to keep smiling and pretending to fit in, and I was so, so tired.

I was desperate for change. Even though I wasn't sure I had the energy to understand the Course, I needed to try before I let hopelessness totally take over. Major miracles were promised as early on in the book as the preface, so I vowed nothing less than a major effort on my part to engage with the material.

AND THUS I dove into A COURSE IN MIRACLES feeling like a drowning person grabbing a flotation device and hanging on for dear life. I packed it in my flight bag and took it with me everywhere I went, reading it on stopovers, sitting in the back of the aircraft alone during long waits parked at airports. Some of the flight attendants asked me what I was reading so I showed it to them. They thought it was kind of strange, and I didn't understand it enough yet to discuss it. But they became used to me sitting alone in the back while they gathered in the front and chatted. It became rare for me to show up for dinner and drinks on layovers; instead, I grabbed a sandwich to eat in my room while I read. Nothing else mattered to me.

Determined to understand this program and having arrived at Calgary base from Vancouver with nearly three weeks of vacation days in my time bank, I decided to take extra time off work to do nothing but concentrate on the Course. Day after day, I ate, slept and breathed this program. I knew it had worked for many others and that it would work for me. It had to.

My days were easy. Waking up at 5:30 or 6:00 a.m. as usual, I sat on the floor of my living room to begin my yoga stretches, as I had for many years, feeling each muscle in my often sore back become elastic again as tension drained away. After several minutes of stretching, I grabbed a coffee and sat on the sofa admiring the sunrise through my large balcony window overlooking downtown Calgary. No longer reading the newspaper first thing, I now reached for ACIM and spent a couple of hours reading before climbing on my exercise bike, book still in hand, notepad nearby, for another thirty minutes.

Each time I read something from the Course that seemed especially pertinent to me, I wrote it in my notebook, along with examples from my own life. Sometimes I had so many notes that it seemed as if I was rewriting the entire Course in my own words.

But each note helped me understand this intense program on a deeper level.

After showering and eating breakfast, I went for a walk to the nearby grocery store or the library or the park. As I walked, I thought through what I'd just read, attempting to get a deeper understanding before returning home to study a few more hours. The Course was touching me on such a deep level that I began to see it as my friend, as a guide that I trusted to help me out of my quagmire. It represented possibilities that I'd only dreamed about: escape from the past; peace and love in my heart, for myself and others; safety; and graciousness on a level I'd never thought possible.

It had been years since I'd allowed myself to stop being on the go constantly and it wasn't easy to convince my type-A personality that, by spending all my time studying, I wasn't being lazy, that I was just taking care of myself. But I found that I was calmer than expected. The minor irritations of not finding what I wanted at the grocery store or someone bumping into me on the sidewalk disappeared. Just believing that inner peace was possible was already easing my mind.

The program was intellectually intense and it used old-fashioned language that I found difficult to understand. It presented some strange concepts: Was it really possible to love everyone? But I was willing to accept that, at that moment, I was capable of only a superficial understanding. I trusted that it would become deeper as I worked my way through the program. In order to help me better understand the Course, I ordered some books and CDs by Kenneth Wapnick from the Foundation for A COURSE IN MIRACLES. Kenneth was one of the people originally involved in the creation of the Course and his work explained the text in layman's terms. This helped.

The Workbook was easier to understand than the Text. It offered 365 lessons, one per day for a year, and I patiently followed each one. At my kitchen table each morning, in my flannel pyjamas with a coffee in one hand and a pen in the other, I wrote out the lesson for the day on a small notepad. After studying it and following the directions, I took it with me when I went out so that I could read it over and over again to remind myself of what it said. I felt good about it, like I was doing something positive, and I never missed a single day of this ritual. As I combined what I learned from the Text and what I learned from the lessons, the messages slowly became clearer. One lesson in particular struck me:

"My mind is preoccupied with past thoughts."

This made me ask myself: Was I looking into the past each time I saw anyone or anything? Was I preoccupied with past thoughts? Of course I was! I viewed everything through the lens of the past. I didn't know how to stop dwelling there or how to stop being fearful that the past would be repeated in the present. I knew that I wouldn't survive another violent relationship yet was terrified that I'd fall into one again. I'd struggled to get out of the past before, without success. I'd told myself to just block it out and stay in the moment but the echoes of my past kept leaking out unwanted and when least expected and the fear gave me panic attacks and nightmares. I didn't want to live like that.

Apparently, I didn't have to.

The lessons had me question the meaning I'd assigned to everything in the world, from the pencil on my desk to the lamp overhead to the ways I perceived myself and everyone else. I had to work at processing the material, and my relationship with it. At times, certain ideas struck me as simplistic or strange. But rather than dismissing them out of hand, I told myself that my way of being wasn't working. My way of black-and-white thinking had gotten me into this mess in the first place and maybe if I changed my way of thinking, I could get out of it. Maybe if I learned how to stop viewing myself so negatively, I could stop unwittingly choosing to be with people who looked down on me and acted accordingly. I really wanted to believe these ideas, so I kept an open mind as I proceeded. I didn't yet know how to put the ideas into practical use, but I did know that I was about to figure it out.

I learned that my understanding of the world was not fact but perception and interpretation. That is, I saw something and I understood it based on my own pre-existing ways of seeing the world. I was positive that I knew what was wrong with the world and how to fix it, and I often judged those who disagreed with me as ignorant. It never occurred to me that I might not have all the facts, or that I might have misinterpreted the facts I did have, or that my 'facts' may sometimes have been based more on what I wanted to believe was true instead of what was really true.

In the past, this had never stopped me from believing that I knew more than I did. But now, this teaching explained how we could each look at an event and describe it totally differently afterwards, and how we could all have such different interpretations of the world. It meant that those who saw things differently from me were not wrong, as I'd believed, but that they just had different perceptions. My judging them as wrong or ignorant for having those perceptions was harmful to them and to me. It was a particularly hard lesson for me to accept. Giving up my 'correctness' left me feeling vulnerable and less able to understand the world around me. And if I couldn't understand it, then I couldn't protect myself from it either. I viewed others as dangerous to my very sense of being and even their different ways of viewing the world seemed threatening. It would be a long time before I learned that understanding the teachings of A Course in Miracles would create such a sense of total safety and confidence deep within me that I would no longer feel shaken by someone challenging my views or feel threatened by my own confusion.

Why had I been so desperate to be right and make others wrong? Nothing good had come of it.

As I read, I learned that defending my beliefs created separation and division based on differences. It was not the Oneness I was seeking to know, a love based on the commonality of being human. The deep level of Oneness I was trying to experience couldn't be achieved by separating people into groups of right or wrong, different races or religions, poverty or wealth, or various political views. The great divide between all groups was artificial, totally made up, and I wondered why I'd accepted these divisions in the first place.

For my part, I intended to erase it by completely ignoring what appeared to be our differences and acknowledging only the love in the heart of each person I met. I wanted what these lessons offered: a deep understanding of unconditional acceptance and the peace of mind that comes with that acceptance. It would take a lot of practice.

The Course showed me just how constantly judgmental I'd been; it came as a shock. I wasn't aware that I'd always been looking for the negatives in people and that, in my mind, I was constantly criticizing everything about them: their clothes, their hair, their conversation, their occupation. Subconsciously I thought that because everyone else was so much better than I was, I'd like myself more if I found fault in them and brought them down a bit from that lofty perch I'd unconsciously placed them on. Of course, it never worked. It never helped me feel better about myself. In fact, it left me feeling worse about myself. I'd never understood this dynamic before.

I'd been attaching importance to things that I had no control over and that were, in reality, unimportant, like what others thought of me. At the same time, I was not recognizing the things that I did have control over and that were important — like what I thought of others. It slowly became unimportant if others looked down on me but very important that I not look down on others. Each lesson built towards the next, and each formed an important step in the direction of understanding the concepts introduced. If I hadn't realized how judgmental I was, I wouldn't have understood why I often looked down on others. I wouldn't have been able to correct it. I wouldn't have known why my judgements were so harmful to others and to me or why offering love to others would heal me, as I was about to learn.

Gradually, I stopped complaining about things I couldn't change and the constant judgmental chatter in my mind began to fade. I couldn't change the things about others that I didn't like. I couldn't make other drivers drive the way I thought they should or make people be more polite or change their beliefs to mine. But, with practice, I could accept them the way they were. When I did so, I began to see my own mistakes in the mistakes of others. I had cut people off in traffic, accidentally or not, and I'd been rude.

I'd always fought against the negative, unattractive qualities in myself. I thought they defined me and didn't realize that what I couldn't accept in myself, I couldn't accept in others, so I judged them harshly. My goal became not to eliminate my negative emotions, but to stop judging them and accept them. I would stop trying to be perfect and accept that my mistakes, and those of others, were just that: mistakes, not inherent badness. I aimed for a complete acceptance of reality, to trust the flow of life and act with grace.

I liked this experiment and my new way of seeing the world. It made me feel good about myself. I was gaining wisdom and inner power that strengthened me.

From the moment I'd begun reading the Course, it touched something in me, something strangely familiar that seemed to go back a thousand years in time. It was a flash of something wonderful, bright and joyful. It was the childhood joy of being in a thunderstorm, twirling and laughing as hail pounded down, lightning flashed and the heavens roared. It was the power of the waves that crashed over me as I bodysurfed naked in the moonlight in the warm ocean off Bali, the force of the rapids in the Slave River as the helicopter I was in landed on a large rock in the midst of the rushing water. It was the beauty of the savannahs of Africa and its lions, elephants, zebras, rhinos, gazelles — a vision that filled me with joy at the diversity of the world and which left me with a deep knowing of the greatness of this earth. These memories were glimpses of an enormous power, something brilliant and awesome, something greater than anything I'd ever known. I wanted to understand this power. I wanted to know how to be truly joyful, how to reach deep inside and consistently find joy. I wanted not the temporary joy from the pleasures of life, but the stupendous joy of sheer existence.

As I read, I knew there was truth here. A whole and absolute truth that I trusted with a surety previously unknown to me. It seemed that I was being told in a thousand different ways how much God loved us. I'd never believed in God's love before. As a teenager, I'd learned of God the Father, an Old Testament God who was harsh, judgmental and violent, a God who'd scared the hell out of me. I'd instantly closed my mind to anything to do with God. I had enough bad fathers already, thank you very much. But now I was learning of a different God, a God of pure love and grace and unconditional acceptance. I warily reached out for more understanding of this God.

I learned that this God loved every one of his creations. That meant He must love and accept me too. This would be the unconditional love that I'd craved so much, that I'd been searching for in relationships — the love that I couldn't find because I didn't know how to offer it to myself or others. I'd never been able to trust love that had been offered to me in the past. It was just too hard to believe that I was lovable.

But because these teachings were so true to me, because they made sense and the love described was so pure and unconditional and profound, it seemed to fill a gaping hole in my heart and I gradually, ever so slowly and hesitatingly, began to accept that love.

"The Thought God holds of you is like a star, unchangeable in an eternal sky." — ACIM T-30.III.8:4

"You cannot understand how much your Father loves you, for there is no parallel in your experience of the world to help you understand it. There is nothing on earth with which it can compare, and nothing

you have ever felt apart from Him resembles it ever so faintly."
— ACIM T-14.IV.8:4

"Look, then, upon the light He placed within you, and learn that what you feared was there has been replaced with love."
— ACIM T-13.IX

I started accepting that God had not abandoned me as a child, that there was no such thing as excommunication. I wasn't the worst of the worst because of what others had done to me. I learned that I never had to ask myself if I was worthy of this love. I was worthy by the very fact of my existence. As I read and practiced, I saw the Course as a love story between the Creator and his creations and I began to see myself as truly lovable for the first time in my life.

15

It's Not Fair!

"The fear of God is the fear of life and not death.
Yet He remains the only place of safety."
— ACIM T-23.IV

M Y BROTHER Mark was so afraid of living that he chose death. I thought I understood his fear and why he did what he did. I was familiar with that awful sense of nothingness and hopelessness at the core of one's being. Growing up around the ever-present threat of suicide, it was hard to learn that life was to be valued and that the earth was not just a torture chamber to be survived. By devaluing life as torture, I had limited my expectations and ambitions, believing that hopelessness was all there was. I'd missed an understanding of the miracle of being that I was now learning about.

I became aware that I was often more afraid of living than of dying and more afraid of people's love than their hate. I was used to being hated; I certainly wasn't used to being loved. It was scary. It created expectations that I didn't understand and felt I couldn't live up to. I'd often viewed myself as fake, especially when others saw me as courageous and strong. If someone loved me for that courage and strength, did that make it real? By believing I was fake, I stayed in my littleness and was blocked from recognizing who I really was and from seeing the love that others offered me.

"Accept your sense of failure as nothing more than a mistake in who you are." — ACIM T-15.VIII

Ego is defined by the Course as the belief in the reality of the false self, of the self we believe we are, not the self we really are. In my victimhood, I'd been seeing myself as so much less than everyone else and was confused on the occasions when my illusion was proved to be wrong. It left me questioning my sanity because I couldn't figure out my own reality.

I learned that I needed to recognize my ego, but not condemn myself for having one.

I learned that, as we release ourselves from our egos, we release the cognitive dissonance that is so painful and stop attempting to live with reality and unreality at the same time. What a relief it was that my Creator didn't view me with the same viciousness that my ego did and that my Creator saw me as I truly am and still had infinite, unconditional love for me. This is the biggest miracle of all.

I began to watch funny movies in the evenings to balance out the intensity of what I was learning. To my surprise and delight, I discovered that movies I'd previously rated as too silly were suddenly hilarious. Finding a sense of humor that had been buried deep inside, I sat on my sofa all by myself in sweatpants and an old T-shirt, curled up in a blanket, a bowl of popcorn nearby, lights dimmed and candles lit, watching and howling loudly at the funny comments and antics. I'm sure my neighbors thought I was nuts. But it was fun and joyful and easy and the world seemed less dark when I was able to laugh at it.

Then, each morning, I plunged forward again into more abstract concepts. I felt I had more to learn before I could understand how to apply the teachings in any practical way.

The Course described two sometimes confusing levels. There was the level where Jesus existed: pure love, kindness, peacefulness and non-judgmental Oneness. This was the only true reality, the level where you understand that you can't hurt someone else without hurting yourself. This was the level that so many of us are striving to reach.

And then the other level, where most of us are now, existing in the seeming reality of our human faults and failures. This was the level I was now attempting to rise above.

On the first level, the Creator saw each of us as perfect, with an inner magnificence that radiated beyond any realms we could imagine. It was a magnificence we couldn't see because of the shadows in our perceptions of ourselves.

This was a stunning new concept but it was also difficult for me to accept as the old tapes kept playing in my head. It was hard for me to believe, in that moment, that I could ever look inside myself and see magnificence. But I wanted to believe in the possibility.

The Course taught that, on the level of Oneness, we are all, without exception, innocent; that we are the pure light of God and nothing else. For the first time ever, I began to think that I was not bad inside and that whatever had happened in my past didn't matter in any real sense because it had not affected who I was at my core. Nothing could make me less than I was or change who I was in any way unless it was to make me stronger, even if I couldn't always see that strength. The past was the past and, other than what I'd learned from it, it was no longer relevant to the present. Acknowledging the past and letting go of it freed my present and future.

I already knew that it wasn't your past that put you in the psych ward. It was your fear of the past and the worry that it would suddenly echo into the present at the worst possible time. This fear had arisen frequently throughout my life. I'd always believed that because the violence of my past had continually repeated in abusive relationships that I'd thought I deserved, that it defined me. Now I understood that it didn't and that I hadn't 'deserved' it.

But now I had a choice. I could see myself as whole or I could see myself as disempowered by what others had convinced me I was. Did I choose to believe that my brokenness contributed to my wholeness or that my wholeness had been destroyed by my brokenness?

Believe it or not, it wasn't an easy choice to make. I could believe what I was reading, or I could believe all the negative things I'd heard and accepted all my life. I knew what I wanted to believe but it would take a lot more studying to really convince me deep inside that it was true for me.

It took all my courage, but I decided to trust. I would immerse myself totally in A COURSE IN MIRACLES and live the teachings, being aware in every moment of what I was doing and thinking and following the steps precisely and deliberately.

I kept reading.

"Could you not look with greater charity on whom God loves with perfect love?" — ACIM T-16.II

IN OTHER words, if God decided that each of us was lovable, who was I to say that someone else was not? I decided to see only the goodness in the heart of everyone I met, to see their essence instead of their actions or words, and to see our commonalities, no matter how different we seemed to be. I would assume the best of others, that they were pure light and that, if they caused hurt, it was not intentional. I would see the light inside them that showed their magnificence and reflect that back to them. I began to practice with everyone I met, beginning with a simple smile of acceptance and continuing with erasing any thoughts of judgement that may have been in my mind.

As I did this small practice, I thought about the people who had so badly hurt me in the past and wondered if I could truly see the light in them. But then I remembered the forgiveness Jesus offered on the cross that had so caught my attention as a teenager, and the forgiveness of the Jewish survivors of concentration camps. Then I knew in my heart that I could forgive anyone and anything, even those who had caused me so much pain. I was far enough along in my understanding of the Course that I knew it was possible. Maybe not easy, but possible. And I was learning that forgiveness was the only path to peace and freedom. I vowed to myself to overcome any difficulties and follow this path completely.

I WENT for my usual walk one afternoon, stopping at a small coffee shop where I ordered a bowl of soup and a sandwich. I was just finishing my meal when a young woman approached me and asked if she could pay my bill. I recognized her from the park near my apartment. As I'd gained new understanding from the Course, I found I was becoming more open to others and less inclined to just rush around and I'd stopped to chat with her several times when I saw her sitting on one of the benches. In spite of her slight handicap in expressing herself and understanding others, I'd enjoyed her sense of humour and lightheartedness. Now, in the coffee shop, she wanted to pay my bill. She told me that, "No one talks to me the way you do. Most people just walk away, but you're nice. No one's ever been so nice to me. Let me pay your bill to thank you." I told her that I liked her and enjoyed her company and that she didn't need to pay my bill to thank me.

The realization that I did like her, that there was nothing fake or shallow about it, affected me deeply. In the past I'd always kept my invisible wall up and silently pushed people away but now, as I looked at others without judgement, I discovered that I really did like people. I saw only the light in them, and somehow they knew their light had been seen. They understood that I had looked past their inner shadows and accepted them unconditionally.

It had an amazing effect on others. They were drawn to me, opening doors for me and offering small kindnesses, even stopping me on the sidewalk to thank me for the smile I'd offered them. And I was struck by how little attention it took to make someone else feel good about themselves. I suspected that my acceptance of who they were may have eased the fears of those who worried about being perceived as not good enough, fears that I was so familiar with. It warmed my heart to know I'd made such a difference to another person. It was proof positive that my efforts to understand the Course were truly worth it.

A funny thing happened when I accepted others as they were. I began to accept myself as I was, very gradually letting go of my many fears. It was a positive C of Catch-22. I accepted others without judgement and, by doing so, accepted myself without judgement. But it was only as I learned to let go of self-judgment that I was able to stop judging others. But it worked. Somehow it all worked.

I no longer judged who deserved a smile and who didn't, or who I should be afraid to smile at and who I felt safe with. Calmness descended on my days as I offered my smiles as gifts from my heart to everyone I crossed paths with.

Some would consider that mindset naive, even Pollyannish. But I wasn't looking for sainthood. I just wanted a better way to live. I felt this new way of looking at others could offer me that. It was all a state of mind, an internal decision to change my viewpoint. I aimed for living a life of unconditional love. Easier said than done. But "Aim for the stars" was my new motto. I told no one of the grand experiment I was undertaking!

THE COURSE told me that I was a changeless core of light.

"It is not you who are so vulnerable and open to attack that just a word, a little whisper that you do not like, a circumstance that suits you not, or an event that you did not anticipate upsets your world, and hurls it into chaos. Truth is not frail." — ACIM T-24.III

That was exactly what had been happening to me. My certainty that I lacked value and purpose had made me feel vulnerable and confused. Everyone else's comments and actions upset me. Even a condescending look could ruin my day. But if I believed what I was reading, then the overly sensitive person I'd always been was just ego and not reality. I didn't know who I really was. It was difficult to believe that I would eventually see myself as changeless and strong, regardless of what others said to me or what emotions cascaded through me.

This idea was new and I didn't necessarily trust it yet. It seemed like wishful thinking. So I only gave up my old beliefs one small piece at a time, and only with proof that this was a better way. Required proof was minimal. The more I studied, the more minor frustrations seemed to disappear. There were moments of easiness to my days and an occasional brief calmness that I'd always longed for. I had a new level of appreciation for the park I walked in after each few hours spent reading the Course. I sat on a bench and, for the first time, truly valued the beauty of the flowers — the roses and petunias and pansies and others I couldn't name — that provided a glorious palette of color and scent amidst the backdrop of the green of the trees and the manicured lawns. I loved the peaceful energy that emanated from the area and I wondered how I hadn't really seen the park's elegance before.

One day I joined a friend for lunch, a colleague who enjoyed Italian food as much as I did, and we sat on the patio while we ate our seafood pasta and people watched. It was a beautiful, warm day and we chatted and joked about families, work and life in general. An hour and a half later, as we prepared to leave, she surprised me with this comment: "You aren't as edgy as usual. You seem more peaceful."

I'd never told her about ACIM, so her comment caught me totally off guard. Wow. After studying for just three weeks, the change in me was obvious. Confirmation felt wonderful. I eagerly went back to reading and studying ways to change my life for the better.

Then this hit me like a ton of bricks:

"I am upset because I see a meaningless world." — ACIM W-12

It occurred to me that I had no clue of who I really was. My inside world was meaningless. As I looked at the outside world when my pretenses were down, it appeared meaningless as well. Why was I here? Why was anyone here? Standing on my ninth-floor balcony, overlooking the busyness of downtown, I watched everyone rushing about their business and saw people as mice running around in a maze. We are born, we live and we die. Why? Was there any purpose to this painful and empty existence? I wanted purpose and a more gracious understanding and acceptance of my existential journey. No more just bouncing from crisis to crisis in a panic.

"God has no secrets. He does not lead you through a world of misery, waiting to tell you, at the journey's end, why He did this to you." — ACIM T-22.I.3:10

I learned that God did not create a meaningless world, that God did not create war or disaster or airplane crashes or cancer. I liked this concept, as it reinforced my choice to believe in the loving God of the Course. The remnants of my confusion about this deity lessened significantly. I learned that I did indeed have a purpose, that it was to face my inner darkness and replace it with love and joy.

A FEW DAYS later, looking out my balcony window at the pouring rain and knowing I wouldn't get my walk in that day, I turned once again to my studies. I learned about the effects of my thoughts and that none of them were neutral. There are no idle thoughts. Each thought contributes to either truth or illusion. Fearful thoughts are all destructive, just as they are all unreal. My fears were totally made up and I could choose to let go of them. I loved this idea — it offered freedom and release. And, as I kept reading, I began to understand just how to obtain this freedom.

"Understand that you do not respond to anything directly, but to your interpretation of it. Your interpretation thus becomes the justification for the response. That is why analyzing the motives of others is hazardous to you." — ACIM T-12.I.1:4

Knowing in my heart that others disliked me, and fearing that they were going to hurt me, I had sometimes lashed out first. I'd grown up hearing how bad I was but did this mean everyone thought of me that way?

Now I questioned that assumption. Did everyone dislike me and were they going to hurt me? I didn't know that for sure. So, what if I stopped planning how I would handle their 'inevitable' attacks on me? What if I let go of this ingrained fear of others and trusted that I wouldn't have to defend myself?

These were questions I'd never asked myself because I was so sure of my world view and knew that I was right. But being right had taken me to some dark places. If I looked at everyone as if they were dangerous, then I didn't see people for who they really were and I missed the goodness inside them. And, if I couldn't see the goodness in others, how could I see it in myself?

When I assumed that I knew what other people were thinking, or why they were doing what they were doing, I passed judgement on them. They were stupid or mean or dishonest. Now I was becoming aware that I didn't know what others were thinking, or why they were doing what they were doing. When they hurt my feelings, I didn't know if it was deliberate and malicious. I didn't know if they understood the depth of the pain they caused.

"Wisdom is not judgement; it is the relinquishment of judgement." — ACIM M-II.4:5

I learned that, with my negative judgements of others, I'd not only been unkind, but unwise, and I began to reach an even deeper level of understanding about judgment. It struck me how arrogant I'd been to think I knew enough about others to judge them as lacking and began to understand that doing so had hurt me even more than it had hurt them.

The Course teaches that other people are mirrors that reflect what we see inside ourselves, even if we don't understand that at the time. So, I was subconsciously judging myself each time I judged others. When I saw someone doing something I'd done in the past, was I mad at them or at me? I wasn't happy to be looking in the mirror. It didn't feel good and made me not like myself, and it kept me from making real connections with others as I tried to hide who I thought I really was.

I gradually stopped thinking that I knew what was best for others and judging their actions and thoughts as good or bad. In fact, I stopped looking at everyone as good or bad in any way and I began accepting them just as they were.

ACIM described that there was a catch to obtaining the gifts of this program. We couldn't heal alone. If we wanted to see the light in ourselves, we had to see the light in others. If I truly wanted to give up the belief that I was bad, then I needed to offer release from that belief to others.

But how would I do that? I thought long and hard before deciding that, with each person I met, acquaintance or stranger, I would consciously shut down any thoughts in my mind about outward appearances and actions and focus only on who they were. I would imagine that I saw a light inside each and, in my mind, acknowledge only that light. It wasn't long before I truly began to see only the light in people. It seemed that once I'd cleared my mind of old ways of judging, a new clarity allowed me to see past the external to the light inside each person.

To my delight, I discovered that I automatically stopped comparing myself to others once I stopped judging. It became less important that others agreed with me. A disagreement was no longer an indictment of my thoughts and opinions and who I was, nor a confirmation of my nothingness and stupidity. Gary had called me stupid so often that I'd believed it. It was his weapon of choice but now I wondered if it just indicated that he was insecure about his own intelligence. Maybe it hadn't been about me at all. The feeling of nothingness within myself was the illusion that I'd always crashed back into, a default state. But with this new understanding, my panic attacks subsided and I felt peace in my heart.

THE realization came that I couldn't understand my own wholeness as long as I was trying to diminish the wholeness of others, even silently, through judgements, criticisms or put-downs. That only kept me stuck in the darkness. There was no dignity or generosity in that. No wonder I hadn't been able to find the grace I was searching for.

In truth, it wasn't easy to give up the specialness of my victimhood and I wavered, constantly going back and forth between reaching for the light and being afraid of it. What the Course promised sounded idyllic, but when I snapped at a clerk in a store who'd seemed to be a bit condescending with me, I realized how superficial my understanding was. And who could possibly understand these concepts on a deep level after only a partial reading? Not me.

Memories had been haunting me and reminding me of my worthlessness, and I took my pain out on the clerk. I was ashamed of myself. But these memories kept popping into my mind when least expected. I felt joy when I learned a new concept but then slid backwards into memories and feelings that upset me.

It seemed to be two steps forward and one step back as I let the light shine on each bit of darkness inside me. But it was hard to give up lies I'd understood as truths for an entire lifetime and recognize the truth that I'd known for only a few weeks. I was so angry and furious at men in general, unable to give up the terror they induced in me. I didn't yet understand that what I was most afraid of was the darkest parts of my past that I hadn't yet had the courage to acknowledge. So I subconsciously stuffed the worst of the dark memories deep inside and refused to look at them, unaware of what that would cost me in the future. I see-sawed, discovering the joy inside me as I read through the Course but not letting go of some of the shadows of the past. It was exhausting.

"Beware of the temptation to see yourself as unfairly treated." — ACIM T-26.X.4:1

My parents hadn't been fair. Gary and Tom hadn't been fair. I had a long list! Poor me. When I saw myself as unfairly treated, then I had to blame someone, thus making others guilty. And it kept me stuck in the darkness of victimhood.

I looked back at all the people I'd judged. It wasn't just my parents I was angry with. It was friends and strangers, corporations and politicians and the entire world. It was life in general. I felt so alone and misunderstood. It wasn't fair! My latent victimhood frequently reared its ugly head. Now the question became: Could I forgive my parents and others for not being perfect? For all the pain and darkness I'd had to go through? Could I forgive the world for treating me unfairly?

If I could forgive, that meant the anger that lay just beneath the surface, the anger that made me lash out at others whenever I was irritated or afraid, would have no reason to exist anymore. The fury that had boiled up inside me, thanks to all those years growing up hearing that I was less than everyone else, could be released.

But unless I understood that I was whole inside, what I had on the outside would never be enough and I would always see myself as lacking and as less than.

"When you are angry, is it not because someone has failed to fill the function you allotted him?" — ACIM T-29.IX.4:1

I'D ALWAYS gotten so angry with people who didn't behave as I demanded they should, who didn't live up to my expectations, even when they didn't know my expectations. I had an idea of how parents and siblings and friends should act. I'd seen the TV show Leave it to Beaver. I had silently, subconsciously, demanded that people live up to such a fake perfection, and was furious when they didn't. How crazy was that? I didn't even know that I had any expectations. I pretended to smile and say please and thank you and all that obligatory rot. I didn't know the anger and frustration that was hidden underneath. I thought life was difficult because of my unlucky start.

But many people have unlucky starts in life, many of them much more difficult than mine. Did they all boil with rage on the inside while smiling on the outside? Who knew? Were their lives as messy as mine? Maybe. There was no point in comparing tragedies, as the severity of the pain was irrelevant. I wasn't special. No one gets out of this life without pain of some sort.

"One of the most important goals we have as students of the Course is to allow our definition of ourselves to be undone." — *Questions and Answers*, Foundation for A COURSE IN MIRACLES, p. 301.

The definition of myself that I'd lived with all my life may have been negative, but the thought of letting go of it was the scariest thought I'd ever had. I was asking God for the truth about who I was, and I was paralyzed by fear of the answer, feeling as if I were leaping into an abyss. Would reality be worse than my illusions? As I attempted to redefine myself, I went back and forth between moments of glorious, overwhelming joy and sheer terror.

But, somehow, I found a bit of courage and slowly progressed as I kept reading the Course and choosing to let go of old beliefs. It was surprising how free I felt on giving up my old ways of seeing myself. I felt I could do anything I wanted once I stopped believing my pain was holding me back and that others looked down on me because of it. All that mattered was how I dealt with that pain; how I looked at it. I could be a victim by sitting in judgement of myself and others or I could free myself by letting it go.

"The moment we see ourselves as victims of someone else, we are giving that person power over us." — *The Journey Home* by Kenneth Wapnick, p. 418.

As the realization that I was continually giving my power to others sank in, I decided that I wasn't going to listen to those who told me my anger at being victimized was justified and that letting go of it was craziness. It wasn't justified. My anger hurt me, and how could hurting myself be justified? I chose to let it go. I was taking my power back.

I didn't need to worry about trusting others anymore, about who was safe and who might hurt my feelings. It was now about trusting, totally and absolutely, the knowledge that I was loved and that that would never change, no matter what. Slowly, a sense of being safe in this world rose within me and I understood that it was time to stop being so defensive with others. They couldn't hurt me. None of the difficulties of my life had truly hurt me. I was still the same person at my core that I'd always been. Now I could see my strength and goodness. Now I could see who I really was. I vowed to never let others define me again.

I could define myself now, thank you very much.

16

Deciding to Live the Teachings

THE entire premise of A COURSE IN MIRACLES is forgiveness. I recall being mesmerized as a teenager by the words of Jesus on the cross asking God to forgive those who were killing him. I also remembered visiting Dachau and reading of the depths of forgiveness demonstrated by some of the Jewish survivors of the concentration camps. It seemed to me that Jesus's message of forgiveness reflected a universal truth, one that was independent of a particular faith or belief system.

But as much as I loved Jesus' words, I didn't really understand how one could forgive such terrible things. And I hadn't really known how to find out more. Until now. The more I studied ACIM, the clearer it became to me that the path to a deeper, more meaningful understanding of forgiveness was in front of me. This was the pathway I'd spent my life trying to find.

I had not a single doubt that I was on the right track, so I dove deeper into these philosophical premises and attempted to understand how to apply each one as I went along.

The Course offers a clear explanation of what's involved in the forgiving process, and why it's so important. As I began to understand that guilt was the unconscious burden most of us carry, I realized that until I could release that guilt and accept my innocence, I would not be free. To forgive myself, I needed to forgive others and to acknowledge that it was fear that had made me react in negative ways: fear that I was less than others, fear that I wasn't good enough. Fear had controlled everything I'd said and done. And it was fear that made others react negatively as well. Knowing this, it was easier not to judge the fearful person who was hurting others and easier to let go of the blame of my fearful self for hurting others.

By refusing to judge and silently offering forgiveness, I could just let go and accept the world and the people in it as they were. I learned that forgiveness doesn't require that I tolerate abuse or put myself in dangerous situations. It didn't mean telling the other person that what they had done was okay when it wasn't. Forgiveness was just letting it go and moving past it. Sometimes love is simply not hating.

At first, I didn't want to let others off the hook for what they'd done. But as I learned more I recognized that there is no healing without forgiveness. And I wanted healing more than I wanted blame; I wanted peace, not anger. What I ultimately wanted was to have no need to forgive because I would not have judged in the first place.

"If you assume correction's role, you lose the function of forgiveness. No one can forgive until he learns correction is but to forgive, and never to accuse." — ACIM T-27.II.10:3

I lost the desire to try to make others understand how badly they'd hurt me and no longer felt the need to accuse anyone of anything. I was choosing to let go of the pain I blamed them for and the judgements that went with it. It no longer mattered because they didn't do the damage I thought they did. They didn't destroy me. As I released their control over me, I felt peace. I was in control of myself.

"He [Holy Spirit] will teach you how to see yourself without condemnation by learning how to look on everything without it." — ACIM T-9.III.8:10

I was learning how to stop condemning myself by ceasing the condemnation of others. To see past my inner shadows, to see the light in myself, I had to see it in others and offer unconditional acceptance. In order to forgive myself, I had to forgive everyone else, the key word being everyone. There could be no exceptions. I couldn't pick and choose who I thought deserved forgiveness, or didn't. This was an all or nothing program. If I held on to resentments, they would have a hold on me. I'd read once that holding on to resentments was like drinking poison and thinking the other person would die. Now I learned that it was through letting go of resentments and condemnation that I could stop condemning myself. By recognizing the light of the Creator in everyone else, I could recognize that light in me.

MY VACATION time was over. I decided that I would literally live the teachings. Having isolated myself so that I could study the Course, it was now time to step out and see how practical my new skills were.

As I headed out to the park one afternoon, a few days before my return to work, I noticed for the first time some of the homeless people I walked by. This was nothing new, I'd seen them every day for years. But that day, I really saw them, and ideas from the Course came to mind.

First there was the Oneness I'd just learned about. If we were all one, then I was no better than they were. In reality, there was no difference between us. They were simply in different circumstances. In the past, I'd seen them as either victims or victimizers, but now I understood I'd been looking down on them, and I let go of my judgments.

I began to smile genuinely at each person, a smile that told them I saw the light inside them, not just their outside appearance. As I did this, day after day, I got smiles back. They seemed to understand that they'd been seen for who they really were and that they were being offered a confirmation of their worth. Once in a while I stopped to chat, to ask how they were doing, and I spent a few minutes listening to what they had to say. Eventually I realized that I was no longer being asked for money. Apparently, my attention was more important than money.

"In this world you can become a spotless mirror in which the Holiness of your Creator shines forth from you to all around you. You can reflect Heaven here." — ACIM T-14.IX.5:1

But smiles were not enough to demonstrate unconditional acceptance. I jumped in my car and headed to the nearest big box store where I bought two dozen men's extra-large sweatshirts, socks, gloves and toques, along with cases of protein bars. I stored all of this in the trunk of my car. The next time I went to the recycling bins to drop off cans and bottles, where many of the homeless hung out, I was prepared. It was a cold day and I saw that many of them weren't properly dressed. I offered warm clothes and a protein bar to each person who wanted it, without judgement of any kind. Their gratitude warmed my heart as I understood that it wasn't just the stuff I offered but the love that went with it that they were so grateful for.

At home, I went to drop off my garbage in the large bin behind my building and, when I tossed the bag in, a head popped up and a young woman who'd been searching for bottles jumped out of the bin. I apologized for hitting her with my garbage and she smiled at me. She was a scrawny young thing, with the ravaged face and damaged teeth of a drug addict who appeared to be not long for this world. She was shivering in the cold and I asked her if she wanted a warm sweatshirt. She walked with me to my car where I opened the trunk and offered her clothes and a protein bar. She grabbed the sweatshirt and put it on, staring at me in surprise and thanking me over and over. As I went to my apartment, she wandered off down the alley. What surprised me the most was how much these small gestures warmed my heart each time and how it raised my self-esteem to reach out to others in an open, loving way, without judgement.

Weeks later, once again dropping off my recycling, one of the men I'd given clothes to came up to me and asked to talk. He told me he'd just been diagnosed with cancer and didn't have much time left. He wanted me to be the first to know. I hugged him and asked him what I could get for him. He asked for more socks. I'd run out but I promised to be back in a few days. When I went back, he never showed up and a friend who worked at the Drop-In Centre told me he'd passed away. When the homeless get diagnosed, it's usually so advanced that they pass quickly. He was in my thoughts for a long time after.

Reaching out to others had helped me more than them. The love I'd shown was given back many times over and I felt like I'd been gifted with something wonderful and exquisite that would stay in my heart forever.

BACK AT WORK, it wasn't long before a challenge showed up. But this time, when I encountered a particularly edgy co-worker, I recognized her perennial grumpiness as a sign of her inner lack of self-worth. Normally when encountering someone like this, I put up an invisible wall, ostensibly to protect myself from their slings and arrows — but as I realized now, I was hiding my disdain and judgement. This time, I stayed open as I pondered how to help her feel better about herself. I noticed how efficient she was and how her organizing skills made the service flow more smoothly. I hadn't noticed this before because I'd always focused on her bad moods. This time, I told her that I appreciated her efficiency and how it eased the workload. Her huge, surprised smile lit up her face and told me how seldom she received a compliment. After that, she opened up to me more than ever before, chatting easily. My other colleagues asked how I'd managed to calm this notorious grouch but when I told them I had merely offered her a compliment, they didn't believe me. "How could it be so simple?" they asked.

And, indeed, it wasn't as simple as a compliment. By being more open with her, without judgment and with no walls of self-defense going up, she immediately knew that I wasn't judging her. That made it safe for her to let her guard down. But I didn't understand these dynamics yet, certainly not well enough to explain them to anyone.

I repeated the experiment with others, seeing something good in each person, knowing that each compliment had to be specific and genuine, not manipulative in the hopes of getting any particular outcome. It was simple, really. When I didn't judge people, even silently, they felt safe to show me who they were. When I helped someone to see her value, I saw some of my own, and we both benefited, just like the Course promised. I was amazed at the perfection of it.

It worked in personal relationships too. In the past, before Gary, I would often lash out at someone who said something negative to me, trying to hurt them as they had hurt me. When dating relationships ended, I listed the faults of the other person I'd been dating, just to let them know they weren't any better than I was. In hindsight, I can't imagine how much pain I'd caused as I tried to destroy those I blamed for my pain. Sometimes my first thought was still to do that when a friendship ended, but now I could stop myself and allow the other person to vent without blasting back at them. I could try to understand why they were hurt and angry. It was hard at first, but it became easier as I recognized that I was seeing my own insecurities in the other person and my defensiveness had nothing to do with them. It seemed unfathomable now that I'd ever felt such a need to destroy others.

17

The Most Challenging Lesson

D URING a phone call, one of my sisters told me that Mom had attempted suicide again a few days before. I was shocked and upset. I'd recognized the depression in Mom's voice with each of our conversations but I hadn't realized how deep it was. I called Mom and told her I'd be there the next morning. Getting up early and jumping on the first flight to Vancouver, I took the bus to Mom's straight from the airport, arriving on her doorstep about 9:00 a.m. I could see as she answered the door that she was struggling to smile. She was still in her nightgown in the dark apartment and my heart broke as I saw her pain. As I opened the drapes to let in the sunlight, I could see that she hadn't cleaned in a long time. Making tea, I asked her what she'd been up to. Her speech was slow, without energy, and she seemed on the verge of crying as she explained that she'd gradually stopped visiting her friends and going out, that her world had become darker and more exhausting. She didn't confess to the suicide attempt and I didn't ask. It was clear that she didn't want to talk about it.

She began to perk up as I told her about the latest compliments I'd received for the sweaters she'd knitted for me and of an offer I'd received to buy one of them. She pulled out the half-finished sweater she was working on to show me. It was a beautiful peach and white angora, knitted with wool that I'd purchased on my last visit with her. I admired every detail as she told me she'd taken it to the wool store to show them and they'd tried to buy it from her. I mentioned her TV shows and some of the funny parts of the latest episodes that I'd watched on layovers and we began to laugh together. She loved hearing about incidents that happened on flights and the weird things passengers sometimes said and did so I dug deep for memories of funny incidents that would help her mood.

I shared a story of a flight from Los Angeles to Calgary where a woman boarded the aircraft with a tiny Chihuahua dog trailing along on a leash behind her. This was before pets were allowed on flights so the crew told her that she couldn't bring her dog on board, to which she replied, "He's a seeing-eye dog because I'm partially blind."

It was the end of a long day for this crew and we were punch-drunk tired. Barely able to control our laughter, and with a nearly empty flight, we let her on. When the same passenger later asked for help getting to the bathroom, we asked her, just out of curiosity, why the dog wasn't able to help her get there. She ever so casually answered, "Because he's blind." And, sure enough, right at that moment he stood up and walked headfirst into the bulkhead.

Well, there was no controlling our laughter at that point and, as one flight attendant helped her to the bathroom, the rest of us retreated to the back galley, howling, with tears pouring down our faces. A blind seeing-eye Chihuahua! That one took the cake. Mom loved hearing every detail.

Then, wracking my brain for something to do that didn't involve sitting in a smoky bingo hall or a casino, I asked Mom if she wanted to go for a drive to Bellingham, just across the US border in Washington State, so that we could shop in the factory outlets. She loved that idea. I rented a car and we headed out. It was a warm fall day and the leaves on the trees were many different colors. There were still flowers everywhere and Mom's mood improved by the minute. When we got to the factory outlets, she spent hours going through every single store, looking at everything. She didn't buy much but she was excited about each bargain she got and, trust me, she knew a bargain when she saw one.

After a late lunch at a restaurant in town, we stopped at Costco on the way home where I bought food to fill her freezer. I had no idea of the significance of the food until I found out months later that she'd told my sisters about it. Mom didn't really care about 'things', but it meant everything to her that I'd bought her food. I realized how hard it had been on her to deal with so many years of hunger, and how a full freezer eased her fears.

Mom opened up to me on the ninety-minute drive home, talking about the past, about things she'd never talked about before. I listened quietly as her memories of the violence and poverty and her hatred of my father came pouring out of her. No matter how uncomfortable her anger made me or how painful her memories were for me, I didn't shut her down. I knew how awful it was to be silenced, not allowed to speak your truth. I determined I would never do that to her. I didn't bring up my own memories because I wanted her to go at her own pace, without me triggering things she wasn't ready for. Interestingly, her conversation confirmed my memories of things that had happened, right to the last detail. I'd never had confirmation before and had sometimes wondered if my memories were accurate. Now I was surprised at just how accurate they were. But Mom surprised me when she said, "You were such a bad child."

"Why did you think I was a bad child?"

"Because, ever since you could walk, you ran away and I always got in trouble with the police and social services when they brought you back."

"Mom, a two-year-old doesn't run away. If a door was left open while you were sleeping, then a small child will just walk out the door."

She was furious and raised her voice. "You have to take responsibility for what you did as a child. You ran away and caused trouble for me."

I decided to let it go but it made me aware of how limited her parenting skills were. She honestly didn't know that children have to be watched all the time. As she went back to talking about my

Dad, I thought about what I knew about her childhood. Her mother had died when Mom was only about eight. My grandmother had been in a tuberculosis sanatorium for a year before her death and Mom and her sister were not even told their mother had died until they were taken to her funeral and saw her in the casket.

Her father eventually remarried and her stepmother had to threaten my grandfather with divorce if he didn't buy his children winter coats, in spite of the fact that he was the wealthiest man in town.

Of course she didn't know how to parent.

When we stopped at Canada Customs as we crossed the border to home, she joked with the customs officer. She told me afterwards, "You know the reason we got through customs so easily? It's because he liked me. You know that, right?"

This was a side of Mom I hadn't seen before. Who knew she was such a flirt?

The next day I began cleaning her apartment, starting with washing the fridge and the freezer inside and out, scrubbing the bathroom, then dusting and vacuuming and finishing with cleaning the windows. While I worked, we talked about politics and what was happening in some of the small African countries and in South America, about economics and how the new federal budget would affect the country, and about various social issues. By the time I'd finished cleaning, we'd solved the world's problems and her place looked cozy again. As she settled into her big chair with her feet on the ottoman and admired her sparkling apartment, I tried to convince her to hire someone to clean for her, but she didn't want a stranger coming into her place. I told her that, in between my visits, she had to keep it clean. I worried about her health and knew that a dirty apartment only contributed to her depression. She'd always kept her home very clean and I knew she'd feel better when things got back to normal.

She looked considerably better by the time I left the next morning and I promised her that we'd make the Bellingham trip every time I visited, which I was now planning to do once a month.

As I was going out the door on my way to the airport, she gave me a parting shot, a bit of familiar motherly advice: "Why do you still look so ugly? Can't you do something with your hair? Why do you wear those clothes? No wonder Gary left you. He was too good for you."

The air was sucked out of me as the stabbing pain of my divorce overwhelmed me. I was suddenly forced to acknowledge that both Gary and my mother viewed me in the same negative way. Instantly retreating inside myself, I silently hugged her goodbye and walked away.

Arriving home still upset at her comments, I decided to figure out a better way of dealing with Mom, a way to keep her comments from hurting me. I was aware that I hadn't totally let my invisible wall down with her. It was too scary to leave myself open to her unexpected comments and to feel that knife in my back. But I wanted to figure out a way to deal with her attacks so that they didn't hurt so much. I wanted to know how to help her without having to bear the brunt of her painful verbal blows. I didn't want to change Mom as much as I wanted to change myself.

I thought of the teachings of A COURSE IN MIRACLES:

"Because you see them as they are, you offer them your acceptance of their truth so they can accept it for themselves." — ACIM T-3. II.6:6

I had to look beyond the obvious, see the good in everyone in spite of the negatives, and then reflect that good back to them so that they could see it too. I knew that her only truth was the light inside her and I knew that nothing was unforgivable, that no one was less worthy of forgiveness than another, and that someone who hurt others did so because they were lacking love. I thought about the lack of love Mom had faced early in life that had allowed her to treat her children as she did and resolved to give her as much love as possible. It seemed very hard, when I was hurting, to accept this teaching, but I decided to test it with Mom.

"There is one particular person with whom we are struggling, who provides our most challenging lessons on forgiveness." — *Questions & Answers*, Foundation for A COURSE IN MIRACLES, p. 235, question 223.

Would this Course work on the person who had caused me the most pain?

For me to totally trust the teachings, they had to work without exception. There were so many faiths that people discussed in terms like, "Well, I believe this part, but not that." But I didn't want a partial faith. I wanted total and complete truth. I wanted more than belief. I wanted knowledge. I would now follow the Course to the letter in my relationship with Mom. I wasn't trying to make her love me, nor did my feelings have anything to do with altruism. It was solely about testing the tenets of this new understanding, of offering her love without expecting anything in return. I knew what a challenge it would be for me to see only the good in her, to offer her pure love when she was at her most angry and nasty, when she was ranting about what a terrible person I was and listing everything she hated about me. During times when I would normally run away from her, offering her love would confirm for me the value of this Course I was putting so much effort into understanding. It would show me if it really contained the complete truth.

I chose to look for the good in my mother and for a way to provide some of the love that she was so obviously lacking. If I was going to use the Course to walk out of hell, I wanted to bring my mother with me. This was my chance to practice unconditional love.

I decided to write a letter telling her all the positive things I could think of. Mom needed to know that she was loved. She didn't seem to love herself and I suspected that she couldn't imagine how anyone else could love her. So I told her over and over again, in detail, exactly what it was that I loved about her. Initially, it was much harder than I thought it would be to get past all of my memories of her negativity and darkness, so I had to dig deeper inside myself. I told her that it meant a lot to me that she hadn't walked away from us as kids and that she stuck it out no matter how rough it got. I thanked her for all the beautiful dresses she sewed using old drapery material, for all the knitting she did, for all the meals she cooked, all the pies she baked, seemingly out of nothing, all the laundry she did with that old wringer washer, and all the floors she scrubbed on her hands and knees. I thanked her for the good advice on surviving in a rough world, for the times she hid us to keep us safe and the times she took my father's brutality in order to protect us from it. I told her how much I admired her intelligence and that, if circumstances had been different, she would have been a politician or a CEO. If the opportunity had presented itself, she would have flown high. I told her how much I admired her humor, her courage and her strength.

It felt good to reach out to Mom in such a positive way and, as I wrote, I was surprised to realize just how completely I was letting go of resentments and truly forgiving her for all the wounds of the past. The teachings of A Course in Miracles had gone much deeper inside me than I'd thought and I now recognized their effectiveness on a level I hadn't understood before. When I was done writing, I mailed it to Mom, fingers crossed that it would help her.

A few days later, I called her and as soon as she heard my voice, she started to cry. "I got your letter. No one ever said nice things like that about me. I keep reading it over and over," she sobbed into the phone. "I thought everything I did was bad and I was a bad mother. I thought I never did anything right."

I reiterated what I'd written in the letter and told her I loved her and that, even though I lived farther away now, I would always be there when she needed me. As I hung up, my relief was enormous.

18

The Miracles Just Keep Coming

"It is not what happens to you but your rejection
of it which causes the dark night of the soul."
— *Dark Night of the Soul,* p. 102

I T WAS early fall and the green spaces in Calgary were an exorbitant display of bright orange, yellow, and green mixed together as the leaves changed color and began to fall. Enjoying the spectacular display of nature, I drove along the streets early one evening. I wasn't sure why I'd signed up for a yoga class; for years I'd been doing yoga daily but I guess I wanted to see what was new. There was a large group of men and women in the brightly lit, cavernous room, chatting and laughing as they introduced themselves to each other, picked up mats and looked for a clear spot on the floor to claim as their own. It was partner yoga. How had I missed that when I registered? I didn't like to be touched by strangers and would never have taken that class had I known. My assigned partner was a woman about my age, tall and imposing, who told me she'd never taken a yoga class before and was excited to be there. Her friendly smile helped me to relax and trust that it would be okay.

The room was quiet as the instructors, a man and a woman in their mid-twenties, began to speak. Their perfectly muscled bodies were a testament to the effectiveness of their teaching and they demonstrated each pose while the students attempted to copy it. The first few exercises were relatively easy and I relaxed even more as we continued.

My partner and I were in the middle of a pose. She was leaning over me while I crouched on all fours, about to stretch, when suddenly her hands were moving over my body—in places they shouldn't have been. Lightly touching my breasts, for the briefest moment, before moving down over my hips and into my crotch, then quickly away. It was a feather of a touch, barely there before it was gone. I froze, unable to comprehend what had just happened. Terrified, I cowered, stopping mid-stretch for only a second before continuing, pretending that nothing had happened. Unable to think clearly or to speak, my mind closed down. I was no longer in a crowded room. I had gone to that familiar place in my mind where I didn't have to acknowledge what was happening, where I was floating away in the clouds. The sounds of the instructors' voices faded to a blur. My body continued to move with the exercise, stiffly and carefully, pretending nothing was wrong.

Then, thankfully, the class was over. I looked around, my biggest fear being that someone had seen what happened. The shame was too much. But I couldn't tell if anyone saw. My brain was not functioning. It was frozen, on autopilot. Refusing to look at my partner, I gathered my belongings and rushed to my car, feeling sick to my stomach. All I wanted was to get home and I kept telling myself: *You're almost there. Not much farther. You'll be safe there.*

And then I was. Safe at home, by myself. I barely made it to the bathroom before throwing up. Sobbing, I lay down on the cold bathroom floor, my head leaning on the edge of the tub, nausea bubbling up inside me as I raged. Not at my yoga partner — at myself, at my reaction to what she did. I froze. What was wrong with me? How could I have let this happen? Why didn't I say something? Do something? Anything? You coward! No matter what I did or said to act like a person deserving of respect, it was all a lie. I was a coward!

My fury knew no bounds as I pounded on the floor, crying, disgusted with myself, wailing at the raw agony inside me. The self-hatred was so very familiar. I knew that this was my fault. She saw something in me, some weakness that allowed her to do what she did. She wouldn't have done that to someone else. She would have expected someone else to speak up, to yell, to complain, to tell her, "Get your hands off me!" But not me. She knew I wouldn't say a word. She saw the weakness of who I really was. Every bit of my new-found self-esteem seemed to be gone in a flash, forgotten in the midst of my pain. As the vomiting subsided and exhaustion took over, I crawled into bed, choosing sleep as my weapon of denial. I would wake up and realize that it had never happened, that it was all a bad dream.

But as I slept, the nightmares began and old memories came alive, detailed memories I'd never allowed into my consciousness. Ugly memories. So real, it was as if they were happening right then, in that moment, with a clarity that terrified me. I was a child again, about five years old, smelling a familiar smell: stale cigarette smoke and alcohol. I heard his laugh, his voice, "The game, remember the game?" I couldn't breathe as he reached for me. It hurt. Silent screams raged through me. Afterwards, his loud, angry voice, "You are an evil child. If you don't stop making me do this, I will have to kill you. I promise I will kill you." Terrified, I didn't know what I'd done. What did I do?

As I came back to the present, I was ragged with exhaustion, disconnected from the world and my normal life. It all became perfectly, unavoidably clear as I remembered every detail of what had happened so many years ago, as I connected the confusing bits of memories that had floated to the surface of my mind over the last many years. This was the ugliness that had been hiding beneath the surface of my consciousness, the ugliness that threatened to drown me in self-hatred, a pain as sharp as a knife in my soul. I tried to shut it off, to think of something else. I tried to deny it, telling myself that it wasn't real. But it was.

For the next few days, I stayed in my apartment, drapes closed to keep the world away. In a fog, I could barely get out of bed.

Someone knocked on my door. I ignored them. In the distance
I heard my phone ring several times before the recording told
the caller to leave a message and I would call them back. I knew I
wouldn't call them back. I knew that I wouldn't survive this pain.

UNABLE to lift myself out of the darkness on my own, I contacted a
therapist. She seemed gentle and kind and we sat in her small, win-
dowless office with the lights comfortably low. I started sobbing
before I was even able to tell her why I was there, before I could
tell her that I had newly recovered memories and that I was having
nightmares about those memories. When I calmed down a bit, she
asked what I remembered and I told her that I was abused, but
I couldn't describe it in detail. It was too raw and painful and I
couldn't let anyone know the awful things that had happened so
many years ago, not even a therapist. In my pain, I didn't have the
courage to do what A COURSE IN MIRACLES taught:

*"The Holy Spirit asks of you but this: bring to Him every secret
you have locked away from Him. Open every door to Him, and bid
Him enter the darkness and lighten it away."* — ACIM T-14.VII.6:1

The darkness of pain and guilt and shame was still there, too
scary to look at, and so I pushed the memories back deep inside.
I believed that I'd forgiven my father a long time ago. I mistook
the fact that I was unable to express anger with the belief that it
had been dealt with, not understanding that I was still afraid. If I
expressed even a little anger, the bitter rage would pour out of me
so hard and fast that I would want to kill him and I would have no
control over that rage.

So, without giving more details, I told her about being called
evil. She told me that I wasn't evil and repeated over and over
again that the abuse wasn't my fault, that I was just an innocent
child, that it was my dad's fault and he was solely responsible for
his actions. But I'd been told for so many years that I made him do
it and, even though I knew intellectually that it wasn't my fault, I'd
been unable to give up on the lifelong belief that I'd deserved what

happened to me. Slowly, I began to understand that my Dad had only called me evil because he couldn't take responsibility for his terrible actions and so he had blamed me.

But even though I saw this, and despite my new understanding gained from the Course, I couldn't yet truly forgive my father, or free myself from his chains, because I couldn't find the courage to look at the details of my past and thus let go of the shame.

I talked about Tom's violence. As I told her about the things he did to me, I was no longer present. The memories came alive and I was back with Tom, lost in the past, trying to protect myself from his blows. I forgot that she was even in the room. At one point, she leaned forward and I jolted backwards in my chair, arms crossed over my head to protect myself, yelling, "No, no, don't hit me." My heart was pounding with fear.

She was shaken by my reaction and told me about Post Traumatic Stress Disorder.

She took a piece of string and told me to use it to form a circle around me, as large or as small as I needed to feel safe and promised that she wouldn't cross the string into my safety zone. It worked, and I felt safe within my circle. At the start of each appointment, I put the string in place before I began talking. I moved on to issues with Mom. Even though I had reached out to help her, I'd been unable to negate her never-ending rants that were seared into my brain: how ugly I was, how no man could ever possibly want me, how no one could stand me and how I'd never have any friends. She had made it clear that she thought I didn't deserve anything good that happened and how bad things would always happen to me. Mom honestly believed what she said and was truly surprised when good things happened to me.

Even now, after all these years, I still didn't like to look at myself in the mirror. I could put on makeup but I could not really, honestly look at myself. I had totally accepted that my mother was right. For one of our appointments, the therapist arrived with a smile on her face and a mirror in her hand. She wanted me to see that I wasn't ugly. But I couldn't do it. I was too afraid that the mirror would only confirm that Mom was telling the truth. In spite of her reassurances that I was in a safe place, no place was safe enough yet.

Eventually, her words began to sink in and curiosity got the best of me. I bought a small mirror and, after a couple of drinks, decided that I was brave enough to look into it. In the bright bathroom light, sitting sideways on the toilet lid, I put the mirror on the counter. Angling it in different directions, first looking at each side of my face, then my chin and forehead and then deep into my eyes, I stared at my reflection.

It was okay. I wasn't struck by lightning and the earth didn't swallow me up. It was actually an anticlimax. From then on, every time I walked by a mirror, I looked. It was mesmerizing, like when a baby sees her reflection for the first time. But it wasn't long before the novelty wore off and I was over it. I thought back to all the years of believing the nasty things that Mom, and then Gary, had said to me, the years of feeling crushed and broken. What a waste!

Before we finished counseling, the therapist asked me one last question: Why had I reached out to Mom and not Dad when they split up?

Mom, I told her, was all alone and suicidal. Dad was with someone, a woman he'd moved in with after the divorce. Mom needed me. Dad didn't. Dad still seemed dangerous to my mental health. Whereas Mom had damaged my self-esteem, Dad had damaged my soul.

SIX WEEKS after our visit, Mom opened the door with a smile on her face. She was excited to see me. She'd prepared salmon and rice and a salad, which was more than welcome after the ten-hour drive through the mountains from Calgary to Vancouver. For the next few hours, she filled me in on what was happening in her life before I headed to my friend Nancy's for the night. Mom was unhappy that I wasn't staying in her tiny bachelor suite, but I was just getting over bronchitis and her heavy smoking was too much for me. The next morning was sunny and beautiful and traffic was light as Mom and I headed to Bellingham. As I drove, Mom started talking about the past again. I listened quietly until she asked a stunning question: "Did your father ever touch you?"

My jaw dropped but I decided that, if she wanted to know the truth, then I would be respectful and answer honestly. I couldn't believe that she'd found the courage to ask me and I was touched that she trusted I would not hurt her with blame or judgement.

I spoke softly. "Yes, Mom, he did."

"Oh my God. I should have known. I should have protected you. I should have known because his own father tried to do that to you kids but I stopped him. I protected you from him. Why didn't I protect you from your father?" Her voice was shrill as she berated herself.

"Mom, how could you stop something that you didn't know was happening?" I responded. "It wasn't possible for you to stop it. Dad is responsible for what he did, not you. I know in my heart that you would have stopped him if you could have. Let go of it. It's all in the past." I spoke gently and calmly, soothingly. It didn't matter to me if Mom knew or should have known what happened. I had let go of my judgments of her.

"You're right. There's nothing I could do if I didn't know. You're right."

It took a while, but she gradually calmed down and started talking about getting groceries and maybe some new measuring cups. She needed new measuring cups. Damned if she could figure out how she lost the last ones. One thing Mom was good at was blocking difficult things from her mind.

I made sure to buy her extra food like fruits and cheeses that she wouldn't normally buy to show her that I loved her in spite of what happened in the past. Then we headed home. The next morning, I phoned Mom, concerned that she was tired out by the long day before. We'd made plans to get together for lunch. It didn't take long before her edginess showed up. When I asked her how she was, she said, "I'm fine but I have something to tell you."

"Okay, Mom, what would you like to tell me?"

"Well, I don't like the way your hair is. You look so ugly. Why do you always have to look so ugly?"

But this time, something had changed inside me. I knew now that what Mom was telling me wasn't true. I wasn't ugly. She was no longer stating a fact; she was just talking for the sake of talking. Her words couldn't hurt me anymore now that I knew they weren't true. It was time to put a stop to them. I'd tried to stop her comments many times before but as long as I believed they were true, she had all the power and knew exactly how to use it. Now I knew how to stop her. "Mom, I don't agree with what you're saying so I'm going to hang up the phone now and I'll call you tomorrow."

There was stunned silence. She sputtered a bit and then said goodbye. I went out for the afternoon and, when I got back, Nancy said, "Your Mom called and wants to apologize." I called Mom back as Nancy watched to see how it all played out.

"I want to apologize."

"Okay," I said.

"It isn't my place to tell you that you're ugly."

I could hardly contain my laughter. "Mom, I still don't agree with you so I'm going to hang up and I will see you tomorrow." Her sputtering was even louder this time.

A few hours later, she called back. "I'm sorry. You're not ugly. I don't know why I said that. Now will you come over?"

"No, Mom. I said I'd come and see you tomorrow. Thank you for apologizing."

I knew that Mom wanted me to spend as much time as possible with her—and so did I—but I couldn't continue to put up with her comments. I knew that, if I went right over to see her, she'd ignore my little boundary exercise. Staying away was the best way I knew to show her there was a price to pay for her grumpiness. It was a new boundary for her and she was as upset as a two-year-old being told she couldn't have a cookie. This was my way of demanding respect. And it worked. The next morning, I knocked on her door and acted as if nothing had ever happened. We both enjoyed the rest of the visit.

When I returned to Calgary, I thought of the past and all the nasty comments Mom had made and how I'd crumbled each time, my warmth giving way to coldness and edginess as the pain burrowed into my heart. But now I truly understood that her comments were a reflection of her own inner pain and self-hatred, not the truth. How could a mother who saw herself as so worthless that she regularly attempted suicide believe that she could create children of any value? How could she not see her children as she saw herself? My beautiful mother, who saw herself as ugly, could only see me, one of her creations, the same way. I was not the only one of her children she told had so much less value than the person they married. She'd always been astonished by my small accomplishments and had trouble trusting my compassion for her. But with my calmly refusing to accept her negative comments, instead of getting upset by them, I realized that my invisible wall was finally down.

I kept subtly and quietly reminding Mom of the goodness at her core and she began to change. Her edginess was gone; calm took its place. There were no more critical comments. She hugged me more often and laughed a lot more. She went out with her friends more often, going downtown for lunch and shopping, and she travelled more, taking long bus trips to Reno and Las Vegas, using her small pension and a few thousand dollars she'd received after the sale of the apartment she and Dad had lived in. Her friends told me how funny Mom was, how she constantly made them laugh with her wittiness and how much they enjoyed her company. She was still insecure and didn't understand how much they liked her, but her confidence was growing. She joined a gym and took exercise classes. She even began dating a man and they travelled together.

I understood just how much she'd changed when we were watching TV together in her apartment and a commercial came on showing a baby crawling across the floor, crying. Mom said, "Oh pick the poor thing up."

I was astonished to hear Mom express compassion for a baby. I was astonished even more when, as I was saying goodbye before returning to Calgary, she hugged me and whispered, "Thank you." I'd never told Mom about the Course in Miracles because she'd always referred to all metaphysics as "woo-woo" stuff, but her 'thank you' now acknowledged and expressed gratitude for the changes these ideas had brought to her life and to our relationship. The miracles just kept coming.

My world was a better place when I knew that anyone giving me a different and negative version of myself was mistaken. Finally, I was sure of who I really was.

Or so I thought. I was unaware of what was yet to come.

19

A New Path

As I continued to study the Course, I gained more control over my emotions and my life. As I stopped worrying about the state of the world, my own world became even more peaceful.

One of the benefits of being in Calgary was that I was once again part of JoAnn's family and invited to family birthday parties and celebrations. It was like no time had passed from when JoAnn and I were children, and we met often for shopping and lunches and joined a gym together. I loved JoAnn for selflessly sharing her mom with me her entire life and for once again welcoming me as part of her family. But I'd never opened up to her or Ann about the darkness of my childhood and I didn't feel comfortable doing so yet. I never mentioned my new understandings from A COURSE IN MIRACLES either. I wasn't ready to share those with anyone.

My relationship with her mother, Ann, who was now widowed and living with JoAnn and her family, had been much deeper and she'd been a bright light in my existence for over forty years. In spite of being away traveling so often, I saw her as much as I could. But I felt some guilt for having taken our relationship for granted over the years. Gradually, I explained some of what I'd been going through as a child, although not the worst of it.

She was horrified, saying repeatedly, "I could have adopted you. If I'd known, I would have adopted you." I thanked her for that wonderful thought.

Ann still loved to laugh and be silly, sometimes randomly breaking out in song and dance, and we had fun as we went for walks in her neighborhood. Armed with sticks, we walked through the park poking at dead leaves and rocks to see what was underneath. There was a freedom between us, the freedom to totally be ourselves with no judgment from the other. It was a calm, quiet, loving relationship like none other in my life.

I also enjoyed my work more and a long-buried sense of humor gradually arose from within. It was easier to laugh and I discovered that I could make others laugh by clowning around on flights. For example, when briefing the passengers at the window exits on how to escape in an emergency, I was supposed to ensure that they understood English. If they didn't, I had to move them to another row, something most passengers didn't take kindly to.

One time, a man in the exit row just smiled every time I asked if he understood me. I wasn't sure if he understood me or how to sort it out, so I simply proceeded with the briefing until I found myself saying: "In case of emergency, this is how you open the window. But don't open it if you see fire because, then, when you slide down the wing, you'll burn your bum." I said it so quietly that he couldn't quite believe he heard me properly.

He responded loudly, "What did you say? Burn my bum? Is that what you said?" His laughter made it perfectly clear that he understood me.

Another time when the airline was offering a choice of dinners, I needed to ask everyone whether they wanted chicken or beef. When non-English speakers looked at me questioningly, I improvised.

"Chicken?" I asked while putting my hands in my armpits, waving my elbows and squawking like a chicken. "Or beef?" I asked while mooing like a cow.

The passengers doubled over with laughter. The only problem was that, upon seeing this, those who did speak English often pretended they didn't so that they could see me make a fool of myself. I didn't care. Clowning around made the flights go faster and I would stand on my head if I thought it would get some laughs. I loved this newfound lightness of being.

I began to work in business class regularly and enjoyed having time to talk to the passengers, many of whom I saw on a regular basis. Sometimes, one of the businessmen was excited about having closed a deal and I liked listening to him tell me about it. There were even times when I came back from vacation and was confronted by passengers. "Where were you? You didn't tell us you were taking time off!" It was nice to be missed and I was happy to regale them with my latest vacation details.

Passengers often told me I'd brightened their day and I began to see myself in a different way, as less uptight and rigid. I liked myself more. So did others, apparently. The light inside me was beginning to shine brighter and I got asked out on dates more frequently. That felt good but I never accepted; I still didn't have the confidence.

One of my regular passengers was a businessman who'd been on my flights every Monday and Friday for over a year. One evening after dinner, he stunned me by suddenly getting out of his seat and down on one knee. "Will you marry me?"

I was speechless. The peals of laughter from the other passengers could be heard all the way into economy class. Was he joking? Was he serious? I couldn't tell. Before I could say anything, I was called to help with a passenger having a heart attack in the back of the aircraft and, with relief and not just a little cowardice, I ran to help. The moment passed but my reaction surprised me. I was very attracted to this man, who was gentle and intelligent and fun, and I loved it when he was on my flights. But now an old familiar panic rose in me and I felt I couldn't breathe. What if I were wrong? What if he wasn't a nice guy?

I still didn't trust my own judgement. Unable to dislodge my fear of men, I couldn't let any man near me. I knew I wouldn't survive another mistake. And so, I walked away.

ONE DAY, a Red Cross ad in the newspaper caught my eye. They needed volunteers to go into schools and community groups to give workshops about various types of violence prevention, including child abuse and domestic violence. I'd always felt an overwhelm-ing compulsion to protect children and I now loved the idea of being able to teach boundaries, to help them understand that abuse was not their fault. Feeling I had a lot to offer, I signed up for 160 hours of intense training over the course of ten weekends.

Partway through my training, I mentioned to my psychologist what I was doing and she was shocked. She told me she'd never heard of someone who was in the process of healing being able to reach out and teach about abuse to others. But to me, it just made sense. A COURSE IN MIRACLES was helping me to depersonalize much of what I'd gone through and to separate my past from what I was learning in the training. I was able to see the abused not as victims but as whole people who needed knowledge and nonjudgmental understanding in order to heal. And, of course, it was about prevention as well.

I was surprised at how comfortable I felt in the classrooms. It was fun and rewarding and the students loved the stories I told, as I wove the life lessons I'd learned as a flight attendant into the safety messages I presented to them. I never said anything personal about my past but, every once in a while, when I was speaking about child abuse or domestic violence, one of the young people would say, "You sure know a lot about this stuff." It made me sad because the youth making the comments obviously knew too much about "this stuff" as well.

I also worked some of the practical teachings of ACIM into the Red Cross workshops. For example, I shared with the kids that they can never really know the circumstances of the people around them. The person sitting beside them might be afraid to go to sleep at night; they might be hungry or bruised. So, compassion was in order regardless of the situation. I told them that no one other than themselves could change who they were on the inside, no matter what happened to them on the outside. They always got to decide who they were and who they would be, and there was never a need to give up their inner power to anyone.

Overall, the feedback was positive and kids often told me they felt safer after the workshops.

After a while, the Red Cross asked me to speak about my work from a volunteer perspective and I was interviewed on TV stations and in the newspapers. Due to the huge number of hours I was putting in, I was also nominated for the Volunteer-in-Profile on CTV, which garnered me a mention on the evening news. It was all very exciting.

When I took copies of the videos to show Mom, she couldn't believe it. "You've got more balls than brains, girl," she exclaimed — her way of complimenting me on my courage.

THE airline industry was in turmoil again. Canadian Pacific Airlines had merged several years previously with six smaller airlines to form Canadian Airlines International and it was now near bankruptcy. We never knew if the doors would be locked when we arrived for work or if our pay cheques would bounce. All employees had taken pay cuts to the tune of several thousand dollars each, with some losing their homes as a result.

The only good thing was that the federal government didn't believe it was politically palatable to have tens of thousands of people suddenly out of work, so it stepped in to arrange yet another merger, this time with Air Canada. After months of tense negotiating, they finally succeeded but it was an enormously stressful time.

Personally, it made me realize I'd had enough and I began searching for alternatives to airline work. My volunteering at the Red Cross gave me new confidence and I continued receiving positive feedback from many teachers, school counsellors and kids. I was a little surprised to discover that speaking in front of groups felt natural and that I loved interacting with both youth and adults. But I wanted to be able to offer workshops that were less clinical and more comprehensive.

At a social event, I was approached by the director of a province-wide organization that hired speakers to give workshops on various topics and he wanted to know if I was available. He had in mind creating a workshop for employees working with children in recreational facilities, with the goals of teaching about child abuse prevention as well as protecting employees from false allegations. I accepted the opportunity and put in long hours preparing my research and making it specific to my audience. Not surprisingly, I was nervous, but my preparation paid off. The audience loved the workshop and I was asked to give other workshops in different parts of the province.

I loved this work. I knew my information well and often presented before large audiences. In spite of being nervous, my message flowed smoothly and I could see that I had the audience's total attention. I wove relevant stories I'd read about different types of situations with children, along with some of my own childhood experiences (never letting on any of it was personal), into the information I'd just researched. I subtly added some of the teachings of A COURSE IN MIRACLES that explained a different way of viewing those who'd experienced abuse. I loved being able to present those who'd been hurt not as broken and different, but as whole, as children (and adults) who needed recognition of their wholeness and their magnificence so they could heal. After my presentations, audience members often told me that they were surprised by the power of my words and that they wished the workshops were longer. They wanted to know who I was and several people asked if I'd written a book they could buy. I promised to write one.

With each workshop I gave, I understood more deeply my own healing. Helping others helped me, just as the Course promised. I'd never planned on starting a business based on the wealth of knowledge I had about violence, but it seemed that the universe was guiding me along with opportunities that I blindly accepted, unaware of where it was all going. It seemed that trusting the Course, and the many rewards that came from that trust, was giving me a burgeoning courage that I'd never known before, although I didn't recognize the extent of it at the time. I was learning to trust my inner guidance as I discovered my purpose in life.

This situation was exactly the opening I'd been looking for, an alternative path out of the airline industry. Resigning from my volunteer work with the Red Cross after five years, I started my own company: Alcyone Presentations, named after the Cousteau ship I'd encountered so many years ago in Vancouver. The meaning of "halcyon days" is drawn from Greek mythology, referring to a time of prosperity, joy, liberation and tranquility, and so the name of my company felt perfect.

My intention was to keep flying and to run Alcyone on the side but I quickly realized how difficult and time-consuming this would be. When I learned that Air Canada was also heading toward bankruptcy three years after the merger, I decided to take early retirement. In the fall of 2002, I gave notice that I'd be retiring in February 2003. I was nervous about making such a big move but also excited. At forty-nine years old, I was full of optimism. I'd miss my colleagues, but not the time changes, jet lag, or Christmas mornings alone in hotel rooms. I looked forward to getting enough sleep and three square meals a day. I felt like I'd been tired and hungry for the duration of my twenty-eight-year career. In the back of my mind, I wondered if I'd even know how to create a normal life for myself.

I invested my energies into my business: I had a lot to learn in a short time. Diving in head first, I joined the Canadian Association of Professional Speakers (CAPS) and attended monthly meetings. I also took safety courses from the Calgary Police Service and workshops from the Human Rights Commission, Occupational Health and Safety, and the Workers Compensation Board. I did all of this in order to make my own workshops as comprehensive as possible. Then, when I signed up for training with a professional speaker I met at CAPS, she suggested I take a stand-up comedy course to learn how to be more comfortable on stage.

With an abundance of caution, I took her advice.

20

The Comedian

THE company was called Cheers and it offered different levels of comedy training. I reluctantly signed up for the beginner's course, knowing I was so far out of my element that it would take every ounce of courage to do this. It was one thing to be on a stage in front of hundreds of people, talking about information that I deeply understood. It was something else entirely to stand on a stage trying to make people laugh.

We were a motley group of seven, most of whom had been told by friends and family that they were hilarious and should be performing comedy. During the next eight weeks, one evening a week, three hours at a time, Cheers owners and instructors, Derek and Melany, taught us the general rules, including what we could joke about and what was off limits. For example, disabilities were only funny if we were the one with the disability, and we couldn't make fun of ethnic groups unless we were part of that group. We learned a lot and got to know each other well, laughing our way through the program, sometimes with tears pouring down our faces, clutching our stomachs. Each time I left class, I couldn't wait to get back for the next one.

The only way to graduate, however, was to perform on stage at the Yuk Yuk's Comedy Club in front of 350 people. The idea really scared me. I held in reserve the backup plan that I didn't have to graduate but I kept doing my best just in case I was able to find my courage. After much deliberation, I decided I couldn't chicken out, so I met with Derek to brainstorm and prepare my routine.

On graduation night, I sat shaking in the dark wings of the stage along with my classmates, waiting for my turn to be a stand-up comedian. I'd sold tickets to friends and colleagues, as well as to some airline managers.

What the hell, I thought. *Let's find out if Air Canada management has a sense of humor.* After all, my jokes naturally centered on what I'd known best for the past twenty-eight years: the airline.

Suddenly it was my turn. The students who'd performed before me had been heckled mercilessly and, as I walked to the microphone, the smile on my face hid the fear in my heart and the churning in my stomach. We'd been trained in how to deal with hecklers but I was afraid I wouldn't remember.

Then a strange thing happened. The hecklers went silent. Did I look so terrified that they backed off? I stood in the spotlight, poised in an expectant silence. I could only see the first rows of the audience but I cast my gaze outwards as if to take in the entire club. Holding my notes firmly in my shaking hand — we were beginners, after all, and allowed notes — unsure of what to expect, I began:

"I was a flight attendant with Canadian Pacific Airlines but it went bankrupt. I was a flight attendant with Canadian Airlines but it went bankrupt. I was a flight attendant with Air Canada but it went bankrupt. West Jet has asked me not to apply."

The roar of laughter took me by surprise and gave me a feeling of power, as if I were omnipotent, larger than life.

"As a flight attendant, I've been taught to smile sweetly at everyone." Turning my gaze from one side to the other, sweeping the entire room with a huge, fake smile, I paused for a long moment before saying loudly, sans smile, "F**k that!"

The audience roared again. My language surprised them and they loved it. The laughter after each joke continued. I wondered how my jokes about airline managers not having the correct body parts and not being very intelligent were going over with my guests since they were sitting near the back and I couldn't see them. After a particularly rude joke, I looked in their direction and asked, "What are you going to do, BJ, fire me?" The audience was laughing and applauding.

I loved it. It was exhilarating. It was a drug and I was now addicted. I immediately signed up for the intermediate course.

Once the show was over, I mingled with the audience and received plenty of compliments on my performance from my guests — my friend JoAnn, my sister Pat and her husband, and friends and colleagues — as well as strangers. The airline managers told me they'd loved it. I couldn't believe it had gone so well and was proud that I'd been able to do it.

When I showed up for a flight two days later, one of the airline managers told me that a crew had arrived home from overseas the previous afternoon and gone to the crew room to find out if the rumor was true: "Did Betty really do stand-up comedy? Did she really use the F word?"

"Yes," they were told, "on both counts." They couldn't believe it.

After finishing the intermediate course, I attended a stand-up comedy course at Humber College in Toronto, whose alumni include comedy greats from SCTV like my instructor, Larry Horowitz. I learned a lot, honing my writing and performing skills. Upon returning home, I performed several more times at private functions at Yuk Yuk's and was spotted by audience member, country singer and performer Ray Griff, who had recently returned after spending many years in Nashville. He invited me to be his opening act during a performance in Lethbridge, Alberta and I jumped at the chance. I wrote some jokes for the locals to add to my repertoire. It was great fun. I loved being part of the group and being treated with such courtesy and respect as if I, as a performer, were someone special. Derek and Melany congratulated me, telling me I was their first student to get a professional gig.

I privately wondered if I was the last student they would have expected to move forward in this way. If so, they never let on. When I'd first started working as a flight attendant, my nickname was "Mouse." Bet no one ever calls me that again. Let the Mouse roar!

AROUND this time, the Alberta government enacted a new law requiring all employees to be trained in violence prevention in the workplace, including domestic violence. I tailored my workshops to the exact requirements of the new law and I was ready when it kicked in. Brochures were printed and I began cold calling.

I was hired by the manager of a small city to train city workers in violence prevention, including how to defuse difficult situations. The fire department, paramedics, truck drivers, clerks and all others took part in the half-day workshops. At the end of each one, using what I'd learned from the therapist, I had them pair up and set a boundary with a piece of string.

Everyone laughed at first but they were soon impressed with what they learned about respecting other people's physical boundaries and how important this was in helping defuse another person's anger. One man in particular got very upset when he realized how he habitually got in people's faces and how this could be misinterpreted as intimidating. He asked the others why they'd never told him he was standing too close when speaking to them and they replied that they hadn't wanted to hurt his feelings. Once again, when the course was over, feedback was very positive.

Nonetheless, I hit a wall. I was finding it challenging to get my foot in the door of the speaking industry, even though there was very little competition in my field. In spite of all the positive feedback I received, my old feelings of not being good enough soon took over. How could I convince others that I was worth spending a lot of money on when I still didn't believe it myself? My insecurities must have shown and I had trouble getting additional bookings. Cold calls, never for the faint of heart, were my biggest nightmare. Every phone call and meeting in which I had to sell myself to others was torture. I tried to erase the doubts to the point where I could at least display confidence in what I was doing, but it was an exhausting pretense and the more I failed with each cold call, the more I believed I was in over my head. I started asking myself: How could I have been crazy enough to think I could do this? How could I think I would know how to run a business? How could I believe anyone would want to hear me speak?

But I pressed on.

"BETTY, OVER HERE."

I spun around, scanning the crowd at the sidewalk café I was walking by, looking for the person behind the voice.

A waving arm flagged me down. It was Jane, an old friend from the airline industry. She was having coffee with her ex, Mary, who was just leaving, and Jane invited me to join her. She'd quit her airline job and was working as a technician doing drafting for a local engineering firm. As I ordered a cup of tea, she described the drafting work she'd done on various buildings around the city.

We caught up for hours, sharing what was happening with our large families, sisters and brothers and nieces and nephews and cousins, and other people we knew in common. Jane had a wacky sense of humor and her storytelling made me laugh until my stomach hurt.

I explained my business to her, about how much I loved speaking to groups and how hard it was to get new jobs. I told her how overwhelmed I was with the business details, partly because of my lack of computer skills. She offered to help me organize my research properly and to create PowerPoint presentations for my workshops. I accepted her help with relief and, over the next few days, she spent several hours reorganizing the information on my computer.

One day she sat in when I gave a workshop to a local company. When their computer system failed mid-presentation, she jumped in to get it running again. She loved the workshop and was full of compliments. It felt wonderful to have moral support and someone to bounce ideas off. From then on, whenever she could get time off, she came to conferences where I was speaking, often mingling with the participants during breaks and later sharing their comments with me. This became a source of valuable feedback that allowed me to improve my presentations. I was still insecure about my abilities but she encouraged me and her feedback slowly seeped in.

Jane had a self-confidence that I found attractive. She knew that she was well-loved and she always expected that people would like her. Her default belief was, "Why wouldn't that person like me?" She knew without question that she had a right to take up space in the world.

I wonder now if I was hoping some of that confidence would rub off on me.

After a time, Jane asked me out on a date, and I said, "Yes." I didn't sense any anger in her, in her words or actions or demeanor, and I felt safe with her. She was warm and caring and easy to be with and it was the first time in a long time that I'd felt so relaxed with anyone. I never questioned the dynamics playing out inside me. It didn't register that perhaps my intense fear of men, along with an aching loneliness, was part of what was driving me towards her. I forgot, or at least neglected, the teachings of the Course regarding the importance of shining a light on our inner fears in order to heal them. Instead, I ran away from facing them.

As the weeks flew by, Jane and I spent a lot of time together. She brought more fun into my workaholic life. She loved comedy and wanted to prepare a workshop called "Comedy in the Workplace," one that we would present together. I liked the idea and when she had the materials ready, we offered it to a focus group before making it part of the Alcyone repertoire. It was an instant success.

I kept studying A COURSE IN MIRACLES and loved that I was able to discuss the concepts with Jane. We shared an interest in metaphysics and often read related books out loud to each other. This was the first time I'd had anyone to discuss these ideas with and it helped me feel less alone on my journey.

Once a month, Jane put a picnic together for us, gathering different kinds of cheeses and fruits, liver pâté, crackers and whatever else caught her fancy at the moment. If the weather wasn't good, we stayed in our pyjamas all day and had the picnic in bed while watching movies. We joined a women's dinner group and met regularly for various social events. We flew to Hawaii mid-winter and relaxed in the warm sunshine. Life was good.

I began feeling more strongly that it was time to write that book that so many audience members were asking for. I borrowed a friend's cabin that had no telephone, internet or TV and camped out for a week. But, as I began to write, I struggled. I'd thought it would be fairly easy but I quickly learned that I didn't want to think about my childhood, let alone put it down on paper. Some parts of it were too painful and ugly and, even though the Course taught that we should shine a light on all parts of our past, I just didn't have the courage. So, I wrote out an overview, really just an outline, and jotted down the past memories that Mom and I had discussed during our many hours on the road during visits. I didn't add many details. When I got home, I took the printed copy and tossed it in a drawer, preferring to ignore the past and just enjoy the present. I was unaware of what a fateful decision I was making.

Over a period of several months, I began to feel an even deeper level of safety with Jane, one I'd never felt with anyone before. My nightmares disappeared and I slept deeply for the first time in my life. Affection no longer felt threatening. If Jane touched me in the middle of the night, I didn't wake up in a panic. I felt secure and slowly began letting my guard down. The walls I'd built around me began to crumble. Subconsciously, gradually, I began to feel like I belonged, like I was entitled to take up space, like I was becoming less of an alien in an unfamiliar world. This process had begun when I studied the Course but it accelerated as I began to feel and realize it in a practical sense. Most people take for granted the restful sleep they get each night but, for me, it was new and amazing and wonderful. Jane was helping me heal in unexpected ways.

THANKS to word-of-mouth and cold calling, invitations to speak at conferences and various corporations and government agencies became more frequent. I invited the media to a workshop I gave to business owners and received repeated coverage of my work on the local cable TV station. Soon, I was interviewed by several newspapers, radio and TV stations and was often interviewed as an expert during news stories about violence. The articles were picked up in newspapers across the country. Upon reading a three-quarter page article about me on the front page of the business section of the Edmonton Journal, a town in northern Alberta hired me to speak at a conference about bullying prevention.

At two different conferences, I was approached by police officers from the audience who told me how valuable my workshops were for defusing potentially violent situations. That led me to join the Canadian Criminal Justice Association and attend their conference in 2006. Two Calgary City police officers suggested I put together workshops for the Calgary school systems and I decided to begin researching school issues. I also met the Ontario Assistant Minister of Justice, who was interested in my workshops for youth correctional employees and probation officers, and we arranged to meet again in Ontario.

Husky Oil hired us to give a full-day session, with me presenting a safety workshop in the morning and Jane and I jointly presenting "Comedy in the Workplace" in the afternoon. We both worked hard preparing for it, as every workshop was custom designed. The participants were attentive and thoughtful as I went through the safety and moved on to the comedy. Jane was at her best and everyone loved her. We ended the day with contests and gifts for the winners.

When I was hired to give corporate workshops in various parts of Alberta and B.C., I contacted the local Family Services branches and offered to give presentations in schools and community centers as a way of continuing my volunteer work. I enjoyed this side of my work as much as the corporate side and felt that I was giving back to Family Services for the extraordinary help I'd been given in Vancouver.

After a slow start, I was finally well on my way with my business. I felt blessed and humbled that I was able to do this work, surprised by a talent that seemed to come from nowhere. Though my life was hectic, I couldn't slow down.

PART III

The Accident

"To hold your magnitude in perfect awareness in a world of littleness is a task the little cannot undertake."

— A Course in Miracles

21

Traumatic Brain Injury

WAKING slowly one February morning, I opened one eye as Jane handed me a cup of coffee and told me that, thanks to a chinook, it was a beautiful, warm, sunny day. A common phenomenon in this prairie city near the base of the Rocky Mountains, chinooks arrived suddenly with warm, spring-like weather in the dead of winter and were welcomed with open arms by most Calgarians. A glance out the window told me the snow had melted and the sky was a lovely clear blue. Too nice a day to stay inside working. We piled into my little Nissan, with Jane driving, and headed out to do some errands. Abandoning our winter coats and boots always brought joy and I felt free and lighthearted as we headed out.

Stopped at a red light, we chattered about the movie we'd watched the previous evening: 50 First Dates. It was an hysterically funny, raunchy and sweet story about a young woman with a traumatic brain injury from a car crash who falls in love with a wacky veterinarian, and we reminded each other of the funniest parts, howling all over again at the silliness of it all.

Immersed in our laughter, we didn't see it coming.

An explosion — a loud, harsh grinding of metal on metal and our car was catapulted forward into the intersection. Time stopped in the stillness as an aura of unreality settled over me. Stars and flashing lights streaked through my brain and a dense fog enveloped me. Then I was outside the car, attempting to stand up, unable to, falling against the side of the car. Someone caught me and put me back inside. The world was spinning in circles and I had the horrible feeling that I was falling, even though I was sitting down. Heaving, I leaned out of the open car door, retching so intensely that my stomach hurt. I heard the commotion as a fire truck, a police car and an ambulance came roaring up. A paramedic reached for my arm as Jane told me, "Go with her. She'll take care of you. I'll be there soon."

The paramedic helped me into the ambulance, gave me a bag to throw up in and then helped me onto the bed. I lay down, holding tight to the edge of the bed, dizzy and heaving. The sensation of rapid spinning in my head was horrible but I couldn't find the words to tell anyone. Another paramedic kept asking me questions but I didn't understand him; in fact, I was irritated that he wouldn't shut up.

The ambulance took me to the hospital, leaving Jane at the crash site, and deposited me in the emergency room where a nurse assured me that a doctor would see me soon. The bright lights and busyness made my head pain, nausea and dizziness excruciating. I wanted everyone to stop talking, to quit bugging me, to be quiet. I couldn't think clearly. I hurt all over. My head and neck were in agony, my back had stabbing pain all the way down to my knees, and my jaw felt like someone had punched me in the face. The dizziness was unrelenting. I held tight to the bed rails, certain that I was about to fall off the edge.

Jane arrived and relief poured through me. A police officer showed up, wanting to check on how serious my injuries were before deciding what charges to lay against the driver who hit us. He stayed only a few minutes, eying my neck brace and the back board I was laying on and asking questions that I didn't understand. Jane and the doctor answered for me. I was given an IV with painkillers and anti-nausea drugs, and after several blurry hours of extensive testing, I was discharged with a diagnosis of whiplash and concussion. It was nighttime and Jane called a friend to drive us home.

I had no clue that my life as I knew it was over — gone, never to return.

JANE unlocked the door to our apartment and I followed her inside. I had the eerie sensation of entering a stranger's home. It was familiar in a weird sort of way, but it didn't feel like home. Leaning on furniture to keep from falling, I walked to the other side of the living room and the balcony doors and looked out over the stunning view of the lights of downtown Calgary. The silence was so nice after many hours in the emergency room.

Jane took my arm and walked me to the bedroom, pulled back the covers and helped me undress and get into bed. The second I lay down, the spinning in my head intensified. It was like being really drunk when, as soon as you lie down, you need to throw up. Trying to ignore it, I finally fell asleep only to awaken a few hours later covered in vomit. Getting up to go to the bathroom, I walked straight into the wall, hard enough that bruises later appeared on my face and shoulder. Jane heard my cry of pain and got up to help me to the bathroom. Then she changed the bedding. I was sitting on the edge of the bathtub, in the dark, when she returned with a glass of water and a wet cloth to clean my face. After gratefully accepting her help, I headed back to bed. Vomiting in my sleep became a regular occurrence that continued for months.

The next morning arrived with a vicious migraine. I was sure there was a knife stabbing and twisting in my brain, a pain made worse by noise and light. My mouth tasted awful and I wanted to brush my teeth but, staring at the sink, I didn't know what to do. I simply couldn't remember how to brush my teeth, turn on the taps, or which tap was hot or cold. Jane found me there and handed me my toothbrush, showed me where the toothpaste was and how to put it on the brush, then how to turn on the tap to rinse my brush. When I tried to turn the tap off, I turned it the wrong way and was sprayed with water.

Jane helped me climb into the shower but dizziness took over and I clung to the wall as the hot water and steam eased my aches. When I leaned back to wash my hair, jolts of pain shot through my head and neck. Quickly exhausted, I eased my way out of the shower by sliding my body along the wall for balance. As I dried myself off, I called to Jane to help me brush my teeth.

"You brushed your teeth two minutes ago," she told me. I didn't believe her. It wasn't possible I could forget so fast.

At that point, I was unable to understand the extent of my head injury and was too confused and numb to feel afraid.

Holding on to the walls and furniture, wearing the sweatpants and T-shirt that Jane had laid out for me, I slowly entered the living room. Jane closed the drapes to keep the bright sunlight from stabbing my eyeballs and sending streaks of lightning to my brain. It didn't work. I automatically lowered myself onto the soft, thick carpet to begin my yoga stretches, as I'd done every morning for over thirty years, but it hurt too much.

And then: Why am I on the floor? I couldn't remember.

The same thing happened when I sat on the sofa to say my morning prayers. Not only could I not remember my prayers, after a moment I was asking myself why I was sitting there.

Already worn out, I went back to bed but every time I closed my eyes, nightmares of the accident repeated, over and over again. The trauma segued into other nightmares, terrifying memories from long ago. I was running from someone who was hurting me. Constantly running, but never quite getting to safety. They weren't clear memories, just jumbled glimpses of the past, of pain and injuries and betrayal.

There were so many things I didn't want to remember.

JANE was also in pain and it wasn't until months later that she was diagnosed with a torn rotator cuff and two fractures in her back. We commiserated together but she continued to care for me. My migraines had returned after many years of absence and now they were virtually constant. Each began with an aura of light in my head and numbness in my left shoulder that spread to my fingertips. It took days for the sharp pain in my head, even in my eyes, to ease.

The migraines made the dizziness worse and it became even

more difficult to walk around the apartment without falling. Then, just when the pain began to dissipate, another migraine would start. Jane took me to an optometrist and we picked out some polarized sunglasses. They didn't stop the migraines, but they lessened the pain and I wore them constantly, indoors and out, as Jane joked about which movie star I was trying to imitate.

Then a friend recommended a doctor who accepted accident victims. Dr. John Van Goor was a kind and gentle man and his warm smile made us want to hug him. My confusing symptoms made sense to him and we left his office thinking we would be okay. After all, it had only been a few weeks. On good days, I could brush my teeth without help.

After a few months, Dr. Van Goor diagnosed me with "mild traumatic brain injury." Mild? Really? Luckily for me, he understood that despite the name assigned to the clinical diagnosis, in truth there was nothing mild about it. He had enormous compassion for those suffering from it, something I came to rely on heavily.

One symptom was a heightened sense of smell. Virtually everything smelled like rotten garbage and I dragged Jane around the apartment searching for what was causing the odor. She couldn't smell anything rotten.

Even fragrant smells were a problem for me. Jane's sister brought her flowers and, at my first whiff of them, I ran to the bathroom to throw up. Even as I was vomiting, I tried to joke about it. "With my sense of smell, I could be like a search and rescue dog."

I was rewarded with a smile but Jane told me later that my words came out all jumbled and she had no clue what I was trying to say.

My life became an endless cycle of doctors' appointments: my general practitioner, neurologists, a medication specialist, physiotherapists, massage therapists, a vestibular therapist, and many more. The vestibular therapist, a dizziness expert, had me do exercises that made the dizziness and nausea worse. She said it was to condition me to it. The nausea made me heave every time but I kept at it, doing the exercises a couple of times a day at home where I also threw up constantly. This went on for months before she told me to stop — that it wasn't working and the dizziness might be permanent.

At that point, I didn't yet understand what a terrible blow the accident had been. On the surface, I accepted the diagnosis of brain injury but, deep inside, I didn't really believe it. My mind was blank, unable to process the practical aspects of my situation and the dangers that my vulnerability presented. It seems that sometimes ignorance is bliss and, as I dealt with overwhelming dizziness and pain and nausea, frustration kicked in and a jumpiness at unexpected noises and movements, but not real fear. I had no clue yet that, as I healed and began to understand more, terror would often reign supreme.

Humor helped Jane and me deal with the difficulties, although every joke now required a long explanation on Jane's part. She began calling me Forrest (after reminding me who Forrest Gump was and why this was funny) and making jokes about my mistakes. I doggedly tried to get back to my routines and, one day, I was on the sidewalk in front of our building, grocery list in my pocket, intending to get to the Safeway two blocks away. I walked slowly, concentrating on every move. Suddenly, I heard Jane's voice from nine stories up. She was leaning over the balcony yelling, "Run, Forrest, run." I burst out laughing.

Some of our friends were horrified when they heard her do this but what they didn't understand was that, as difficult as life had become, I really believed that my injuries were temporary, so the jokes were funny. And laughter had become a saving grace.

Getting groceries was hard. I couldn't remember how to choose the right food. One day, on the edge of complete exhaustion, I stood staring at the bin of potatoes in front of me. A young employee approached me and asked if he could help.

"I need potatoes, but I don't know how to choose them," I told him.

"Let me pick out the very best potatoes in the bin for you," he offered.

He proceeded to put potatoes in a bag, then offered to help me get anything else I needed before carrying my groceries to the checkout cashier. In my ocean of difficulties, his kindness stood out.

I couldn't understand money and was confused by the different bills and coins. Unable to tell a twenty from a five or a ten, I ended up holding out my wallet to let the clerk take the money and give me change. I would have used my debit card but I couldn't remember the PIN or how to use the machine. Weeks later, we received Safeway gift cards from family. They became a godsend.

One day, I returned from the grocery store, happy to have successfully brought home food.

"Look!" I said, proudly. "I got groceries!" Looking at what I bought, Jane informed me, "We don't eat any of this stuff." My shoulders slumped as it dawned on me that I'd messed up again.

Walking outside made my dizziness worse. The ground often felt like it was shifting beneath my feet. I realized for the first time that sidewalks aren't always perfectly flat but slightly slanted for draining purposes, usually toward the street. The slant that most people would never notice was hugely exaggerated to me because of the dizziness. I would unconsciously follow the slant, startling more than a few drivers as I unwittingly stepped off the curb toward them. When Jane was with me, she was constantly grabbing me back from the edge. I also tripped on curbs because there was a big difference between where I saw the curbs and where they actually were.

Another time, I had an appointment a few blocks from home. It was a beautiful sunny day and I slowly made my way along the busy sidewalks. Halfway there, I encountered a construction site and I didn't know what to do. It looked like the sidewalk was open. It seemed that there was a lane just for pedestrians and, so, after standing back trying to figure it out, I walked into that lane. Suddenly, out of nowhere, a construction worker grabbed my arm, yanking me out of the lane. He proceeded to escort me across the street against the traffic light, halting five lanes of cars.

Crying, I struggled to understand how the sidewalk had turned into a dangerous place. Jane explained later that I'd wandered into the lane used by cement trucks to access the site and I'd been in serious danger. Of course, there had been a sign warning people to stay away but I hadn't been able to understand the words on it.

One cloudy day as I headed out on an errand, I took along an umbrella, an old-fashioned kind with a large, curved handle. As I walked, I realized I was leaning on it like a cane. It made me feel more centered and eased the constant nausea and the feeling that I was falling. It also helped me feel where the sidewalks and curbs were, giving me a sense of stability that I hadn't felt since before the accident. It prevented the slight staggering that had me constantly bumping into things and seemed to help with the stabbing pain in my lower back and legs.

I bought a cane. It didn't prevent all my falls but I felt safe as I no longer followed the slant of the sidewalk into oncoming traffic or tripped on curbs. My physiotherapist was happy to see the cane, telling me that she rarely recommended them because the idea of needing a cane was so upsetting to people that she let them slowly figure it out for themselves. I understood how devastating the idea of needing a cane was. Using it presented an enormous incongruity in how I saw myself as physically active and strong and healthy. And I never quite came to terms with it. That couldn't be me using a cane! I was too young, only 54! I tried to pretend that I didn't really need it. I tried not to lean heavily on it, to stand tall and act as if it wasn't really there. I knew this was the shallowness of my raging ego but I couldn't quite get past it.

My normal coping mechanisms were gone. I couldn't remember my prayers or focus long enough to meditate. Each time I tried, I quickly forgot why I was sitting there. The words in my copy of A COURSE IN MIRACLES were all jumbled and made no sense. Exercise was impossible because pain flared up with even the simplest of movements. This was particularly challenging, as exercise had always been my saving grace. Pushing my body to its limits helped whenever it had seemed that my mind was being pushed to its limits, whenever my fragile sense of self felt threatened. But now I couldn't go to the gym or even do yoga.

I cried constantly. There was a wall between me and the rest of the world, as if I was in a bubble. It didn't help that I had tinnitus, ringing in my ears, that added to the sensation that I was separate from everyone else, alone in my own foggy world. Even with all the help I received, I felt isolated.

I got easily lost when I was outside. Even though I'd lived in the same place for over eight years, I became confused as soon as I was more than two blocks away. Forgetting that I had a cell phone and could call for help, I often sat down at the nearest bus stop and cried. For the first time, I hated that I lived downtown. Cars, bicycles and motorcycles went whipping by and fire trucks, ambulances and police cars screamed past. There were people everywhere. It was sensory overload and panic often took over.

I kept losing things when I was outside. Shopping bags I was carrying disappeared by the time I got home. As I got off the bus, other passengers often called out to me, "Your purse! You left your purse!" Sometimes stores or coffee shops called to say they had my purse. It was always, without exception, returned intact. But the three cell phones I lost within a month never made it back into my hands.

One day, I heard a knock on the door and opened it to find a courier offering me an envelope containing my keys which I'd recently lost. No charge. A month later, it happened again. Who knew that all those small donations over the years to the War Amps group with their key tag program would result in this assistance now?

22

A New Reality

"I'M FINE" became my new mantra. Once in a moment of grandiosity, I decided to bake muffins, unaware that I had no clue about which measuring spoon was a teaspoon and which was a tablespoon, or whether I'd added an ingredient once or three times. It wasn't until I was putting away all the ingredients that I realized I'd used Coffee Mate instead of flour.

It was one mistake too many that day and I called Mom in Vancouver, crying.

"I'm sure they're fine," she told me. "Give one to Jane." She dutifully ate one and said they tasted good. Months later, I learned that after I went to bed, she'd tossed them in the garbage.

Jane quickly learned to cut open any meat before eating it after discovering that the food I "cooked" was often raw inside. I didn't know if food had been in the oven for five minutes or fifty, nor did I remember to set the timer. Most of the time, I didn't even remember I had a timer.

I constantly broke dishes, not understanding that three plates were heavier than one. Once, I broke six small bowls in one go. After every crash, Jane would yell, "Get out of the kitchen now!" and she would rush in with the vacuum cleaner. We went through a lot of dishes.

I pulled hot dishes out of the oven and instantly forgot they were hot, putting my bare hands on them. We went through a lot burn cream.

I cut food using a large knife, not knowing that the blade was upside down. When I pushed down on the blade to slice the food,

I sliced my palm instead of the food. We went through a lot of bandages.

I can do this, I told myself, as I looked at a large pile of laundry. Our washer and dryer were apartment-size stackable and had to be hooked up to the kitchen tap. Concentrating hard, I followed the steps: Connect the hoses, turn on the tap, put soap in the washer, load the clothes, push START.

Relax.

Fall asleep.

Wake to the sound of the drain hose unwinding like a wild snake from the back of the washer, flopping around in all directions, spewing soapy water on the floor, ceiling and walls.

Oh no! I'd forgotten to hook up the drain hose.

There was so much water on the floor that I called Jane, who was at an appointment, and twenty minutes later her brother was at the door with a carpet shampooer to suck the water up before damage was done to the apartment below. Unsure if I should laugh or cry, I did both, with laughter quickly turning to tears.

He gave me a big hug before leaving and, when I recovered enough, I went to put the clothes in the dryer and saw that I'd run an empty washer. I'd added soap but no clothes, which were still in a pile in front of the machines. I started over.

It took great concentration to do the simplest things. Putting on makeup was complicated. I couldn't get the order of things quite right and I forgot to comb my hair in the back. Once in a while, Jane stopped me on my way out the door and combed it for me. Clothes were a problem too. Who knew how confusing and entangling a bra could be? Or how much it could hurt to put on your socks? I couldn't tell if my clothes matched and I was afraid that I'd look like a crazy woman. Jane said not to worry about it, just hold out a hat and hope that people on the street offered money. Very funny!

I wore the same clothes constantly, unaware of when they were last washed but unable to decide what else to wear, forgetting that I had more clothes in the closet. Every few months, I went on a search to discover what was in my closet and dresser drawers. One day, I found a beautiful sweater and when I showed it to her, Jane said, "I gave you that sweater for Christmas last year." I didn't believe her. I was certain I'd never seen it before.

I was obviously no longer able to drive and Jane's injuries made driving too painful for her, so our wonderful neighbor, Helen, drove us to appointments as often as possible. Being a passenger in a car terrified me, no matter who the driver was. Every time I saw another car nearby, both of my hands clutched the dash and my right foot repeatedly stabbed an imaginary brake. A car twenty feet ahead appeared to be one foot ahead. I cried constantly and couldn't wait to get out of the car. Dr. Van Goor told me I'd lost my depth perception.

As the months flew by and my brain ever-so-slowly began to heal, I became more aware of how vulnerable I was. It was terrifying to get lost so easily, to not understand what was happening around me, to have no sense of time or space, to not feel grounded in any way. It was exhausting. This was an entirely different reality for me, one I had no way of understanding. It wasn't until years later that I truly understood the teaching of A COURSE IN MIRACLES — that our apparent reality is not reality. Time is not linear and space is not concretely defined. Every time I tried to put a glass in the cupboard and smashed it into the shelf because the actual shelf was higher or lower than I thought it was, this sense of unreality became stronger. It was scary.

In effect, I could no longer rely on things I'd previously taken for granted. The ring of the phone made me jump but when I answered it, I couldn't make sense of what was being said. I would forget whom I was talking to and hang up, mid-conversation. My favorite TV shows were confusing. I couldn't understand the words and everyone seemed to be speaking too fast. Even in person, I had trouble following conversations. I asked Jane questions, then got snappy when I couldn't understand her answers. At the time

I had no clue that the problem wasn't her. It was me.

I still tried to joke with my friends but I didn't realize that the jokes came out as sarcastic and rude instead of funny. Nobody laughed anymore. I had no filter and no sense of social graces. If I thought something, it came out of my mouth. Subtlety was a word from the past. I found people's emotions confusing and when I was told by friends that I'd hurt their feelings, I didn't know why they were upset. Even when it was explained to me, I still didn't get it. I felt awful knowing that I'd hurt people.

The only 'good' part of this was that my own feelings were not easily hurt. If someone was offensive or mean to me, I didn't know it. If an insult was hurled at me, I smiled. The intentions behind the words were beyond my understanding… unless an insult was blatant, in which case I cried for days, wondering why anyone would want to hurt me. Months later, when I was attending the Brain Injury Rehabilitation Center, my injuries were measured and I came in at the 10th percentile for understanding emotions, the lowest possible mark. It showed constantly. No matter how much I tried to explain what I meant, I managed to hurt people and, consequently, I lost several friends along the way. It got to the point where I was afraid to say anything because I felt so horrible when I discovered that I'd hurt people's feelings. It was even worse than having my own feelings hurt and I couldn't seem to repair the damage. So, I isolated myself even more.

LATE one summer evening, when we were returning from a rare visit with friends and Jane was putting a lock on the car steering wheel, a man approached me. Eyeing the steering wheel device, he asked, "Do you remember me?"

When I told him I didn't, he said, "Two years ago, you gave me warm clothes when I was cold. So now I'm going to stay by your car all night to protect it. If anyone touches it, I'll kill him."

"Thank you, but don't kill anyone," I replied. "It's just a car."
I'd forgotten that for years I'd handed out warm sweaters and

gloves and hats to the homeless around my downtown apartment. It turned out, however, that the recipients hadn't forgotten and wished to repay me. Some of them had seen the damage to the car before the repairs were done and knew that I must have been injured. Now, when I took out the garbage, those who hung around the bins looking for bottles approached me to lift my garbage into the bins for me. When I neared my apartment building carrying groceries, they often took my bags and carried them to the outside door while asking me how I was doing. I realized just how much my small gifts had meant to them over the years and I was touched by their thoughtfulness.

I quickly learned that my level of awareness depended totally upon my state of rest. The minute I reached a tipping point of tiredness, my brain stopped working. I had no warning of when it would happen, even mid-conversation, when I was working hard to translate thoughts into words, and then instantly the thoughts became a blur and I was babbling. I decided to stop trying to force myself out of bed when I was still tired and instead allow my body to tell me when to sleep and when to get up. It helped a lot, once I accepted that I needed at least twelve hours of sleep each night.

Acceptance was extremely difficult for this former workaholic.

Music helped too. It had always touched my soul and eased my pain. Now it hinted at memories of previous times, of my travels around the world and of great experiences. The familiarity of it helped to ease my fear of my vulnerability. On the days I had no migraine, I played it at full volume, overjoyed that I could re-member some of the words to the songs, with no awareness that my neighbors might be fed up as I played the same music repeatedly, trying to remember more with each playing. Music was more healing in those moments than I knew.

We also had a kitty — she added grace to my existence. Tiny, white with black marks, beautiful and elegant, she followed me around, copying every move I made, even sometimes imitating my yoga stretches. I loved her dearly. She never left my side, even when

I was vomiting. I relied on her cuddling when fear and confusion and nausea took over and I wondered if I'd ever be okay again.

THE insurance company sent us many forms to fill out, along with a cover letter requesting permission to access employment history, medical, chiropractic, massage, counseling and dental records and other information they could get, going back five years. The letter was vaguely threatening, telling us that, if we didn't give them what they wanted, we might not get proper medical care and there might be other repercussions.

We took the forms to Dr. Van Goor who told us not to sign anything, but get a lawyer. It hadn't crossed our minds that we'd need a lawyer. He recommended several and, once home, we chose one and made an appointment. A few days later, we were sitting in Barry's office and he was reassuring us, telling us he would inform the insurance companies, ours and that of the man who hit us, that he was our lawyer and would now deal with all the paperwork. He and Jane joked a bit as I sat there in a thick fog, unable to answer many of his questions, but we left his office feeling relieved, knowing that he would decide which demands from the insurance company were reasonable and which weren't.

I was worried about my work. As a professional speaker known for my high energy, I had to be able to think fast and speak clearly. I was booked to give several workshops that had been prepaid. Each one was custom designed for each client and involved many hours of research and organizing, but I hadn't finished the research for some of them. Each time I tried, my back pain prevented me from sitting for long, the words were confusing and the light of the computer screen drove me away. Reluctantly, I cancelled two of them and refunded the money.

One day the phone rang. The woman on the other end of the line identified herself as a human resources person for a large oil company — a company I'd been trying to get hired by for months. I couldn't understand most of what she was saying and I knew that what I said came out jumbled and confused. Not surprisingly, she hung up. I wasn't even able to get her name to call her back.

Jane went back to work part-time, in spite of her pain. Our savings were being rapidly depleted and we were stressed about credit card payments and having to return more prepayments for workshops I wouldn't be able to give. But we told ourselves everything would be okay, that the case would be settled soon.

At one point, whenever I went for walks, a man followed closely behind me, even getting in my face at times, leaning close to me when I was standing in line at a store and then following me out onto the street. It began to happen almost every time I went out. In the car, Jane told me there was a vehicle following us. We met friends for lunch and one of them said she couldn't understand why the people at the next table were so intent on hearing what we were saying.

Jane looked over and said, "Those people were driving behind us on the way here. They must be from the insurance company."

Our friends were shocked, but we weren't. We'd been told that insurance companies do this. It didn't bother me at first, because I thought it was good if cheaters got caught, but after a while it just became creepy. It gradually dawned on us that these 'stalkers' weren't looking for proof that we were injured but instead proof that we weren't. Their job was to catch us doing or saying anything that could be twisted into evidence that we were faking our injuries. In point of fact, their "getting in my face" was nothing short of intimidation.

And it worked because I did feel intimidated. I wondered how I could know the difference between a real stalker and the insurance company stalkers. In my safety courses, I used to teach about how dangerous stalkers could be. Tom, of course, had served as my own personal example. Now, even though I knew the insurance people didn't intend physical harm, I began to feel vulnerable. I was followed everywhere, day after day, month after month, year after year.

It was hard not to get paranoid. I saw a news story about an insurance company in the US that hacked into an injured man's computer to try to catch him cheating. I wondered if that could happen here. Another friend mentioned that perhaps the insurance company had bugged our apartment. I knew it was ludicrous but, just in case, I sang along a little louder than usual, in my normal off-key, screeching cat kind of sound whenever I listened to music. Take that, you stalkers!

23

Missing My Mom

I T WAS winter of 2007, ten months after the accident, and I was missing my Mom. My sense of disconnection from her was one of the hardest parts of my head injury. In fact, it was the one that made me feel most isolated. Because of the state of my mind, I was no longer able to laugh and joke or talk about what was happening in the world. We'd tried having our usual political conversations on the phone but I just couldn't keep up. I couldn't understand her point of view and was unable to explain my own jumbled thoughts.

And even if I could have managed to express myself clearly, my efforts to read newspapers and magazines and books only allowed a very basic understanding of what was happening. I could no longer make sense of details and I either quickly forgot them or grew confused. My brain was full of bits of information that were stripped of any context. Time frames were a challenge; I couldn't remember if something had happened last week or last year. I often pretended that I understood but Mom knew when I was bluffing and it was hugely disappointing for both of us.

Oh, how we missed my brain cells.

Jane and I used my airline passes to fly to Vancouver to see her. We took her shopping and to the casino. Mom and Jane had always enjoyed their time together and this was no exception as they laughed and joked and had fun. I quietly retreated to the lobby by myself, unable to stand the flashing lights, ringing bells, clanging machines and noisy crowds of people. I didn't have the heart to tell them how awful this experience was for me and how shut out I felt by the situation. Through the confusion in my mind, I knew that Jane must need a break from my neediness and I was happy to see her having fun.

Mom and I were no more able to connect in person than on the phone and in hindsight, I suspect that she was much more devastated by seeing my injuries in person than she let on. She didn't know how to be motherly in this situation and it was easier for her to give her attention to Jane. Her way of dealing with pain and fear had always been to pretend that everything was normal. And so, for a couple of hours, she and Jane did just that.

The trip wore me out. I flew home exhausted and devastated, realizing that my days of flying to Vancouver, or anywhere else, whenever I wanted to, were long gone. I'd been traveling constantly for all my adult life and losing this ability hit me harder than most of my other limitations. My wings had been clipped and this wasn't a limitation I accepted graciously. I isolated myself more often, depressed and tired, rarely going out unless I had to.

Jane was overwhelmed by my confusion and neediness and my struggles to cope, not to mention my edginess when I was frustrated. It was hard for her always having to repeat herself, knowing that, in five minutes, I wouldn't remember what she said and would keep asking the same questions over and over again.

Her world had been shattered just as much as mine and she approached me one day, upset. "I can't work. I can't ride my bike. I can't even lift my nieces and nephews in my arms. I can't do anything I used to do."

I felt her enormous sorrow as she spoke but all I could say was, "I'm sorry."

"We used to laugh all the time," she continued. "Our humor is what held us together. But now you don't understand jokes anymore, even when I explain them. You aren't the person you were before the accident. I've lost my best friend and I don't know what to do now."

I didn't know what to do either.

She told me that one of her friends suggested she leave me, that my injuries were so severe that she'd be justified in walking away, that no one should have to cope with my problems. She was offended by the comments and told the person so but, in spite of her assurances, I could feel her withdrawing from me and it hurt like hell.

I could see how depressed she was and, as time went on, I felt her withdrawing even more, barely speaking for long periods of time. I knew that her pain was intense as she awaited major surgery to fix some of the damage to her torn shoulder muscles, and I tried to be understanding and not bother her. She spent a lot of time sleeping and when she was awake, she went out to the neighbors' or her family. She had dinner with me most evenings but was out the door even before the dishes were cleared off the table. She stopped driving me to appointments or for groceries or helping with cleaning and she often refused to even answer me if I asked a question.

Our upstairs neighbor, Helen, stepped in and drove me to appointments and took me to the laundromat the mornings after I threw up in my sleep. Helen also brought me groceries when I was too sick to go to the store and hugged me when I couldn't stop crying. I asked Jane several times over the next few months to go for counseling so we could try to work things out but she refused to even talk about it. So, eventually, I stopped asking.

Jane hadn't actually moved out but she had left me. She was the one person in my life whom I'd totally trusted in every way. And now she was gone. I felt abandoned and terrified of being on my own.

As I sat alone in the apartment, I realized that the most difficult part of this new situation was that I would have to think for myself. There was no one to turn to for explanations, to ask, "What does that mean?" I'd seldom watched a TV show without asking Jane to explain it. I began to know just how much I'd asked of her in translating the world for me. Some days, I wondered why Jane had left me. Other days, I wondered why she'd stayed as long as she did.

Just over two years later, Jane officially moved out. She tried to explain why she'd backed away from me, telling me how difficult I was to be with, how much work I was to look after, how my mood swings were tough to cope with. I understood why she was telling me this. She wanted me to know that she wasn't a bad person. She was just overwhelmed with my problems and her own pain as well. I knew how big her heart was and that she wasn't a bad person, and I thanked her for her patience and kindness and thoughtfulness, meaning every word of it. But once I was alone, I cried.

I have eventually come to understand that, in a sense, I'd been in a relationship with Jane for the wrong reasons. Jane had given me a feeling of safety for the first time ever and her love had helped me heal from some of the trauma of my past. I'd loved her for that. But what I didn't understand at the time was that, subconsciously, fear had been a major driver in the relationship — namely my fear of men. This was not a good basis for a relationship.

A year after she left, she gave me a letter apologizing for not being stronger and saying she wanted to be friends. I thanked her, saying few couples could have gone through what we did and come out the other side in one piece. We've been close friends ever since.

It was spring 2009, about 18 months after our visit to see Mom, and I called her in Vancouver for one of our weekly chats. She told me about the path she'd taken that morning for her walk, talking about the blossoms on the apple trees and the brightly colored flowers that were everywhere. She was 84 and still liked to go for long walks around her neighborhood, now relying on her walker. Summer was her favorite time of year because she could wander in the sunshine and enjoy the outdoors. She told me how much she loved stopping by her usual shops to say hello to the staff and to chat with neighbors who were also out and about. It was the busyness and the noise that she loved the most as she slowly made her way along the commercial thoroughfare of Kingsway.

As she described it all to me, she casually mentioned a momentary loss of balance she'd felt while walking and how her left side had been numb, but just for a few seconds. Afterwards, she'd felt fine and kept on walking.

I felt a spike of fear. After twenty-eight years of first-aid training as a flight attendant, I knew the symptoms of stroke well.

I tried to keep my voice calm as I said, "You need to get that checked out to make sure you didn't have a stroke. Please, Mom, go to emergency right now."

She was quiet for a moment before saying, "No. I'm fine."

I pushed. Mom had always listened to my guidance before but, ever since my accident, it seemed she no longer trusted my advice. And I couldn't just hop on a plane anymore to make sure she was okay.

Several days later, Mom stunned me when she called to say that she was moving to Edmonton to live with my sister Margaret. It was very unlike her to make such a major decision without me. But I tried to ignore my hurt as I struggled to understand. I wondered if she was worried that maybe she'd had a stroke and was afraid to live alone anymore. But the more I thought about it, the more grateful I was that she would be close to four of my sisters and their families. Within a week, she was settled into her new surroundings in the suburbs.

I called Jane to tell her what was happening. She loved Mom and she offered to take me to Edmonton, a forty-minute flight away, to visit her while my sisters were gone for several days at a family wedding. I was hoping I'd be able to convince Mom to go to the hospital to get checked out.

We arrived in Edmonton on a hot summer day and hopped in a cab. The second I walked in the door at Margaret's, it was obvious that something was wrong. Mom said she couldn't see properly. Afraid that it was another stroke, I called an ambulance. At the hospital we learned that, yes, it was a major stroke and she had just lost over fifty percent of her vision. We also got confirmation that this was her second stroke within the last few weeks.

My heart broke.

Mom was amazingly upbeat. My sister Cathy arrived at the hospital and Mom now had an audience. She'd always loved an audience, and her wittiness and crazy sense of humor were on full display. She and Jane joked about how, when Mom washed dishes now, only half of each plate would be cleaned since she'd only be able to see half the plate. Margaret and Cathy joined in the fun. They'd never seen this side of Mom.

The doctors couldn't believe the laughter coming from her room either. Each time one of them came in to check her, she told them she knew exactly why they were there: They liked her so much they couldn't stay away. She flirted outrageously with every male that entered the room.

Mom didn't yet understand the reality of her situation and I wanted to just wrap my arms around her to protect her from the pain that such an understanding would eventually bring.

After many hours at the hospital, we took her home. Margaret flew out the next morning and Jane and I spent the next ten days taking care of Mom, cooking and cleaning, doing laundry, getting her to appointments and shopping for what she needed. The doctors had told us that the strokes had done a lot of damage and Mom didn't have much time left. So we put all our energy into giving her whatever she wanted, which was going to the casino and bingo.

Jane took her. The unfamiliarity of Margaret's home and where things were, and the energy it took to take care of Mom, left me with migraines and vomiting. While they were out, I just lay on the sofa, numb.

I loved knowing they were having so much fun when they came home laughing and joking, Mom bragging about her winnings at the slot machines. We spent our evenings watching her favorite

TV shows and old movies, eating popcorn and listening to her fill us in on the latest Hollywood gossip. Then Margaret came home and it was time to head back to Calgary.

NOVEMBER 9, 2009: 5 a.m. The phone woke me up. Mom had passed.

A few months after my last visit with her, my sister had called to let me know Mom wasn't doing well. She'd been having trouble breathing and had been moved to palliative care. I'd known since her second stroke that she didn't have much time left but I wasn't prepared for how hard her loss would hit me.

Several years later, when I was able to think a bit more clearly, I reflected on the changes that A COURSE IN MIRACLES had brought to my relationship with Mom and the true enormity of its gift of forgiveness and love. My Mom and I had risen from the depths of despair, in our separate lives and our relationship. For the last thirteen years of Mom's life, we'd had a wonderful relationship, with a love that was powerful and deep, cleansed of issues that had marred it in the past. Without those shadows dragging us down, we'd each been totally free to be ourselves, to laugh and joke and have fun in a way we'd never known before. Every single promise made by the Course had been fulfilled. This miracle was more than I'd ever hoped for.

But I wasn't ready to let her go. It was too soon. Our good times had been too short after so many years of a difficult relationship. For the last two years since the accident, I'd been thinking that I'd get better and then I could connect with Mom again, but now that would never happen. Sorrow overwhelmed me, literally incapacitating me. I was too shattered to even attend her funeral in Edmonton, too raw and vulnerable in my pain to go anywhere. Staying in my cocoon at home, wrapped in blankets, sobbing, I was distraught, unable to find any emotional balance. Jane, feeling her own sorrow over the loss of Mom, was there for me, letting me know I wasn't alone, making tea and doing whatever she could to ease my pain. I cried constantly for weeks.

24

Rehabilitation

IN JULY 2008, the Brain Injury Rehabilitation Centre (BIRC) called, months after my doctor sent in the application. Finally they had space for me and I was overjoyed. After giving me numerous tests, it was clear that I would benefit from their programs and I began to attend the center three hours a day, three days a week. This quickly became four days a week when they realized how much help I needed.

Part of the work involved sitting with a volunteer for hours, looking at words and sentences and then numbers, trying to get them to make sense. We quickly gave up on the numbers; I just wasn't able to process them. But I studied words and sentences day after day. After a while, there were occasions when I was corrected by a volunteer for the way I'd strung my words together into a sentence but I argued the point with them and was, occasionally, proven correct. Apparently, my inner grammar nerd hadn't been as affected by the brain injury as the rest of me.

Going to BIRC exhausted me. The mental exercises were more draining than any physical exercise and I was absolutely sure at the end of each day that I would not have the strength to return the next day. But I forced myself to show up, wanting to take advantage of every bit of help I could get.

Jodi, a BIRC worker, took me to apply for medical welfare and the food bank. I hated that I needed help. Jane hadn't officially moved out at that point and we had lived on our savings for over eighteen months with little income. I'd had to return thousands of dollars in deposits from clients and Jane's return to work hadn't lasted long, as her pain overwhelmed her. We could no longer pay the rent or cover the costs of medication. I was devastated that my life had come to this.

Four days every week, I walked the seven blocks each way to BIRC. My dizziness and pain flared up on the walk but I didn't have enough money to take the bus. I counted every step: two blocks to Safeway, two more blocks to the underpass and then three more blocks to BIRC. Each time I wondered if I would have the energy to stop at Safeway on the way home and get the groceries we needed. Most of the time, I didn't. My exhaustion and pain were worse than my hunger.

It's now mind over matter, I told myself, and vowed to handle the situation with as much grace and dignity as I could muster. I was going to put a smile on my face each day, no matter how much I was hurting, and try to enjoy the walk each time. Sometimes I didn't succeed in hiding my pain but most days I did and felt better for it. Apparently, so did others. I often forgot that I was smiling as I gritted my teeth and persevered; when someone on the street smiled back at me, it was a nice surprise. A tall, good-looking man in a suit, carrying a briefcase, walked by me every single day, going in the opposite direction. One beautiful summer day, he stopped me, smiling as he touched my cheek with his finger and told me, "Every day you smile at me as you go by, and some days that is the only smile I see. Thank you." His words warmed my heart and made my efforts worthwhile.

BIRC provided a wealth of information. One of the most un-settling things I learned was that my exhaustion would probably never ease, that it was due to the extra effort required to understand what people were saying and to perform the tasks that were so easy for others to do automatically. That part of a brain injury seldom gets better. I learned lots of tips on how to get organized: how to line up my makeup on the counter in the order I would use it; how to plan my grocery shopping so that I didn't buy too much to carry; how to plan my days so that I didn't try to do everything at once and then pay a price later when my pain flared up. I was told to use sticky notes and I put them all over the apartment. On the door was a note reminding me to take my purse, my umbrella and a coat. Another one told me to take my keys and cell phone. On the kitchen cabinet were notes telling me how to do laundry — how much soap to add, how to sort the clothes and what the cleaning symbols on the clothes meant. Some notes had cooking instructions. On good days, I even remembered to check the notes.

I put an important note of my own on the fridge door: If it was suddenly ten or twenty times harder to do the things I do every day, would I rise to the occasion? I read that question every morning, vowing to do my best and, every evening I asked myself if I'd risen to the occasion that day. This helped me, because I recognized how many days I did rise to the occasion. And on the days when I complained too much, I renewed my commitment to do better.

Jodi convinced me to apply for Income Assistance for the Severely Handicapped and for a federal disability pension. Both were for permanent injuries. I'd been struggling to admit that I might never fully recover but, when Dr. Van Goor filled in the applications and wrote that my injuries were indeed permanent, I had to accept it.

I told Jane not to call me Forrest again; it wasn't funny anymore.

Jodi took me to apply for Access Calgary, a shared driving service for people with disabilities. To my great relief, I was accepted. I came to love the taxi drivers who were specially trained to deal with people with disabilities. They were some of the kindest and most thoughtful people I'd ever encountered. Most of them were immigrants and many of them had been doctors, engineers, architects and teachers in their homeland. Many of them had left war zones and starvation behind and were grateful to be in Canada. I loved listening to them talk about their countries and they told me they enjoyed hearing about my own travels, especially my trips to Africa and the Middle East, where some of them were from.

Some of my distant memories were still intact and we could chat about places we'd seen in common. They were kind about the fact that I was confused and they never seemed to mind that, even after having a wonderful conversation on a previous trip, the next time I saw them I had no idea who they were or what we'd talked about. Some gently reminded me of our previous discussions, but even then, I didn't usually remember. I got frustrated with myself, especially when I saw the disappointment on their faces.

In this sense, Access Calgary meant a lot more than just rides. It was an opportunity to socialize with people from all over the world. I encouraged the drivers to talk about history and geopolitical situations relative to their countries of origin and I always wanted to know more. I knew I wouldn't remember but I loved hearing it nonetheless. One of the drivers was from India and, after I told him how much I loved Bollywood music, he never failed to put in a Bollywood CD whenever we were alone in the car. "Louder!" I'd command as I swayed in the backseat to the raucous music while he sang along from the front. We always arrived at my front door laughing. Many times, with other drivers as well, when we reached my destination, we both declared that the trip was over much too soon and that we would have liked it to last longer.

Even though at BIRC they told us not to talk about the past, believing that we should just move forward, I felt like I'd lost my sense of self since the accident and so it helped to talk to the drivers about who I used to be and the things I used to do. I felt such sorrow over that loss. I had so completely identified as a flight attendant, as a traveler and a comedian, and then as a professional speaker that I wondered who I was now without those things. I couldn't even read the books I used to read or watch the TV shows I used to enjoy. It's frightening not to know who you are. My friendships with the drivers helped immensely.

On good days, I didn't use Access. I took the bus or train, in spite of often getting lost.

Jane called it my terminal independence. There was a bonus.

I learned of the true kindness of Calgarians. I was always offered a seat, even when the buses were crowded, and most often young people were the first to jump up when they saw my cane. I'd always been impressed by our youth, ever since my days of volunteering with the Red Cross, and this only added to my admiration.

Sometimes, I had to suppress my laughter. One day, when I was about to cross the street, a young man of about sixteen dashed out ahead of me, dramatically standing spread-eagle in the middle of the nearly empty street, telling me, "It's okay to cross now. I'll make sure you're safe." I profusely thanked this young hero.

Another time, I was on the train and it had just pulled into my station. There was a tough looking young man in the car with a bald head, tattoos and an intimidating manner. There'd been silence ever since he boarded and I could tell that people were afraid of him. I waited to get off as others went by me. When he reached my seat, he stopped so that I could get off before him. I smiled and said that I'd wait because I moved more slowly than others. He insisted that others would wait for me and put his arms across the aisle so that no one could get by. I thanked him and got off the train ahead of him. As I walked down the street, he walked in front of me and kept turning around to see that I was alright, smiling to reassure me. It was proof, if I needed any, that who people are on the outside didn't always reflect who they were on the inside.

IT WAS early December and I had another appointment with a medication specialist at the hospital. Access Calgary dropped me off and I found my way to the doctor's office as usual. But as I was leaving, an alarm went off and I panicked. A nurse explained it was just a fire drill but I still had to work to stay calm in the midst of the shrill piercing noise. Once in the elevator, I managed to hit the wrong button and, when the doors opened up, I found myself in the basement. Here the alarm was accompanied by red and white flashing strobe lights. There was a Christmas bazaar set up near the elevator and people swarmed around tables cluttered with sale items.

The lights and noise terrified and confused me and I felt vulnerable. My heart pounded in my chest and I struggled to breathe. But the elevators no longer worked. Tears pouring down my face, I searched for but couldn't find the stairs. My panic was mounting because the Access Calgary car was my ride home and I couldn't miss it.

And then an angel appeared: a woman in a winter coat and boots shopping at the tables stopped and asked me, "What's wrong with you?"

"The noise, the lights — I have to get out of here. I don't know how to get out of here." She took my hand and led me up the stairs to the Access entrance.

My ride was there and I climbed in, heart still pounding, panic still overwhelming me. A young disabled man was sitting beside me and I began speaking to him slowly. I showed him my brightly colored key chain. He was excited by my attention and, in return, he shared with me his toy car. We chatted amiably, quietly, and the distraction removed me to another world, one in which all that mattered was a brightly colored toy and a new friend. I was incapable of functioning normally at that point and, putting myself on the level of the child-like young man beside me, I was a bit distracted from the fear, allowing me to shut out the scary world around me for the twenty-minute drive. My panic gradually eased and, with it, the painful pounding in my chest, as my sense of being in terrible danger receded. The shrieking alarm and flashing strobe lights had instantly made me feel I was in a war zone and that danger was imminent.

Since the accident, I'd been jumpy and edgy when, in my confusion, I couldn't understand what was happening around me. Incidents that seemed small to others, such as a fire alarm, left me terrified that I was about to die. All my life I'd relied on my instincts to keep me safe through many dangerous situations but I was no longer able to understand my instincts. The fight or flight response was always near the surface in me, ready to be triggered.

The driver looked at me curiously when he heard me speaking on the same level as my young friend, and he seemed to understand that I wasn't doing well. He asked no questions of me, telling me he'd have me home soon, and his kindness soothed my pain. Thankfully, I didn't even have to provide him with my address; he knew exactly where to take me.

At home, I changed into pyjamas and curled up in a blanket, unmoving in the silence and the darkness except for the shaking that took hours to ease. Kitty joined me under the blankets, curled up against me. I wanted to stay in this cocoon of safety forever and never have to navigate the wilderness that my world had become. I was later diagnosed with Post Traumatic Stress Disorder and that diagnosis helped me understand why I was never able to let my guard down, why I couldn't trust what was happening around me, why the nightmares had returned so ferociously, and why I was terrified in cars and when I heard noises that I couldn't understand. For many years following the accident, the PTSD controlled me. It has turned out to be the most difficult of my injuries.

A COUPLE of close, long-time friends told me constantly that I was fine, that I was no different than before and that they couldn't tell I had a brain injury. Their intentions were clear when, for example, if I couldn't find something, they'd say, "I lose my keys sometimes too." Or, after yet another fall, "I sometimes lose my balance too." When I tried to explain some difficulty I was having or asked for help in understanding something, they tuned me out, not hearing what I was saying, essentially telling me "It's not that bad."

I knew that they had no clue how hard I worked to understand them when they were talking to me, or simply to navigate life day by day. When they told me I was doing "great" and that nothing was wrong, even when they could see that I was struggling to understand what they were saying, they thought they were being encouraging. This upset me. It trivialized the enormity of the changes in my life and my struggles to cope with them. I wanted to yell at them, "How would you feel if you couldn't understand what was happening around you? If you couldn't remember what was in your cupboards or your closet, so that you constantly had to look through them each time you needed something? And you knew that, when you found it, you'd forget again in five minutes. How would you feel if you constantly cut yourself, or burned yourself, or got lost or couldn't shop or drive or cook or do anything right? Stop telling me that my brain injury will heal if I'll just do crossword puzzles. Stop treating me like I'm refusing to do that just to piss you off. I don't have the energy or the smarts to do crossword puzzles. Stop trivializing this horror show I'm living right now. My whole world is upside down. I'm scared and I need to talk about it but if you deny it, you are denying my reality and it makes me feel crazy. I don't need to feel crazier than I already do." Their comments were like telling someone with a broken hip to just go for a run and it would heal.

I didn't want them to dwell on the changes in me. But when I was particularly frustrated and crying, I wanted them to acknowledge it. I desperately needed both understanding of my reality and compassion — not denial. So, I became defensive, thinking that they didn't believe what I was telling them about how hard it was. After all, brain injury is the invisible injury.

I began to distrust that those closest to me would be honest when I really needed them to be. When, a few years later, my lawyer asked me to bring someone who knew me before the accident to a meeting in his office with a forensic psychiatrist in order to confirm the changes in me and the daily difficulties I faced, I didn't trust that these friends even saw my difficulties. They'd been so busy denying how confused I was and how I was unable to do the things I used to do, I believed they truly didn't understand. So, I chose Jane's sister to join me.

Later, some of these friends told me how hurt they were that I hadn't asked them to go. When I explained why, they were surprised. Of course, they told me, they saw the enormous changes in me. They had only lied about what they saw in order to encourage me. But being lied to was one of my worst triggers, and they didn't understand that their lies had hurt me.

On the one hand, my situation was not unique. This is a common complaint of people suffering from brain injuries. On the other hand, at the time I had no clue that my irritation was intensified because these well-intentioned friends were inadvertently repeating the lies I'd been told all those years ago as a child. The abuse never happened, nothing was wrong, white was black, down was up and what I was experiencing wasn't real.

I knew that it wasn't fair to judge them. How could they possibly know what I needed? Most people have no clue about brain injury. But rationality was no longer my strong suit and the situation made me isolate myself even more.

I kept trying to figure out who I was now. I knew who I wasn't. I wasn't a professional speaker or a stand-up comedian. I watched recordings of my stints at Yuk Yuk's and I couldn't understand my jokes anymore, even though I'd written them myself. And people had laughed at them so they must have made sense.

I wasn't someone who could understand politics or social issues or economics. I couldn't even read about them anymore; the words and sentences were too jumbled.

Numbers still didn't make sense. I couldn't compare prices or add or subtract in my head, and I still had to hold my wallet out to a clerk to pay for things. I used to love numbers and was so quick with figuring out math that Jane had once asked me if I was autistic. Now I couldn't even play solitaire.

I kept thinking I'd go back to who I'd been before but it wasn't happening. I'd lost myself. Not only was this frightening, it also left a horrible emptiness inside me. My introspection naturally turned to existential questions: If I couldn't define myself, did that mean I was nothing? This feeling of nothingness was all-too familiar from my childhood.

A COURSE IN MIRACLES had been a saving grace for me up

until the accident. I'd studied it for thirteen years. I'd thought those teachings were so ingrained in my psyche that I couldn't possibly forget them. But where were they now?

25

Wholesale Dishonesty

ONE year after the accident, my lawyer called to tell me that my insurance company was refusing to pay my medical bills and was sending me to an independent medical examiner (IME), a forensic psychiatrist. Jane was out of town but the neighbor who saw me off that morning dropped a small recording device in my pocket, knowing that I wouldn't remember anything of what was said at the appointment. It recorded every word.

Little did I know that this was the first in an odyssey of difficult appointments that nearly broke me entirely. I'd thought I'd already reached that limit but the worst was yet to come.

It was February and I trudged through deep snow and freezing winds to get to his office. Walking in the door, I barely had my heavy parka off before the doctor began explaining why his office, inside and out, had so many security cameras and recording devices. He had received threats from former clients and was afraid for his life. He actually told me that.

I saw his fear firsthand when the mailman stopped by. Although he was clearly dressed as a mailman, he was asked to identify himself into a microphone while the doctor watched him on a bank of cameras. After asking many questions, the doctor finally let him deliver a registered letter.

I was taken to a back room with a small table on which he had placed the file he'd received from the insurance company. There were two chairs placed against a low window that was only inches from my face when I was seated. Bright, blinding sunlight poured in — deadly for anyone with a brain injury and migraines.

Our session began with him speaking slowly, barely above a whisper, and with exaggerated politeness. He told me that if I didn't understand him, it was because I had a hearing problem. "Which ear has the problem?" he asked.

I knew that my hearing was just fine. Then, he suddenly switched to a loud, fast and aggressive voice. The fog in my brain slowed my thoughts and I struggled to understand his questions. When I told him that he was speaking too quickly, he ignored me, leaving me no time to think or to filter what I should or shouldn't say. I wanted to limit my answers to only what I absolutely had to say, but I couldn't figure out how to do that. All I knew was that my lawyer had told me I had to answer all questions. So I did.

He continued with rapid-fire questions. Do you pray? To what do you pray — a tree? Do you like people? Do you shoplift? Do you lie? Are you envious? Are you a perfectionist? Are you cheap? Are you a packrat? Are you angry? Do you procrastinate? Then: "What would you do if Jane were killed?" I gasped, but then he repeated it and demanded an answer.

"Has there ever been a suicide in your family?"

I told him about my brother.

"Has anyone in your family ever been charged with a crime?"

I knew there were records of my Dad's fraud charges.

He pounced. "Fraud in the family — no wonder you're a professional speaker."

I didn't understand the connection.

He kept pounding away, asking me the same questions over and over again and I was quickly worn down. The hours passed by slowly and the appointment ended up being four and a half hours long. I complained several times about my back pain, telling him that the chair I was sitting in was bad for someone with a back injury. He shook his finger at the chair and said, "Bad chair."

I replied, "You need a psychiatrist." It was the only clear thought I had that day.

He demanded details about my history. When was your first sexual encounter? What was your age? Where did it happen? Who was it with? How many one-night stands have you had? How often have you had sex since the accident?

It was a horrible invasion of privacy and I kept asking him what any of these questions had to do with the accident. But he ignored every objection, continuing his rapid-fire questioning as my confusion got worse.

Was there ever child abuse? Was there hitting? Choking? Kicking? Broken bones?

Hospital visits? Was there sexual abuse? Was it touching or intercourse? How often? How old were you?

He was a man focused on sex and his questions sickened me. I'd never told anyone what had happened to me as a child. Even when the sexual abuse memories had returned after that awful yoga class seven years before, I hadn't discussed the details with my therapist and I didn't have the courage to accept the Course in Miracles teaching that I should shine a light on all the shadows deep inside me. It had been too terrifying to look at the details of the past and so I'd once again blocked it all out. Yet, here was this stranger callously probing the most painful memories in my psyche, making ugly comments, wondering aloud why the abuse had happened to me and if I'd been a bad child.

I'd spent years telling myself that it wasn't my fault. But now this professional psychiatrist insinuated that it was. He'd touched a raw spot — so raw that shame flooded through me as I sat there, horrified that he'd validated the old fear of my inner badness. The memories reminded me that I could not hide who I really was and I felt myself beginning to crumble under the weight of shame and guilt.

I had that same feeling of helplessness I'd had as a child when I heard the bedroom door open in the middle of the night. I heard my Dad's voice: "This is your fault. You are evil."

Exhausted and unable to understand that he was manipulating me, I shifted into dealing with the situation exactly as I'd done fifty years earlier. I detached, becoming meek and submissive, escaping into never-never land. I felt that familiar terror but I couldn't allow myself to acknowledge that anything was wrong. As a child, I had to do exactly as I was told, no matter what. The cost of doing otherwise was too high.

So now I stopped protesting the psychiatrist's questions and docilely answered each of them the best I could. The monster of my childhood now wore the guise of a psychiatrist who was paid thousands of dollars by an insurance company that would do anything it took to avoid paying for injuries, including breaking me into little pieces.

After four hours of questioning and personality testing, he asked me what my goals were for the future.

"To be a better person," I answered.

"I've never heard that answer before," he said.

I was totally unable to explain what I meant. What I wished I could have said was, "I want to come out of this awful experience of pain and confusion and degradation with some degree of dignity. I want to learn how to deal with what's happening and not let it change me into someone who's bitter, who buys into victimhood and sees the world as a dark and fearful place. I want to come out of this stronger and wiser."

But it would be years before I could articulate these thoughts.

While in his office I'd done a good job of dissociating, denying my pain, and blocking from my consciousness what was happening. It wasn't until months later, when I read his forty-page report, that I remembered some of the details of what he'd put me through. His report never mentioned the emotional manipulations or subtle accusations that he used to break me down. He excoriated me as a liar, claiming that I made up the child abuse because I liked attention and that I also made up my injuries from the car accident. He lied, writing that I'd never once said I had back pain and that it was obvious that my cane had never been used. He claimed that I was just trying to make money from the accident. Therefore, no medical treatment was needed and there was no reason for me not to be back at work. He warned that, if I decided to challenge anything in the report or to complain about him to the College of Physicians and Surgeons, I "ought to consult a lawyer."

It was obvious to me that I wasn't the litigious one. As I later listened to my recording of the appointment, it was also obvious to me that I wasn't the liar.

In my naïveté about insurance companies and IMEs, it hadn't occurred to me that the psychiatrist wouldn't believe me — or that he would simply ignore the obvious symptoms of brain damage and physical disability. I thought my condition was obvious, and I had medical records that illustrated this even more clearly than an interview could. But what upset me the most, I realized later, was that the psychiatrist had expertly played on an old fear my dad had put into my head: "If you tell, no one will believe you."

When I told my lawyer that I had a recording that confirmed the psychiatrist had lied, he didn't want to hear it. He said the psychiatrist couldn't testify in court because all the judges knew he had no credibility. When I discussed this report with my doctors, they told me that the only purpose of the interview was to intimidate me so that I would walk away from the lawsuit. One of them told me that another patient had committed suicide because of similar treatment.

But the day after reading the report, I was able once again to block out the memory of what this doctor did to me, just as I had compartmentalized events in my mind as a child. I knew how to pretend bad things never happened. Even after reading his dishonest report, I tucked it away in my mind and pretended it didn't exist.

A few months later, I received a cheque from my insurance company for $12,000 (despite the fact that my insurance contract stated that they had to pay up to $50,000 in medical bills) and a letter stating that, due to the psychiatrist's report that there was nothing wrong with me, they were closing my file. My lawyer told me that they were refusing to answer his letters and phone calls and were ignoring his attempts to contact them. He said, "We are already suing the other guy's insurance company. Do you want to sue your own as well?" His opinion was that it wouldn't be worth it and so I dropped it. It was the only money I'd receive from either insurance company until the case was settled seven years later.

AUGUST 2009. I was ordered to attend a hearing for discovery and Jane came with me. For two days, I was grilled by the insurance company lawyer. I was nervous about making mistakes and worried that my words wouldn't come out right, that I'd be too confused to think clearly about my answers. My memory was so fuzzy that I could have eight days of vicious migraines and vomiting, and then two good days without them, but when I was asked about getting migraines, I wouldn't remember the sick days and answer, "No, I haven't had any migraines."

I also had a lifelong habit of minimizing my pain. So I was unaware when my answers weren't always factual. I was shocked by the amount of personal medical history that was demanded, going back over thirty years. I detested the invasion of privacy.

As the hearing continued into the second day, panic began building inside me. They referred to the psychiatrist's report, reminding me of how negative it was, and my thoughts went to him stating I was a liar many times over. Did they believe him? Did they think I was crazy or that I would just lie about everything? Did they not understand that I was incapable of lying, that I couldn't think fast enough to tell a lie? My heart pounded as fear swamped me. None of it made sense to me.

I didn't understand my increasing panic. My belief in my inherent badness, which was resurrected by the psychiatrist, was surfacing in a horribly frightening way, clashing with the calm self that I wanted to present. I felt like a fake and was afraid of being discovered. I had to keep pretending. The thought of them seeing who I really was terrified me so much I could hardly breathe. I kept thinking: *There's no air in this room. Why is there no air?*

I couldn't figure out why the opinions of the lawyers were so important. It would be months before it dawned on me. The situation was an echo from many years ago. I needed the lawyers, and eventually a judge, to acknowledge that I was telling the truth, the same way that the policeman did when I was fourteen. It was also important that I not be found to be lacking, to be less than everyone else. I couldn't stand the thought of it. Fear triumphed over common sense. No one could understand my turmoil and my lawyer kept telling me to relax, that none of this was personal.

How could it not be personal? They used every piece of personal information they could against me. How could it not be personal?

I was ordered to provide more than a hundred additional documents. They wanted my day timers, paperwork from my business, records from doctors, chiropractors, massage therapists and psychotherapists for the last twenty years. After the second day of questioning, I was worn out and feeling beat up. I went home and crawled into bed. The next day, I tried to organize the paperwork that they demanded but, when Jane walked in and saw that I was getting it all mixed up, that I was totally confused and frustrated and crying, she took over and spent many hours putting it all together. Once it was organized, we slipped back into our separateness.

IN APRIL 2010, a mediation meeting was arranged between the insurance company and Jane and me. I was hopeful that, after three years, this legal process would finally be over.

Sitting around a large table in the conference room in my lawyer's office, I was shocked when the insurance company lawyer, who'd seemed reasonable during the hearing the previous year, became nasty and threatening.

"You won't like what will happen to you if you don't accept this settlement offer," she said. "You have no idea how ugly it will get." I couldn't understand why she was so different this time. When she went into another room with the insurance adjuster and mediator, my lawyer explained that she was just acting tough to impress the insurance company. I took it personally, feeling betrayed and attacked. Combined with an overwhelming sorrow for all the losses of the past few years, her mean-spiritedness was too much and I crumbled into pieces, sobbing and feeling broken. Once the tears started, they wouldn't stop. My lawyer and Jane looked on helplessly.

The mediator, who'd been going back and forth between the two rooms, returned with a final offer from the insurance company. I was upset at how low their offers were, not understanding that my self-esteem was wrapped up in how much the insurance company thought I was worth. I sank further into depression with each low offer. I knew that it was stupid to even think of taking the offer and my lawyer told me not to, but I accepted it anyway. I was out of energy and I just wanted out. But the insurance company refused to accept my acceptance unless Jane settled too. She refused and we walked away. Little did I know just how vicious the insurance company would be when they followed through on their threats.

At home, I tried to sort it all out in my head but I had no perspective and blamed myself for not being stronger, for crumbling so constantly. I knew better than to let other people control me like that and I hated myself for being so weak. But what I didn't realize was that one of the most difficult parts of my brain injury was the loss of my ability to read people. I no longer knew where they were coming from, what they meant when they said things, when they were being honest or dishonest or when they were joking or serious. It scared me to be so taken by surprise by the lawyer's nastiness and it reinforced my feelings of vulnerability.

The lawyer followed through on her threats and, in July 2010, I was sent to another IME, a forensic psychologist. I spent two days with his assistant, being tested for four and a half hours each day. By the third day, when the psychologist himself interviewed me, my efforts to focus had left me exhausted. I didn't tell him that I'd had nightmares about the appointment and that my backache and headache were worse than usual. He had a copy of the forensic psychiatrist's report and he, like the other doctor before him, concentrated on my childhood. I couldn't handle another dive into my inner darkness and started crying, telling him my childhood had nothing to do with the accident. He said it did. He demanded details of the most difficult parts of my past as he rapidly typed on his computer keyboard, looking up only to glare at me with distaste, as if he could barely stand the sight of me. He was cold and arrogant and intimidating, constantly telling me, "The other doctor didn't believe you."

I kept replying, "The other doctor is the one who's not telling the truth."

He was snappy and rude, repeatedly cutting me off mid-sentence. There was nothing professional about the interview.

When his lengthy report arrived many weeks later, it referred to the previous doctor's assessments as fact. It was full of nonsense. He stated that the injuries were in my mind and that, if I'd been told I had no injuries, then I wouldn't have had any. He seemed to believe in magic, stating that my injuries would disappear if only I believed him when he claimed they didn't exist. His dishonesty was disheartening.

Putting his report on a stack of legal papers in the apartment, I tried to distance myself from the case, at least for the moment. Once again, I turned to A COURSE IN MIRACLES, knowing there were answers in there that would help me cope. But the words were still jumbled and didn't make sense. Struggling with bitterness, I became bitchy and snarly, taking my pain and fear out on others.

It wasn't really about the money, although I was worried about my future. It was about the horrible, nasty, debilitating, degrading process. Telling myself to let go of my fears, I tried to trust that I would be okay. Sometimes I succeeded; most of the time I did not. Turning to Dr. Mahon, the wonderful psychologist from BIRC, I spent many hours in her office as she gently guided me out of the dark place that I had parked my heart.

I turned to music, nearly wearing out the CDs of Amy Bishop, whose beautiful sound touched a place deep inside me. And my favorite classical music brought back such warm memories that it also instantly soothed me, lifting me up when I was down and calming me when I was panicked. I used laughter as a balm, watching more movies — the sillier the better — and often turning on the family channel to watch children's movies. They were easier to understand and kids really know how to be silly. A friend told me to watch 50 First Dates again. I had no memory of having seen it twice before and now I watched it again several more times, understanding a little bit more each time, laughing at every single line, feeling joy that I could finally understand jokes. I often wondered if the neighbors thought I was nuts, sitting alone in my apartment, laughing so loudly.

Maybe I was nuts.

"Am I crazy?" I asked Dr. Mahon.

"Of course you are," she said. Then, after a long pause, "We all are."

26

Overwhelming Darkness

SEPTEMBER 2010. The phone rang and my lawyer told me that the insurance company was sending me to yet another forensic psychiatrist. I hadn't yet healed from the emotional pain caused by the last IME. Jane couldn't believe that this was being done to me yet again and offered to pick me up when the appointment was over. She'd been offering to help more lately and I gratefully leaned heavily on her that day.

Access Calgary took me to the appointment but, when I arrived at the address on the south side of the city, I was confused. The nondescript building had barbed wire along the roof, security cameras on every corner and reinforced windows. It looked like a prison. My Access driver didn't want to leave me there and, in fact, told me not to get out of the car. I comforted him by saying I'd be okay, without having any idea whether or not I would be. He walked me to the front door and held it open as I entered. Inside, I found an empty reception area with a sign saying, "Ring the bell," but I couldn't find a bell. I looked all around before giving up and taking a seat. I was unnerved, unsure if I was in the right place. I was tired and feeling confused before even beginning the appointment. Maybe, I thought, I shouldn't have sent the Access driver away.

A woman entered from outside and asked, "Why are you here?"

"Are you an employee?" I asked.

"Yes," she replied, showing me her ID badge. "Were you in an accident?" She began asking a lot of questions. I was confused, not sure why I was being asked for all this information in the reception area, remembering only that my lawyer had told me to co-operate with the process. Thanks to the thick fog in my brain and my previous experiences with IMEs, I was seriously intimidated. Jane wasn't coming to get me for several more hours and I had no way of leaving if I needed to.

Then she asked if she could pray for me. This struck me as seriously weird but I didn't want to start off on the wrong foot so I said "Yes," thinking she would go home and pray for me later. But that wasn't what she had in mind. She told me to close my eyes and then launched into a long rant about Jesus healing me. It was a very long prayer, maybe two full minutes. Finally, she finished and left the building. Though I'd been polite, I found the whole thing very offensive. I was getting more and more worried about what kind of nut job the insurance company had ordered me to see.

Finally, a short, chubby man came into the reception area and introduced himself. He took me to his small, cramped office in the back, which was a dirty mess with stacks of papers spread over chairs, a table and a desk. As he cleared away room for me to sit, his first words were, "We're going to talk about your mental health issues."

"I don't have any mental health issues."

"Oh, yes, you do. You have depression."

"Everyone has depression at some point in life."

Anger flashed across his face, but by this point, I was getting mad as well. The whole situation was insane. "Why do you need so much security?" I asked him. "Are you afraid of your patients? The other forensic psychiatrist is afraid of his patients. Are you like him?" I added that I was offended his employee had asked me personal questions in the reception area and made me sit through her prayer. In truth, I was trying to find my bearings, trying to sort out what was going on there.

He blew up and told me I had to leave, that he would reschedule my appointment because of my bad attitude. I wondered what kind of psychiatrist kicks you out of his office for asking a question.

"No. I'm here now and I'm not going to reschedule." I was so tired that the thought of rescheduling overwhelmed me and I didn't know why I should be inconvenienced by his temper tantrum. It was one of the stupider decisions in my recent history of stupid decisions. I had no clue how vulnerable I was, how my tiredness was affecting the way I was seeing things.

He told me to sit in the reception area while he decided what to do.

I called Jane, sobbing as I told her what had happened and she told me to hang up while she called our lawyer. Then she called me back to tell me that the insurance company lawyer, who had arranged the appointment, was being called as well. Apparently, there were lots of laughs in my lawyer's offices because I'd asked the doctor if he was just like the other one. I didn't know how hated that first psychiatrist was by his colleagues and what a huge insult my question was. I wasn't quite as amused as they all were. I was afraid and worn out, finding it almost impossible to cope, and I couldn't stop crying. What few personal boundaries I might have had when I walked in the door were now demolished.

The doctor was ordered to proceed. He explained that the building had so much security because of other work being done there. He said he'd been offended that I'd compared him to the other psychiatrist and added, "I'm sorry for telling you to leave."

My momentary rebellion was thus quashed. This doctor, who had seemed just like my dad with his anger and rudeness and arrogance, had apologized, something my father had never done. It took the wind out of my sails.

I had no way of judging his sincerity, of knowing just how intolerable this process was, of having any perspective on what was happening. My sense of self had been crushed long before the appointment began and now I was beyond exhausted.

He asked me for intimate details of my life. I answered all his questions without considering what I should or shouldn't say; I had no real ability to discern what was necessary. It took enormous mental effort to think of the answers to his questions and I felt like a lump of clay being molded through hours of relentless questioning. Just as the other doctors had, he dwelt on the abuse and violence I'd experienced. He continuously dragged me back and forth between the past and present, asking for details about the child abuse and then asking about Tom's violence and then going back to my childhood, until I was so confused that I had no sense of where I was or what I was there for. As he pounded away with questions, I became numb, offering him whatever thoughts came into my mind and, as the ugliness of the questioning intensified, I relived the abuse in detail yet again as the agony of the past whirled inside me.

Crushed by the weight of it all, I felt smaller and less whole with every comment he made.

I sobbed continuously, a victim again, feeling every pain I'd ever felt as if it were a fresh wound. It blended with guilt and a sense of the inconsequence of my life.

He was very good at his job. He smiled at me and pretended to care while he crushed my soul. I didn't even understand what was happening.

We took a break and he walked me back to the reception area. Still crying, I called Jane and told her how difficult it was, how lost I felt and how awful the pain inside me was. She told me that I would be okay, that I'd been through worse, and that I was the strongest person she'd ever met. I felt better after talking with her.

I was thirsty and wanted a soda, but I couldn't figure out how to use the soda machine. I studied the machine but didn't know where to put the money in, what coins to use, or even what kind of soda to get. I couldn't remember what kind of soda I used to drink and none of it looked familiar. It was just too complicated. The doctor came into the reception area and, seeing me staring at the machine, showed me how to get a soda before taking me back to his office for more questioning. That small kindness, in the ocean of cruelty of that day, became exaggerated in my mind. For a brief moment, I felt less lost and afraid.

Then we were back to the questioning and I retreated into my-self again. In my mind, I was begging him to end this hell, to let me go.

Finally, after four and half hours, he told me we were done and I felt so grateful to him because it was over that, when I called Jane to come and get me, I told her what a nice man the doctor was for helping me get a soda and for letting me go. Years later, I would see it as my own version of Stockholm syndrome.

At home, I crawled into bed and stayed there for two days be-fore going to see Dr. Mahon, who helped me deal with the horrible emotional pain. She told me that every time I began to heal from the PTSD, one of the insurance company doctors reinjured me, triggering the trauma, the nightmares and the terror from the past all over again. I asked her if I would heal from it and she said it was possible that I would always have PTSD and, therefore, the chance of it being triggered again would always be present. With the pas-sage of many years, although I have not been able to entirely elimi-nate the triggers, the principles of A COURSE IN MIRACLES have allowed me to minimize them and reduce their control over me.

Needless to say, when the doctor's report arrived six months later, it proved I'd been completely suckered by his pretense of kindness. Things I'd said were twisted or exaggerated, and he in-vented legal issues with my family and even a previous back frac-ture, none of which had happened. He claimed that things like being unable to remember how to brush my teeth weren't from a brain injury but from dementia. He didn't explain how I suddenly developed dementia at the exact time of the car crash. He quoted the psychologist's report, which quoted the other psychiatrist's report, in effect making him just like the other forensic psychiatrist whom he'd professed to be so different from. He didn't mention the difficulty I'd had in understanding his questions or how often I asked him to repeat himself or how irritated he got with me because of it. And, of course, he didn't mention the heavy security or the strange employee saying prayers for me or the fact that he initially kicked me out of his office. I guess he just forgot all that.

In hindsight, I wish I'd just walked away when he kicked me out of his office. I wish I'd been able to stand up for myself. I wish I'd acted with some self-respect, not just accepted what I'd been told. Not recognizing the extent of my confusion, I blamed myself. It was an old habit, one I thought I'd outgrown, of blaming myself for the actions of others without recognizing my own incapacitation. It was a habit that made me feel small and dark and afraid of my own shadow, someone without dignity or grace.

I spent many hours with Dr. Mahon working through the difficult emotions overwhelming me. Eventually, it would seem ironic that these IMEs, professionals who took a vow to Do No Harm, did so much harm to injured people that they sometimes caused patients to commit suicide and they were accusing me of being the one with mental health issues.

NINE DAYS after that appointment with the forensic psychiatrist, my lawyer called to tell me that he was sending me to an IME of his choice, a doctor who specialized in physical medicine and rehabilitation. From the moment I arrived at his office, I knew that this would be different. He was distant but respectful, informing me that he wasn't interested in my childhood, only in my present injuries, and pointing out that until the accident it appeared that I had been fully functioning, working as a professional speaker, a job that required physical stamina and excellent memory. He listened carefully to each of my answers to his questions and I never at any time felt bullied or manipulated. I could literally feel the tension drain from me as I understood that I was not about to be attacked.

He asked questions the others hadn't and, as I listened to myself tell him how I was no longer able to work out at the gym, go hiking or horseback riding or snow shoeing, I recognized for the first time how limited I'd become physically and what a huge change it was for me. This accident had been devastating in so many ways. When his report came back, it was unbiased. He disagreed with the other IMEs, stating that my injuries made sense with the type of accident I'd had. His honesty renewed my faith.

This proved to be a somewhat brief respite. In December 2010, just nine weeks later, I was ordered to see another insurance company IME for two days of testing. She was a physiotherapist, a tall, square, intimidating woman with a loud voice and aggressive body language. She scared the hell out of me.

I sensed in her a viciousness beyond anything I'd seen in the other IMEs. She snapped out her questions, demanding details about my childhood abuse, my brother's suicide and my mother's death. Then, when I couldn't answer quickly enough, she repeated them rapidly and loudly until I felt like she was yelling them at me. She asked about my sex life, my activities and my income, arguing with me about how much money I was getting. And, repeatedly, at least five times, in her booming voice she asked:

"Why aren't you working?"

"Why aren't you doing comedy?"

"Why are you using a cane?"

I had to wonder if all these insurance company IMEs went to the same training school.

Sometimes, while I was answering a question, she would talk over me and ask a different question. I couldn't keep up and wondered what it all had to do with physiotherapy. She questioned the PTSD diagnosis, telling me, "I don't believe that you have PTSD. That doctor is wrong." Her arrogance amazed me.

This interrogation went on for over four solid hours. The grouchier she got, the more I apologized for not understanding what she was saying. I kept hoping that, if I apologized, maybe she'd be nicer to me, a little less brutal. You'd think I'd have known better by that point.

I tried to answer her questions but I was so thoroughly intimidated that I kept forgetting what she'd asked me halfway through my answer. She became irritated, sighing loudly, leaning over me in her threatening way, telling me several times that the insurance company was not going to pay for any of my physiotherapy, massages, psychotherapy, brain injury rehabilitation, or anything else. I would have to pay every penny of my medical expenses myself. "EVERY PENNY!"

She gave me a form that asked for pain measurements from 1 to 10. Beside the 10 was the handwritten word, "suicide". This seemed to indicate that, if my pain was anywhere near a 10, I would be saying that I was suicidal. I'd never seen a form with that written on it before. I rated my pain as less than it was just so no one could say that I was suicidal.

Finally, after five hours, we were done for the day.

The next day, I woke with a migraine and nausea but showed up for my appointment anyway. I was determined to get through it the best I could. She began by asking me, again, why I wasn't looking for work, why I wasn't doing stand-up comedy and why I was using a cane. Then she told me that I wasn't allowed to use it during the appointment.

Without the cane, the dizziness got worse. I constantly felt like I was falling over and that I needed to throw up. I made several trips to the bathroom, heaving with nausea.

She had me lift weights but as they got heavier over time, I told her they were too heavy and my pain was getting worse. She ignored me. I had no way of understanding if her demands were reasonable or when I should say no to her. I was too numb to know that it was even possible to say no to her. I co-operated, as I'd been told to.

She told me to walk on the balance beam, but I fell repeatedly. She finally stopped the test because I couldn't do it. Then, after four intense hours, she gave me one last exercise: to crawl on my hands and knees on the floor at her feet, back and forth, back and forth. I finally collapsed on the floor, curled in a ball, sobbing. "No more, no more! I can't take any more!" I cried, "Please, no more."

My back pain was stabbing and burning and consuming every

ounce of my energy. The dizziness and nausea had me spinning. She stood over me, smiling, and said, "You could have quit at any time. Obviously, you had no trouble doing this." Looking up from the floor, I saw a brute, devoid of any human qualities, cold and vicious.

When I left to go home, she laughed as she said goodbye, putting her hand out to shake mine. My skin crawled as I touched her hand. This appointment wasn't about testing. It was an assault. I went home in enormous pain. When I told my physiotherapist what she did, he shook his head and said he couldn't think of any good reason she had me crawling at her feet. Dr. Van Goor was furious, telling me that ordering me to crawl at her feet was about power and nothing else. Then he gave me stronger medications to help with the pain. Over time, it became obvious to me that she hadn't just aggravated my injuries, she'd actually injured me. I didn't know if it was incompetence or intention, but it didn't matter.

When I read her IME report later, I wasn't surprised that it was so dishonest.

A few months later, Jane was ordered to see the same physiotherapist but when she was told to crawl on her hands and knees, she was prepared. She asked the physiotherapist to demonstrate and, as she was crawling along the floor, Jane stood over her, shaking her head and saying, "No, I don't think so."

Why couldn't I have thought of that?

Thanks to the additional pain, I was now more restricted in the amount of exercise I could do and less able to go for walks or do my stretches. My tiredness worsened, which in turn affected my cognitive abilities, increasing my confusion. The setback was tough to deal with. In June 2012, I had a back procedure done in hospital to ease the pain from this new injury.

Emotionally, I sank to a new low. Jane called regularly and tried to help. She brought me groceries when I was too exhausted to go out and, more than once, she came over to fix whatever I'd done to the TV remote that prevented it from working. She was very patient.

I was not, however. I snapped whenever I was frustrated, which was often, and then apologized repeatedly. She kept saying it was okay, that she knew it was the brain injury and the pain. "You were never like this before."

Stuck in survival mode, I was becoming more self-centered. I knew how unfair I was being, but I couldn't think faster and I couldn't keep up. In a constant panic, feeling vulnerable after being under attack by IMEs, it seemed that the world was swirling around me and that I was alone and in danger, unable to protect myself. On the days when the migraines and the dizziness took over and the confusion was at its worst, I wondered if I'd even survive.

Darkness settled over me like a heavy weight that was suffocating, sapping my energy and will. I rarely left the apartment or spoke to anyone and I was unable to concentrate on books or TV. I slept a lot, but the nightmares returned full force, so many nightmares that they clashed inside my head and I couldn't keep them straight. Shadowy figures filled with rage chased me. I ran, but never got away. I killed my dad but he never died. Tom was stalking me, threatening me, his hands were wrapped around my neck, choking me. Even when I was awake, the fear had me cowering. I didn't want to get into a car because I knew it was going to crash. I didn't want to go for a walk because I jumped at every sound. The ring of the phone seemed ominous and I was afraid to answer it, afraid that the insurance company wasn't done with me yet. I lay on the sofa, covered in a blanket, hurting inside and out.

Ragged and edgy, I was angry at the world and everyone in it. I wanted to feel forgiveness in my heart but I didn't. I felt hatred for others that I couldn't seem to let go of. I was swamped with hatred for myself, and with guilt. The IMEs, even the physiotherapist, had confirmed my nothingness, writing negative forty-page reports about me. The accident itself was an indictment by the universe. All the evidence pointed to my defectiveness. I woke each morning wishing I hadn't, wishing I'd just passed away in the middle of the night.

I knew now that my past would forever echo into my future. There was no escape.

I began to give up, thinking that, if everything I'd ever done in my life to become stronger and more in control hadn't helped, then there was no point to it all, to this struggle to make sense of the world. Because, at that point, it made no sense at all. My basic belief in the goodness of people seemed idiotic and insane. The world was not what I thought it was. I was shaken to the core by this discovery.

I remembered as a child telling myself that I wasn't evil, that my parents were the problem and that life would get better as soon as I could be on my own. But a little bit of me hung on to the darkness inside, unable to quite believe in my innocence. It now seemed that the little bit of me containing the darkness was actually the whole of me. There was no other part of me that was real.

27

An Honored Guest

I visited Dr. Mahon regularly and she kept reminding me of who I really was. In the hell of my pain and depression, I finally realized that I'd allowed the insurance company and its minions to turn me back into a victim, powerless and worthless. I saw the patterns and commonalities of the tactics used during the legal process. The insurance company doctors and physiotherapist were all bullying, controlling and intimidating. They deliberately brought up dark childhood memories that invoked feelings of worthlessness, using the manipulative tactic of repeatedly reminding me of the terror from my past — a tactic similar to that of domestic abusers — as they tried to get what they wanted, which was to intimidate me into dropping the lawsuit. By the time they were done with me, I'd felt undeserving of any insurance settlement.

The doctors and the physiotherapist had touched on two triggers deep within me. The first was: "If you tell, no one will believe you." The first IME's report confirmed that as it said that I made up the child abuse because I liked attention. The second: "This is your fault." was shown in the IMEs comments insinuating blame, telling me I must have been a bad child. Even after all the years of being told it wasn't my fault, I'd never been able to totally believe it. In touching these sore spots, the IMEs had known exactly what they were doing.

When a friend and I discussed the lawsuit, it was clear I couldn't quite wrap my head around the viciousness of it all, how normal it was for some of these professionals to openly lie when they wrote their reports. I was confused by the dishonesty inherent in the system and I couldn't quite understand how these particular IMEs and lawyers and insurance company adjusters could be so lacking in any moral center that they deliberately harmed injured people just for the sake of money.

"Everyone has a price," my friend told me. "They're just doing their jobs."

At home, I thought about it for a long time before deciding that I disagreed. Saying they were just doing their jobs allowed people to use the lack of integrity in the system to justify their own lack of integrity and ignore the responsibility we each have to treat others with basic honesty and respect. Were those who used the sexual abuse of a small child as a weapon against the vulnerable grown child any less depraved than the child molester himself?

On September 20, 2011, my lawyer again sent me to another IME, this one a forensic psychiatrist from Vancouver, well known and respected in his field. We met in my lawyer's office. He had asked me to bring someone to the appointment who knew me before the accident so that he could ask her about the changes in me, and Jane's sister Marlene was with me. The doctor was kind and thoughtful, telling me that my childhood issues were not related to my injuries now, and he recognized from the other IMEs reports how badly I'd been treated by them. He told me to stop letting others treat me so rudely.

"I can't tell when others are being rude to me," I told him. "I don't know what rude looks like. I know it makes me feel bad, but I don't know why."

The extent of my cognitive issues was showing. He described how my symptoms totally backed up my brain injury diagnosis, even listing my mood disorders as being common to traumatic brain injury. They were biological, not psychological.

His report, which arrived a few months later, questioned the other IMEs reports, disagreeing with them and explaining that they made no sense. He pointed out their obvious biases and errors and then described, in great detail, the incompetence of the IMEs, debunking, piece by piece, the negative reports so thoroughly that it left me wondering how the other IMEs had been granted licenses to practice. He stated that, instead of my malingering in order to gain something from the insurance company, as the other IMEs had suggested, I had significant losses from the accident: my business, my relationship, my home, many friends and my entire lifestyle.

Relief washed through me as I realized that other professionals recognized those reports for the shams that they were.

As THE legal wrangling took a break, I was able to start the healing process. Slowly, my mind became a little clearer and I had greater energy than I did before. I went to the care home more often to visit Ann, who was now ninety-eight. I loved seeing her and was always surprised when, in spite of her dementia, she remembered my name the instant she saw me and said, "Betty's here!" with a delighted smile.

One thing Ann had taught me on the first day I met her, when I was just seven years old, was that, when I was with her, I always needed to be totally present. When I visited her now, she un-failingly asked me if I was tired. If I said, "Yes," she insisted, "That's not okay. You can't be tired. You came here to be with me. You can't be tired."

So I had learned to be fully present with her, regardless of tired-ness, confusion, hunger or pain. She wanted all of me and nothing less during our time together. Our relationship was amazing because of that demand. It possessed a depth that wasn't present in so many of my other relationships, a depth which others hadn't been able to understand. It brought quality to each visit, an intensity that wouldn't have been there otherwise. When I'd been a young child with a tendency to regularly dissociate, the demand to be present taught me how to focus, a gift I hadn't been able to fully appreciate until many years later.

There were times when it would hit me out of the blue exactly what it was about Ann that I loved so much. One day, when the weather was hot and muggy, we were sitting in the crafts room and I watched Ann and the others paint with watercolors. Ann loved to paint and that day she created a beautiful red robin against a green background. When it was dry, we decided, we would hang it on the door of her closet in her room so she could easily see it from her bed. As we finished up, volunteers in the care home brought ice cream to the residents. While many of the residents asked, "What about me?" before they got theirs, Ann did just the opposite. "What about her?" she asked, when she saw someone else hadn't received hers yet.

Other days, as she walked along the hallways, she loved to slyly pat men, strangers and acquaintances alike, on the bum, startling more than a few of them as she used her walker to propel her tiny frame away from the scene of the crime, snickering and laughing.

So, in part I loved her because she was constantly cheerful and rarely complained. I loved her glass half-full way of thinking. But the more I visited Ann, the more I understood the depth of my love for her, and our love for each other. Ann didn't love me just because I was her daughter's friend. She loved me apart from anyone or anything else. And I loved her back. We had wonderful discussions. Normally she was very confused but, on our last several visits, she was quite clear.

One day, not remembering that she'd ever met Jane, she told me that her one wish for me was to find a boyfriend. She couldn't stand the thought of me being alone in life with no one to look after me. So she started giving me dating tips:

"Smile at every man you meet."

"Never look grouchy."

"Don't tell a man you have any injuries."

"If you get confused when you are out to dinner, go to the bathroom so he won't see it."

"Ann," I said after that last one, "If I go to the bathroom, I'll get lost trying to find my way back to the table and then he'll know for sure how confused I am."

She wasn't quite sure how to help me with that.

Each visit brought more tips and more laughter. Ann thought my brain injury was the funniest thing ever. Whenever I couldn't remember something, she told me, "You're just like me. You could be my roommate." I laughed along with her.

I took her to the karaoke singing on Friday afternoons. Ann had never paid much attention to music before but, now, she began to love it. The music touched her heart in the way I'd hoped it would and she enjoyed it right to the end of her days. Standing with her walker, she swayed to the beat of each song, yelling to me, "Louder! Sing louder!" as I swayed along with her, belting out the tunes.

Ann was the only person in my life who had ever told me to "sing louder". The music united us in a new, deeper way. We laughed and hugged and enjoyed every minute together. We had so much fun that many days she danced her way back to her room.

How many of us, I wondered, could know that the end was in sight and yet still have the grace to dance our way towards it?

There was another element to our visits now, a peacefulness and calm that came from the security of knowing we'd been friends for over fifty years. Ann had never been one to express love openly, believing that everyone close to her should just know that she loved them and that she shouldn't have to say it. But now she began to tell me how much she loved me several times each visit. She would sit in front of me and, with one hand on each side of my face, pull me in close so that her forehead touched mine.

"I love you like a daughter," she would say. "You have always been my daughter."

Every time, my heart soared. And I would reply, "When I was little, I always wished you were my mom. I love you too."

She smiled broadly each time and I wondered if she knew how her love was now healing the pain inside me. I reminded her of the times we'd had together over the years and the memories warmed both our hearts. She knew that I could see inside her heart and I knew that I'd been an honored guest in her life. The magnitude of the love between us was beyond description, possessing a new, spiritual quality that filled my heart with joy every time I visited and the feeling stayed with me long after the visits were over. It began to lift me out of the darkness I'd been dwelling in. It was a deeply healing love. The pain of Mom's passing and the losses of my relationship and business and cognitive abilities became less stark; the edges were smoothed as Ann once again rescued me from darkness, just she had first done over fifty years ago.

Ann passed away peacefully on January 4, 2014, at the age of 99. She was, and had always been, the sunlight in my life.

28

The Writing Process

I T HAD been seven years since the accident. I kept visiting Dr. Mahon and, through our discussions, my inner pain eased as I got more clarity about my situation and what the insurance companies had done to me. At some point, I emphatically announced that I would never again allow unscrupulous people to degrade me, to use my past as a weapon to control and manipulate me. I knew that A COURSE IN MIRACLES could help me learn to become invincible to the machinations of others. Memories of the calmness and peace of mind that I'd gained from my original studies of ACIM returned and I knew now that the Course could once again help me regain my sense of dignity and grace. But I had to go deeper this time.

I once again immersed myself in the Course teachings, studying the lessons, one per day for 365 days. For the first time since the accident, I was able to get a basic understanding of what I was reading. There was a familiarity to it all and I was happy to realize that I remembered some of the Course. I began to feel a calm I hadn't felt in years.

Around the same time, Dr. Mahon told me that, after hearing so many bits and pieces of my life story, she was having trouble with the timeline, with putting events into a chronological order that made sense, and she asked me to write out some of my story for her. I remembered that I'd begun writing it seven years earlier, just before the head injury. But I'd been unable to go into the shadows, into the nitty gritty, to honestly look at the past. I kept asking myself: What if I looked at all the pain and realized that what had happened was my fault? What if there was something inherently wrong with me? What if I deserved the violence and hatred that seemed to permeate so much of my life story?

The Course talked about shining a light on the shadows inside us, about how we need to look at every detail of our lives that we haven't wanted to look at, those scary details we hide from ourselves and others, the ones we think are too nasty to see the light of day.

"When what you have dissociated is accepted, it ceases to be fearful." — ACIM T-10.II.1:6

Dissociation is denial. The Course promised there was nothing in my past that was too dark to look at, nothing I needed to deny. I would be safe as I undertook this journey. And what was more, shining a light on my darkness would free me from it permanently.

"Do not leave any spot of pain hidden from His light, and search your mind carefully for any thoughts you may fear to uncover. For He will heal any little thought you have kept to hurt you and cleanse it of its littleness, restoring it to the magnitude of God." — ACIM T-13. III.7:5

I decided to truly trust this time, to not let fear paralyze me, to not let any more of my life be wasted looking backwards in fear instead of being present in peace. It was like deciding to jump off a cliff and it required every ounce of courage and trust I possessed to believe that I'd land safely.

I also decided that I would not just write out a chronology; I would write a memoir.

Grandiosity at its finest! Who knew that writing a memoir when one has so little memory would be such a challenge? Well, pretty much everyone.

When I told my friends that I was writing a book, some of those familiar with the thick fog that enveloped my brain said, "Of course you are." That kind of verbal pat on my head made me feel like a mentally disabled six-year-old who has just announced, "I'm going to be an astronaut." Of course you are.

Still, I wrote.

As I looked over what I had written before the accident, I started adding small details that came to mind and my memories expanded bit by bit. I slowly remembered, for example, all those long discussions with Mom on the drives back and forth to Bellingham.

But the process was much more difficult than I expected. Writing took all my energy and, in order to concentrate on it, I had to concentrate less on life. I stopped trying to cook meals. I ate only the most basic of foods and only when a headache told me I was hungry. I stayed home day after day, no longer going out with friends or shopping or doing anything else. I closed the windows and drapes, even in summer, to avoid distractions. I didn't have enough energy to both write and maintain a social life, so I decided that, since my social life was already barely existent anyway, I'd just leave it that way until I finished my writing. It was too important that I heal before getting into new relationships. I soon realized that writing had become part of the healing process.

At first, my thoughts came out scrambled, almost indecipherable. It was hard to find the right words, then shuffle them around in a sentence and then shuffle the sentences into paragraphs. Sometimes, after I'd written and then reviewed a paragraph, even I couldn't understand what I'd been trying to say. Other times, upon reviewing a page I'd written, I would discover the same thoughts written twice. By the time I'd written to the bottom of a page, I'd forgotten that I'd already written those thoughts at the top of the page.

But I worked hard, studying every paragraph over and over until I had the right words in the right order, then going over each page to be sure that the paragraphs fit together. It took weeks to get the words on each page flowing, not smoothly, perhaps, but clean and clear enough that, if I read it aloud to a friend, she would have some idea of what I was trying to say. Even so, it would still happen often enough that the friend would send me back to the drawing board saying, "I'm sorry, but it makes no sense."

Sometimes, the friends became protective when reading about my childhood. One good and kind reader was angry, telling me he wanted to kill my father. His anger offended me. It was, I'm sure, the last thing he wanted to happen. But it seemed like he was telling me that I wasn't smart or strong enough to understand that I should be angry. His anger felt somehow controlling and disempowering of me, as if he weren't letting me deal with my issues myself, as if he were hijacking my feelings because he thought he knew better than I did. To his credit, he understood this when I explained it to him; he even thanked me, saying that he now better understood why his daughters got so upset with him when he tried to control some of their issues as well.

I knew that some people saw forgiveness as weakness but, in truth, I had come to see it as the opposite. It was real strength. By accepting the darkness in my life as well as the light, I became whole and I felt strong. But, if I let another's anger upset me, then I picked up the pain of the past that I was working so hard to let go of.

I continued writing and the problems with my process continued. My time frames were confused and my thoughts were fleeting. I continually lost my focus and had to stop because I couldn't remember what I'd wanted to say. There was no context or continuity, just loose thoughts that poured out of me onto the pages. The efforts to concentrate on my writing and my world exhausted me and I was often drained after only an hour of writing.

And there were other issues, in a way more technical, but ones that still reflected the impact of my brain injury. When I took it to the library, the writer-in-residence pointed out that my story had no description. I hadn't written, for example, that flowers were red and the sky was blue, or that a particular character was wearing blue jeans and a black jacket, and so on and so on. My world was too limited to be able to see colors and details. It was all grey to me.

I'd had no clue until she told me that the greyness wasn't normal.

I took this advice to heart and, on the days when I did go out, I forced myself to focus:

The leaves on that tree are green.

That flower is yellow.

The water is green.

I walked through the park slowly, cane in hand, sunshine on my face, concentrating on every detail, making notes in my ever-present notebook. Over and over again. It took more than a year of practice to be able to describe colors and shapes and sizes, a year for the greyness to recede.

Piece by piece, my thoughts slowly came onto the page, still very jumbled but with the potential to make sense. My progress was very slow but steady as the days went by in intense, nonstop concentration, as new understandings about my past and about who I am now continued to reveal themselves to me. It was hard work, as I struggled through the migraines, nausea and back pain, in an attempt to clarify my thoughts. None of it came easily. But I was healing spiritually on a level I'd never known was possible. I was climbing my own Kilimanjaro.

Many days, the fog in my mind was too thick to allow me to write and the keyboard wouldn't cooperate. Normally a fast typist, when I was tired, my typing had so many errors I had to give up, convinced that gremlins had taken over my keyboard. Entire days were lost to exhaustion and I was unable to get enough clarity to do even the basic activities of life, like getting groceries or doing laundry. I never knew before that such exhaustion was possible.

This project owned me. Sometimes I wrote as if possessed, as if my life depended on it. I tried to focus on other things but my mind belonged to my story. When I finished writing each day, my thoughts continued to bombard me, so I began to scribble them in a book. They were jumbled thoughts that I had trouble unscrambling the next day. I learned not to write after 3:00 p.m. or I wouldn't be able to sleep because my mind would be too busy.

Sometimes I still couldn't sleep and I'd need to jump out of bed and go write down the thoughts that were swirling in my head.

I had to embrace my fear every step of the way, not in an attempt to conquer it but to accept it, and in doing so to disempower it. My writing forced me to meet my inner darkness head on. This darkness wasn't just a history of what others had done to me. It was also made up of the guilt and shame I felt. It was enormous and scary.

After the accident, I'd forgotten that fear is a choice. It had become a habit again and I'd let it control me instead of me controlling it. But now, I remembered that unconditional acceptance was my goal. Acceptance of whatever was happening every moment of every day. Acceptance of everyone and every-thing, past, present and future. I put the word "Acceptance" on another sticky note on the fridge.

"Look then, upon the light He placed within you and learn that what you feared was there has been replaced with love." — ACIM T-13. IX.8:13

I set a goal: To be able to look at the details of my life in an objective way without suddenly feeling that I was back in the middle of it, reliving it, having nightmares. I promised myself that I would open all those compartments in my mind and shine a light on every darkness, that I would have the courage to follow through on this project.

So now, bit by bit, I confronted that darkness, looking deep inside, slowly working my way through each shadow to get to the light. It wasn't easy. Memories came forth that I would have preferred to leave buried, memories that were much more detailed and painful than I'd ever admitted to before. Sometimes they were so painful that I had to run to the bathroom to throw up. In spite of my good intentions, it was as if I was reliving every detail of my past. And I frequently froze, unable to write for long periods of time because I was too terrified.

Sometimes, when memories got more difficult and exhaustion

and confusion increased, I felt like I was walking on the edge of a knife. As my writing forced me to confront all the details of the insanity of my past, as I balanced on that sharp edge, I often felt bat-shit crazy. Other times, I wondered how I could possibly be so sane.

But each time I reminded myself of my promise, that saved me from the darkness on the days when I couldn't see any light, when I couldn't remember my purpose. There were many, many such days. But as I slowly undid the pain of the past, I unwrapped its suffocating grip on my consciousness. I forced myself to move forward and the blocks eased as I slowly made progress. The only reason I needed to look back at the past was to uncover the grace it contained. That was who I was — who I am. Not the shadows and the darkness as I'd once believed, but the light in the center of it all. I gradually reached a point where each bit of darkness no longer dragged me down, where what I was writing about was just something that had happened, something that was no longer wrenching and painful. It just was.

I'd always believed that the darkness that was me on the inside was also on the outside. I'd tried to erase it. Diet, exercise, clothes, make-up. I'd tried to be perfect. But if I didn't change my thoughts about who I was on the inside, the outside would never be good enough.

One night, as I slid into a deep sleep, I had a dream. I was all alone, climbing a sheer rock face. I'd always thought that people who did this were nuts. But here I was in my dream, climbing this rock face, partway up and terrified. I kept freezing, and the raw terror felt excruciatingly real. I was afraid of falling, afraid of dying, unable to move for long periods of time. I kept telling myself that I had no choice but to inch forward. Eventually, I managed to work my way off the rock face and climb down from the cliff. Still dreaming, I turned around and looked back and saw a wide ledge about ten feet below where I'd been climbing, a ledge that would have protected me had I fallen. I had been in no danger and all the terror had been a waste of time. I could have just enjoyed the climb without fear. The message was clear, and I woke myself up with my laughter.

29

The Gift

I stood at the front door of my seniors' apartment building looking out at the freezing cold and snow, preparing to step out into winter as I headed to the nearby bus stop. One of my elderly neighbors was standing next to me and she reached over to pull the hood of my coat over my head and tighten my scarf around my neck while checking to see that I'd remembered my gloves. When she was done, she kissed me on the cheek and whispered, "I love you." I whispered it back and headed out the door.

It was 2014 and my lawsuit against the insurance company was finally being settled, seven years after the accident. Left in a position where I could no longer afford the rent on my downtown apartment and unable to work, I'd turned to Dr. Mahon for help in deciding what to do. As we sat in her comfortable office, tea in hand, we discussed my future. She suggested I move into one of the government seniors' buildings. Accepting that I had no other options, we discussed how to find the right place.

Dr. Mahon recommended the Jewish Centre. "It's very diverse and open to all denominations. It's well-regarded and it's across the street from the reservoir, with hiking paths and forest."

I liked that. No longer able to hike up mountains, on good days I still loved to do long walks on the pathways through parks.

"It also has a gym in the attached community center. You don't even have to go outside to get to it."

An added bonus was that someone from Jewish Family Services worked out of the seniors' center two days a week and would offer the limited help I needed to get by. I was ready to sign on the dotted line and so I applied to move in. An interview with Albina, from Family Services, was arranged and I immediately liked her. Apparently, it was reciprocal and I was put on the waiting list.

The move was accomplished with the help of a moving company and two friends, Cindy and Jane. They ordered me to stay out of the way while Cindy, who had done all the packing for me at the old place, did all the unpacking at the new place as well as cleaning and arranging my cupboards. Jane set up my computer and electronics and put together shelving. Both provided moral support, as that nemesis of the confused — unfamiliar surroundings — threatened to overwhelm me.

I had wonderful neighbors. On one side were Volodymyr and Lidiya. When I asked them to please let me know if my music was too loud, Volodymyr replied, "If I hear your music I will dance with my wife."

On the other side of me was the beautiful and elegant Laila, who would sometimes bring me her wonderful cooking and baking as I concentrated on my writing to the exclusion of all else. It wasn't long before I knew that this was home.

Over the next several months, I leaned heavily on Albina, whose kindness and thoughtfulness repeatedly saved the day as I struggled to understand bus schedules and find my way around. She helped me fill out government paperwork and changes of address and other forms and applications. She, a nurse by trade, even pulled slivers from hands that I couldn't get out on my own and offered me advice about the burns and other injuries I'd managed to acquire. The building manager, Barb, was also generous with her time and understanding, as well as her heartwarming hugs, and I loved her sense of humor.

Many of the other residents were from Eastern Europe and some spoke only Russian or Ukrainian. Having lost my ability to learn new languages, we sometimes had trouble communicating but it wasn't long before we were friends and they told me I was family. They were an affectionate bunch and their love comforted me and brightened my days. I was totally in love with all of them. Eventually, I realized that the lifelong hole in my heart that had always had me searching for love was filled by these wonderful people. I hadn't been used to having so many people tell me they love me and show affection. But without me knowing it, the emptiness inside me was disappearing.

Until, one day, it was totally gone. A Course in Miracles had taught me that unconditional love has to come from inside as I recognized the love of my Creator in my very soul. But the external love also fills a hole that I'd never thought would be filled. Another miracle to add to my long list.

I'd come full circle, an irony that was not lost on me — from the writings of the Jewish survivors of the concentration camps that had helped me begin a life-long journey of self-discovery, to living in the Jewish Centre over forty years later, in the midst of the most loving group of people I'd ever known.

Days of writing had turned into weeks, then months, then years. I'm glad now that I didn't know at the beginning that it would take over eight years of unrelenting focus to put my story on paper. But the process was healing, I felt release with each look past the shadows. The nightmares gradually disappeared. The echoes of the past were growing fainter, losing their strength, and the control they had over me was being lifted. The freedom felt wonderful.

I understood the past in a totally different way now. I recognized all the times I'd blamed myself for the actions of others and I saw that I wasn't responsible for what everyone else did. The mistakes I'd made along the way made sense now. They were reactions to the awful things I'd believed about myself. I took responsibility for the times I'd hurt others but I no longer accepted that I was a terrible person. And, as I offered forgiveness to others, I no longer accepted that they were terrible people either. The world was full of people at different stages of their spiritual journeys. Who was I to judge anyone else's journey?

I wanted to view the past as something that just happened, of consequence only for the good I received, the knowledge I gained, the opening of my heart and the awakening of my soul.

Could it really be this simple? Apparently, yes it could.

As I reached this understanding, sorrow briefly welled up inside me, making me want to howl in pain as I acknowledged the details of the things that had hurt me. My biggest sorrow came with the realization of the extent to which fear had controlled my life for so long. It had terrorized and paralyzed and controlled me. Fear of the unknown. Fear of fear. I had let it cheat me out of so much - out of seeing who I really was and who others really were, out of loving fearlessly and frequently. All because I hadn't wanted to look at my shadows.

The light came on as I understood the final piece of the puzzle that is A COURSE IN MIRACLES. Everyone is wounded in some way — some loudly, some silently. If I didn't look at my wounds, if I hid them, then I lost the identity that had formed because of the wounds. Even when a wound heals, there is a scar. I had read that, with forgiveness, each scar becomes a gift of knowledge and understanding and strength. But as long as I didn't acknowledge the wounds, I couldn't see the gifts. When I originally began studying the Course, I'd wanted to learn forgiveness so that I could move forward in life. But I didn't understand that you can't forgive what you don't acknowledge. My life had always been compartmentalized and, in the past, I only opened one part at a time when I needed to. I was too afraid to look at the whole. But now, the Course was promising me that it was safe to look at all of it. What was more, the Course was telling me that if I didn't look at my wounds, if I hid them, then I lost that part of my identity that had formed because of the wounds. Why would I want to keep those parts? Because from them had arisen my inner strength and wisdom. These were gifts, no matter the circumstances from which they had arisen.

The IMEs had focused on the most raw and painful moments of my past, as if I'd been damaged beyond repair, as if I had no value, instead of focusing on the strengths I'd gained from those very issues.

But they wouldn't have been able to do so if I hadn't believed, deep down inside, that they were right. The IMEs were like sledgehammers, repeatedly knocking me back into my past and out of my comfort zone. It had taken several years and the teachings of ACIM before I recognized the gift in that darkness.

The further I went in my understanding of my life, the crazier I looked to others. Some people expected me to stay bitter and angry, especially with the insurance company, their IMEs and lawyers, and they often seemed disappointed when I didn't. They didn't understand that I knew, even through the fog in my head, what I was doing. I consciously chose not to become bitter. It was not easy to let go of my anger, but love is letting go of hate. I chose love.

This was a fully informed choice. I'd been a cheerful and positive person before the accident but now, when I was happy, people thought it was because of the brain injury, that I was too injured to know how dark the world was, like a child with Down's syndrome who, in his <ignorance', loves everyone. Maybe it isn't ignorance or his condition that makes him love everyone. Maybe he is simply experiencing pure, unfiltered love. In my case, I consciously chose to experience that love.

The brain injury had put a wall of fog between me and the world. But now I saw how that wall had forced me to look inside myself. I'd always thought my life was just a bunch of random events, things I'd reacted to rather than things I had any control over. I thought life just happened to me, that I had accidentally and coincidentally become who I was. Now I was finally free to recognize my courage. I'd never acknowledged that I'd acted with courage. But now I saw that every act of courage in my life was built on top of the last one and had created strength and grace and dignity in me. I realized that every trauma, past and present, had made me who I am today and I didn't need to pretend that it had never happened or that it wasn't that bad. When I embraced everything in my past, I became giddy with self-acceptance. I'd looked deep inside and survived.

After decades of being imprisoned by fear, I began to see myself differently. I was light. I was gifted with the light of God, as every single one of us is. All the things about A COURSE IN MIRACLES that I'd previously understood on an intellectual level became true at the heart level. I felt the truth. I knew it.

As I healed each small bit of pain inside me, I felt happiness. I was the child dancing in the thunderstorm, the child who had just learned how to tie her shoes and who knows that she is totally brilliant. The child who announces with each new discovery, "I'm wonderful! I'm amazing!"

Joy burst out of me as a lifetime of darkness was released. I'd gone from someone who continually condemned herself to someone who recognized her magnificence and wanted to share her ecstasy.

As my old beliefs were stripped away from me, I became a blank canvas. I'd been seeing the world through my personality but as my personality changed, my world looked different. I became different.

Others felt it too.

I recall a time when I was outside waiting for my Access ride to pick me up for an evening of music at the Calgary Centre for Spiritual Living. My ride was late because traffic was a mess. When it arrived, the driver helped me into the van, which already had an elderly couple inside. The husband sat up front beside the driver and his wife sat in the back. I climbed in beside her and immediately sensed tension in the air. I began to speak gently, saying hello to the couple and asking how they were doing. They saw my cane and asked me why I needed it, a common question by users of Access. I told them about my accident.

I instinctively knew my purpose this evening. They needed my calmness. As they asked why I was living in seniors housing, I explained that I'd lost everything — my home, my business, my relationship and more.

The wife was instantly angry. "Your partner left you? What a dog!"

"No," I quietly said. "It was very difficult for her to cope with my brain injury. She believed she wasn't strong enough. She's not a bad person. She was in pain as well. I forgave her."

"Really," the wife asked me, "you forgave her?"

"Yes. If I hadn't, then my anger would hurt me more than anyone else. By forgiving, we are good friends now. I believe anything can be forgiven. We just need to recognize our own strength."

She began to talk about how they were going to the birthday party of their young grandson but were in terrible pain because they'd lost their granddaughter to a drunk driver the year before. Now they found themselves unable to move on. My thoughts went to the young grandson who was expecting his grandparents to be very excited about his birthday but who would be hurt when they were unable to lift themselves out of their grief.

The wife put her hand on my arm and held on while she asked me many questions about forgiveness, about why and how we should forgive, and my calmness began to work magic on her. The tension in the van eased. The driver kept smiling at me in the rear-view mirror.

As I climbed out of the van at my destination, she grabbed my arm again as if to pull me back in. "So anything can be forgiven?" she asked. "Yes," I replied.

"Some people just aren't as strong as others?"

"Here's the secret," I told her, "We are all strong. It's just that not everyone recognizes the strength inside themselves."

"Oh," she spoke softly. "I like that." She thanked me over and over again. As the driver walked me to the door, he told me, "I knew you could help them. I just knew it."

I had no memory of having ever met that driver before but he certainly remembered me. He must have been my driver when I'd subtly reached out to people many times before. I walked into the center feeling I'd just received a gift.

30

Knowing Oneness

WINTER 2014. It was freezing cold and the wind was howling as I boarded the train on my way to an appointment with one of the many professionals that I needed to see regularly. I was late because I was confused and had gotten on the wrong train and wound up in the northeast instead of the southwest. Then I had to turn around and come back to get on the correct train. Finally arriving at the proper station, I hunched against the wind, trudging as quickly as I could through the deep snow.

I looked forward to these appointments with Charles. In the warmth of his office, with my coat and scarf tossed on a chair, coffee in hand, we talked and joked and laughed. Over the last several years, I'd developed a comfort level with him that I'd never had with any man before and I felt totally accepted for who I was, injuries and all, with no need for the pretenses or the walls that had seemed so necessary with men in the past. I knew how much I'd missed male energy. Not the macho stuff, but the strong, gentle energy of men who were confident enough to not need macho pretenses.

He was so attractive, with his blue eyes and kind smile, gracious manner and easy laugh. He was flirtatious and I flirted back, surprising myself. In the past, I'd always ignored flirts. But this was more than a flirtation on my part. My heart was involved. Aware that his eyes followed me constantly, I felt attractive for the first time in a long time and I found myself thinking of him often. Unsure if I was reading the situation properly, it scared me a bit. I kept telling myself that the attraction wasn't real; that I was just reaching out to the first man with whom I felt comfortable and safe; that I was lonely and lost; that this was just an illusion in this damaged brain of mine. It wasn't long, though, before I decided that, if this was an illusion, it was a nice one and I was going to enjoy it.

Eventually, I was told by Dr. Mahon to be careful with my heart, as there is a line that professionals are not allowed to cross. So, I reined in my feelings as best I could. I knew that the relationship couldn't go further but I still enjoyed seeing him and couldn't resist the occasional flirtation.

Thinking about it later, once the appointments were no longer necessary, I was astonished to realize that, for the first time in memory, I was truly free of my fears surrounding men. I'd opened my heart to Charles in a way that had never felt safe before, even with Gary, and I knew that it wasn't just Charles with whom I felt safe now. I was getting asked for dates by other men and the absence of fear felt new to me as I enjoyed the occasional dinner out. I was still cautious, and Charles had a hold on my heart for a long time afterwards, but I was delighted at this new comfort level with men. I had to ask myself many times: Is this even possible after a lifetime of being afraid? Is it real?

I knew the answer was yes because I could literally feel the freedom that comes from releasing fear. For the first time, I recognized the enormity and true extent of my healing over the past several years. The joy this realization brought bubbled up inside me.

THE ACCIDENT wasn't an indictment by the universe. It was an awakening. Each time I was forced to look at the pain of my past, I was made to stop hiding from it. The lesson was repeated over and over until I learned that I couldn't escape it. I could no longer pretend. I had to face it. So, finally, instead of fighting the darkness inside me, I embraced it. When I stopped judging it as bad, it no longer controlled me. The perceptual shift offered by A COURSE IN MIRACLES freed me. I was no longer enslaved by the pain and fear of my past. I understood this when I realized that I'd truly forgiven my father. I no longer saw him as a monster but as a human being that God loved every bit as much as He loved every one of us. I had transcended the pain and forgiven, reaching the perfect stillness inside myself that allowed me to see beyond anything negative. The point of perfect acceptance.

I felt a sense of deep connection, like I belonged, like I mattered. I'd come alive with a new calmness thanks to my new way of seeing the world. It affected every part of me: how I dressed, how I walked, how I presented myself. I was no longer pretending. I had disconnected my self-worth from anything outside of me. The memories that had previously packed a punch and seemed so awful no longer had power.

A man once told me, upon hearing my story, that he had no reason to complain because he grew up in a loving family and lacked for nothing. He didn't understand his pain, he said, and thus judged himself harshly for it. But I understood his pain. It was the pain of feeling alone and alien. It is in every one of us at times, to varying degrees, without regard to circumstances. It is the pain of feeling separated from our source, of not understanding who we are, our magnificence, and the deep unconditional love and acceptance of God. It is an agonizing pain, deep within our souls that seems to go back thousands of years.

But it is pain that can be turned into joy, into peace and calmness and love beyond anything each of us can imagine exists. It can turn into a warmth of the heart that helps us view the world around us and the people in it through a different lens.

ONE EVENING as I lay in bed with my eyes closed, about to drift off, a vision appeared to me and an unfamiliar light began to shine inside me, lighting me up in a way I'd never known, bringing feelings of overwhelming peace and love. It was a cone-shaped light coming directly from my heart and expanding outward, beyond time and space. I saw magnificence in this loving light — my own and everyone else's.

In essence, I saw myself walking into the light and merging with it, dissolving into it. At first, I was reminded of the stories I'd read of near-death experiences, where there was a bright light and feelings of calm and peace, and I thought it was a sign that I was dying.

But I wasn't near death. It was simply a beautiful experience.

I wondered: *Why should I have it? What did it mean?*

The next morning, the warmth of the previous night's experience was still with me and I clearly recalled every moment, still without understanding.

But as it recurred night after night for weeks, I slowly began to realize what it was. As I was deep inside that beautiful gift of light, I finally got it. I felt the powerful merging of the light that was me melting into the light of God. I was becoming one with my creator and all others. I knew, in a deep way, beyond the intellect, that we are all one and that there is no separation. I'd known for years that the light of God was not somewhere out there, up above and apart from me, but within me, deep within me. And that we are all one, part of God and each other. But I'd known this only in an abstract, intellectual way. Until now.

I was, for the first time in my life, knowing Oneness. The magnificence of it. The limitless perfection of it. I'd believed for years that everyone's sole purpose was to realize the light of God, first in ourselves and then in others. We can't truly understand our purpose on this earth if we don't understand who and what we are. Now I recognized that it was a much broader love of self. It had the bright light that was me merging with the bright light that was God because I was but an extension of God. Pure love. Nothing else.

This new understanding brought me a deeper sense of peace and joy than I'd ever known. I've proceeded ever since with an unwavering knowledge that I'm deeply loved and part of everyone and everything. That everyone else is whole and must be seen as whole, not just an assemblage of broken parts and pieces from their past as I'd seen myself for so many years. We are each so magnificent that words do not do us justice. We truly are divine light. The joy inside me, the liquid sunshine, is a constant, unwavering presence just below the surface, unaffected by what's happening in any given moment.

Several months later, I opened A COURSE IN MIRACLES to a random page and saw a paragraph I hadn't noticed before:

"*Everyone has experienced what he would call a sense of being transported beyond himself. This feeling of liberation far exceeds the dream of freedom sometimes hoped for in special relationships. It is a sense of actual escape from limitations. If you will consider what this "transportation" really entails, you will realize that it is a sudden unawareness of the body, and a joining of yourself and something else in which your mind enlarges to encompass it. It becomes part of you as you unite with it. And both become whole, as neither is perceived as separate. What really happens is that you have given up the illusion of a limited awareness, and lost your fear of union. The love that instantly replaces it extends to what has freed you, and unites with it. And while this lasts you are not uncertain of your identity, and would not limit it. You have escaped from fear to peace, asking no questions of reality, but merely accepting it. You have accepted this instead of the body, and have let yourself be one with something beyond it, simply by not letting your mind be limited by it.*" — ACIM T-18.VI.11:1

ACKNOWLEDGMENTS

Thank you, JoAnn Wells for your friendship, for generously sharing your mother with me for over 50 years, and for inviting me to be part of your family. Your friendship has changed my life for the better and I'm so grateful.

Thank you, Lynda, big sister, for working so hard to be the mother we all needed while still a child yourself, and for once again stepping up after my brain injury. I love you.

Thank you, Cindy McPhee, my earthly angel, for your love. You were the light in my darkest hours with your understanding and generous heart, with your compassion and humour.

Thank you, Wendy Oryniak, my person, for your love and kindness, for always being there for me.

Thank you, Dr. Mary Mahon, brilliant and much-loved psychologist specializing in brain injury and trauma, for your love and guidance, for seeing something good in me that I couldn't see for myself, for creating a place of safety in the midst of trauma. Your encouragement in writing out my story led to a healing I'd never believed possible.

Thank you, BIRC girls: Melany, Sharon, and Angela. Your friendships brighten my life.

Thank you, Jean Houston and Peggy Rubin for your many years spent mentoring so many people. Your kindness and love have helped me grow closer to my full potential.

Thank you, Elect Yourself Salon participants and especially the Zoomers, for your beautiful and loving spirits, for your unfailing belief in me and your constant support. I treasure each of you.

Thank you, Cathy Price, massage therapist extraordinaire, for your vision and love in encouraging me to write this book in the early days when it seemed so impossible and for your support during the many years it has taken me to complete it.

Thank you, Jennifer Deleon, volunteer co-ordinator at Southwood Hospice, for your thoughtfulness and understanding as you helped me learn how to volunteer with the patients in your care, as you helped me to understand that I still have purpose and something to offer others.

My gratitude and love for their unending support and belief in me go to: my beautiful niece, Jessica Piscopo, friends Pat and Ken Christie, Janice Desrosiers (whose thoughtful listening in the early stages helped so much), friend Barbara Davenport, and many others who have encouraged me along the way.

Thank you, gifted editor and friend, Chris Nelson, for your vision, deep insights, patience and guidance over many years that helped me to see this project through. Thank you, editor and friend, Myrna Riback for guiding my story, and editor Dorothy Irwin, for helping me to finally see details and colors in the midst of the fog in my mind. It changed everything for me.

Thank you, D. Patrick Miller, of Fearless Literary, for your energy, integrity and skill in helping me finally get my book on the shelves.

Made in the USA
Las Vegas, NV
27 January 2022

42439349R00163